THE NOVEL AFTER THEORY

The Novel After Theory

JUDITH RYAN

COLUMBIA UNIVERSITY PRESS   NEW YORK

COLUMBIA UNIVERSITY PRESS
Publishers Since 1893
NEW YORK   CHICHESTER, WEST SUSSEX

Library of Congress Cataloging-in-Publication Data
Ryan, Judith, 1943–
   The novel after theory / Judith Ryan.
      p.   cm.
   Includes bibliographical references and index.
   ISBN 978-0-231-15742-1 (cloth : alk. paper) — ISBN 978-0-231-52816-0 (electronic)
   1. Fiction—20th century—History and criticism. 2 Fiction—21st century—History and
criticism. 3. Knowledge, Theory of, in literature. 4. Philosophy, French, in literature. I. Title.

PN3503.R87   2011
809.3'9384—dc22
                                                                    2011001285

Columbia University Press books are printed on permanent and durable acid-free paper.
This book was printed on paper with recycled content.

Printed in the United States of America

c 10 9 8 7 6 5 4 3 2 1

References to Internet Web sites (URLs) were accurate at the time of writing. Neither the
author nor Columbia University Press is responsible for URLs that may have expired or
changed since the manuscript was prepared.

Contents

Acknowledgments

The Novel After Theory was conceived in a course on contemporary fiction that I began to teach some years ago. At first, it was a general course on recent novels, but I soon heard myself uttering the words "the novel after theory." The course acquired a subtitle, and I started mapping out the future book. I am immensely grateful to the students who took the course and the teaching fellows who discussed the material with me at planning meetings. With their help, my ideas began to take clearer shape.

Doris Sperber was an expert research assistant, always ready to locate yet another item in the library, order a book by interlibrary loan, or photocopy the many articles I needed. I appreciate very much the work she put into this project. Charlotte Szilagyi meticulously checked notes and bibliographic references, making many helpful suggestions for neater and more elegant ways to present information. Christopher Pitts's sharp eye and care for detail were invaluable at the line-editing stage. Do Mi Stauber created a thoughtful and effective index. During my stay at the Deutsches Literaturarchiv Marbach in March 2009, I was fortunate to receive the advice of Ulrich von Buelow, who facilitated my study of Sebald's manuscript of *The Rings of Saturn*, and Nicolai Riedel, who enabled me to consult a number of books from Sebald's personal library.

The Germanic Studies program at Rutgers University invited me to give a talk on the German-language material in this book in the fall of 2003; I am grateful to William Donahue and Martha Helfer as well as to the donors of the Rodig Lecture and the students who participated in the discussion. In the spring of 2007, I gave a version of my remarks on Sebald's *The Rings of Saturn* as the Grilk Lecture at the University of Michigan; I profited a great deal from the discussion and would like to thank Fred Amrine and the audience for their helpful suggestions.

Conversations and email exchanges with colleagues at Harvard provided useful information and intellectual support. Special thanks go to Verena

Conley, whose profound knowledge of French poststructuralism was invaluable; John Hamilton, who pointed me in the direction of *Sweet Charity* and informed me about geographic features of the Traunsee; Christopher Johnson, who shares my passion for W. G. Sebald; Martin Puchner, whose conversations about Coetzee persuaded me to include several of his novels; Eric Rentschler, a fellow admirer of Pynchon's work, including the songs that are Pynchon's trademark; and John Stauffer, who encouraged me to read *Infinite Jest* and looked at a preliminary draft of my ideas about it.

For permission to reproduce four lines from Dylan Thomas's poem "The hand that signed the paper" (*The Poems of Dylan Thomas*, ed. Daniel Jones [New York: New Directions, 2003], 75), I wish to thank New Directions Publishing Corporation for U.S. and international rights, and David Hingham Associates for U.K. rights. I am grateful as well to Editions Rodopi for permission to reproduce a shortened and adapted version of my essay "'Lines of Flight': History and Territory in the *Rings of Saturn*," in *W. G. Sebald: Schreiben ex patria/Expatriate Writing*, ed. Gerhard Fischer (Amsterdam: Editions Rodopi, 2009), 45–60. The Taylor and Francis Group, LLC, a division of Informa plc, has kindly granted permission to include a modified version of my article "After the 'Death of the Author': The Fabrication of Helen Demidenko," in *Cultures of Forgery: Making Nations, Making Selves*, ed. Judith Ryan and Alfred Thomas (London: Routledge, 2003), 169–185. Finally, I am grateful to the German department at Rutgers University for permission to use a heavily revised and expanded version of my remarks in the Rodig Lecture of 2003, published in the *Rutgers German Studies Occasional Papers No. 5* (2006), with a foreword by William Donahue, 5–25.

As usual, my husband Larry Joseph read numerous versions of the manuscript as they emerged from the printer, talked through many aspects of the book as it progressed, and supported the project from start to finish. Vanessa Ryan was a savvy adviser on computer problems, but even more importantly, she read through the entire final version, commenting on points of detail as well as on matters of larger import. Without the two of them, this book would doubtless still be languishing in my files.

Two readers for Columbia University Press gave invaluable advice that helped to clarify numerous points and strengthen the overall argument. My heartfelt thanks go to them. I also owe a large debt of gratitude to my editor Jennifer Crewe, whose early interest in the project and encouragement during its final phases were crucial.

THE NOVEL AFTER THEORY

Introduction

Knowing Theory

Fiction and Theory

In the last third of the twentieth century, a new strain emerged in postmodern fiction, first in France and then in other countries. Soon, an entire array of novels had appeared that might be said to "know about" literary and cultural theory. Some build on theory, some argue against it, others modify it in important ways. Not all of these novels wear theory on their sleeves: readers may be surprised to discover that theory has infiltrated novels most of us just "read for the plot."[1] Identifying moments where theory remains camouflaged and where it becomes visible in literary texts is one way to take the measure of contemporary culture. We remain ambivalent about whether to accept or resist theory. But in one way or another, a remarkable number of novels is substantially informed by theory. How did this state of affairs come about, and what does it portend?

To begin, it is important to understand what "theory" has come to mean in recent decades. Throughout most of the period following World War II, "literary theory" referred to the systematic study of literature, including both its nature and its function. It involved categorizing intrinsic features such as style, imagery, narrative modes, genre, and the like. Some studies of literary theory also paid attention to extrinsic aspects of literature, such as its relation to various contexts, and to different angles of approach that could be taken to understand literary texts. Usage began to shift substantially in the early 1970s, when ideas developed in Europe made their way into Anglo-American university curricula. The term "theory" expanded substantially beyond what had previously been meant by "literary theory." As it became naturalized in the English-speaking sphere, it came to refer to recent European thought that was by no means restricted to the literary field. Many of these theories emerged from history and the social sciences rather than the humanities. Not only did these theories come from France and Germany, they tended to use dense language that many readers found alienating and intimidating. Debates about the ideas and the terminology used in this type of theory soon broke out, and observers began to speak of these controversies as the "theory wars." Although the term "literary theory" is still used in connection with the new theories, it extends the notion of the literary very broadly. This is perhaps the reason why "theory" came to be used as a blanket category.

Rather than treat this entire panoply of thinkers, *The Novel After Theory* focuses on a small group who, despite the often counterintuitive nature of their thought, have had a major impact on contemporary fiction. This approach necessarily means omitting many other types of theory: not only the Frankfurt School, but also second-generation theories like postcolonialism and queer theory.[2] I focus on the French thinkers who initiated poststructuralism and in whose work the paradoxes of such thought appears in sharp profile because of its experimental nature. "French theory" in this sense is a less baggy term than one might suppose: after all, most of the thinkers knew and interacted with one another, and many of them contributed to the same journal, *Tel Quel*, founded in 1960. The student revolution of 1968 brought the debates about theory to a head and motivated a radical rethinking of traditional ideas about literature and social systems. *The Novel After Theory* looks at a series of case studies drawn from several languages and cultures that track the conversation between poststructuralist thought and the fictions that respond to it.

The most obvious type of novel that "knows about" theory is the comic novel set in academia. The academic novel often satirizes theory, appealing at once to an inner and an outer circle of readers. David Lodge's *Small World*

(1984), with its extravagant parodies of contemporary literary scholarship, is a case in point. The character who bears the main burden of the attack on theory is Morris Zapp, a scholar who has already abandoned an entire list of different ways of thinking about literary texts, including—among others—the mythical, the Freudian, the Jungian, the Marxist, the existential, and the archetypal.[3] Now he has come to the pompous (but not actually meaningless) belief that "every decoding is another encoding" (*Small World*, 29). Looking back at Morris Zapp's scholarly effusions from a vantage point of over twenty years, it is hard to imagine quite how obscure they appeared at the time of their first publication. In Lodge's amusing depiction, the MLA Convention remains recognizable, but in the meantime, we have seen much denser utterances than Morris Zapp's. Malcolm Bradbury's *Doctor Criminale* (1992) is also closely informed by recent theory, but it addresses a readership more familiar with the specific forms this theory takes.[4] The title refers to a fictive theorist called Bazlo Criminale. At first, the narrator believes he can rely on a book on Criminale written by a certain Codicil. But it turns out that Codicil's book was actually written by his assistant and thus, in a sense, is an "authorless text" that needs to be read carefully for "the omissions and elisions, the obscurities and absences, the spaces and the fractures, the linguistic and ideological contradictions" (*Criminale*, 285). In *Doctor Criminale*, a lighthearted manner is cleverly dovetailed with precise and detailed representations of French poststructuralist theory. Here, too, the setting is a conference, this one convened at an Italian villa vaguely reminiscent of the prestigious Bellagio Center near Lake Como. In the course of this hilarious novel, we come to understand that seriousness does not always achieve the best results. Indeed, a charming young woman named Ildiko teaches the narrator very effectively to become "a little bit Hungarian"—in other words, more willing to allow the kinds of slippage that practitioners of deconstruction love to discover in texts. In terms of reader expectations, *Doctor Criminale* addresses an audience that is somewhat more informed about theory than the readers of *Small World*.

Academic novels are not the main focus of *The Novel After Theory*,[5] but they do provide a useful gauge to the spread of theory among a readership that extends beyond the university and includes readers who may not have seen a college campus—and certainly have not studied on it—for many years. Campus novels capitalize on the unfamiliar and often overblown character of much recent terminology to create their most humorous effects. To adopt the title of a collection of essays about theory, we could say that the fundamental gesture of such novels is one that defines them as coming "after strange texts."[6] Not all writers of such novels are critical of literary theory in its entirety: often, they tread a fine line between sympathy with the new ideas and an understanding of their off-putting aspects. In their different ways, David Lodge and Malcolm Bradbury are good examples of this balancing act. Both write scholarly books and essays about literature and literary theory, but they see through the pretentious style of much theoretical writing. They and other writers of campus novels have done much to bring the controversy over theory to the attention of a larger public. The penetration of theory into fiction goes well beyond the academic novel, however.[7]

In fact, I first began to conceive this book when working on a novel that is not set in academia: Patrick Süskind's *Perfume* (1985). The more I thought about the novel, the more it seemed to engage directly with debates about postmodernism that emerged in the late 1970s.[8] The novel appealed equally to a general and a more specialist readership; it made rich use of multiple and often contradictory discourses; and its treatment of history vacillated between the public and the private, nostalgia and irony. Above all, *Perfume* appropriated literary tradition in piecemeal fashion, creating a dense web of allusions, quotations, and stylistic imitations. It was almost as if recent attempts to define the postmodern had provided a recipe for the novel's composition. Was *Perfume* an isolated phenomenon, I wondered?

The Novel After Theory traces the reflections of theory in a fairly broad range of narrative fiction. The focus is on novels that, coming after the major theoretical works of the late twentieth century, are informed by theory, build on theory, and take issue with it. Some "novels after theory" urge us, implicitly, to think theory through and identify parts of it that need to be adjusted, overhauled, or outright abandoned. But the novels can and should be read, understood, and enjoyed on many other levels as well. *The Novel After Theory* exposes the theoretical layer in these works, but it does not aim in any way to reduce them to that layer alone.

Theory plays many different roles in the contemporary novel. Some texts refer to theory or theorists in their titles: Gilbert Adair's *The Death of the Author* (1992) and Patricia Duncker's *Hallucinating Foucault* (1996) are examples of this group. The reader is expected to recognize the reference in the title: this gesture gives the book its initial allure. Other novels drop allusions to modern theorists in a seemingly casual or even teasing manner. How seriously should we take such allusions? Is an invented title like "the Deleuze and Guattari fake book" in one of the most hilarious chapters of Pynchon's

Vineland (1990) just a nonce joke, or is it a hint to a larger presence of the French theorists in the novel as a whole? Another made-up title supposedly by the same pair in David Foster Wallace's *Infinite Jest* (1996) provokes a similar question. In the same vein, the French novelist Camille Laurens shows one of the main characters in her novel *Romance* (1992) carrying a volume called "Séminaire"—an allusion to Lacan's famous open seminars in which he developed his ideas, an intellectual institution known to educated French speakers even if they never set foot in the seminars themselves. A number of the writers treated in *The Novel After Theory* are academics by profession: A. S. Byatt is a former professor of English, Umberto Eco is a professor of semiotics, W. G. Sebald was a professor of German, and J. M. Coetzee a professor of literature. Other novelists who engage with theory have little to do with the world of academia: one might think here of Don DeLillo and John Banville. Many of the writers we read for pleasure—in addition to those already mentioned, one might add Margaret Atwood—are familiar to one degree or another with recent theory.

The Novel After Theory does not aim to demonstrate that contemporary novels can be read through the grid of current theory. That has been done often enough. Indeed, most introductions to theory present it as an array of different approaches to literary study, a perspective remote from that of at least some of the thinkers who have come under the capacious umbrella of theory today. In university courses, theory is often studied as a method for application, and students are asked to write analyses of literary texts from the vantage point of various theorists.[9] This is not the goal of *The Novel After Theory*. What this book aims to do is show how novelists themselves engage with theory. The works chosen for discussion do more than merely fit neatly into the frame of one theory or another. In many cases, indeed, the novels draw eclectically on the ideas of several theorists at once. In some instances, however, a novelist's connections with a particular body of theory are well known. Although one of the most prominent theories of our day has to do with the "death of the author," and even scholars who do not subscribe to this notion observe an earlier injunction to distinguish between the author and the narrator of a text, I do not refrain here from referring to the person of the author when that person is relevant. It would be ludicrous, after all, to suppose that Julia Kristeva's novels bear no relation at all to her psychoanalytic theory. It would also be silly not to acknowledge that Marguerite Duras read texts by Lacan and Derrida. Similarly, J. M. Coetzee's essays show that he is well read in Foucault, and W. G. Sebald's essays refer in their notes to Foucault and Deleuze and

Guattari, among others. In these two instances, extrinsic evidence confirms what can also be deduced by close analysis of the narrative texts.

In contrast, it is possible for a text to "know about" theory even when its author does not admit to knowing it or has had no verifiable access to specific theoretical texts. In some instances, the intellectual climate, from current ways of thinking to fashionable use of language, seeps into texts without their authors' awareness. It is hard to remain completely immune from what is "in the air." The best example of this phenomenon is Don DeLillo's *White Noise*, which is widely seen as showing affinities with Baudrillard's theories of the simulacrum and its function in consumer culture; yet there seems to be no extrinsic evidence that *White Noise* is actually in dialogue with Baudrillard. The similarities between the two writers' ideas certainly owe much to contemporary discussions about the impact of media on our lives; yet it is difficult to imagine that the two lines of thought took parallel tracks without any sort of overlap or intertwining. One of the trickiest problems addressed in *The Novel After Theory* has to do with writers who know theory but resist it. A. S. Byatt, for example, takes a cautious position toward theory. She is familiar with the work of several theorists: she has read Hayden White, she knows Roland Barthes, and she admires Michel Foucault's early work *The Order of Things*. She even locates the "germ" of her novel, *The Biographer's Tale* (2000), in her "first reading of Foucault's remarks on Linnaeus and taxonomy in *Les mots et les choses*."[10] Her novel *Possession* (1990) had treated contemporary theory in a more critical and often parodic vein through characters who represent a variety of different theoretical positions: Roland, a former devotee of Barthes and Foucault from his student days in the '60s; Leonora Stern, a brash American feminist with a fascination for sexual symbolism and an interest in the thought of Hélène Cixous; and James Blackadder, a writer of literary biographies. The approach to theory is very different in *The Biographer's Tale*, in part because of the narrator Byatt chooses as the main lens of the story. Phineas G. Nanson, a dissertation-writer who has decided to abandon postmodern theory, nonetheless remains sympathetic to certain forms of French thought, not only those of the early Foucault but also those of Barthes's book on photography. The problematic treatment of archival research and the relation between fact and fiction in this novel is also indebted to poststructuralist conceptions. *The Biographer's Tale* does not advocate a return to a simplistic view of historical fact. In her collection of essays, *On Histories and Stories* (2000),[11] where Byatt speaks in her own voice, she gives a generous assessment of contemporary theory, although she confesses her continued admiration for F. R. Leavis and her former teachers at Cambridge. She is not happy, for example, that many scholarly studies today quote more frequently from theoretical works than from primary texts, as was the case when she was a student. Above all, she deplores the way in which the academy's fascination with theory has led critics "to make writers fit into the boxes and nets of theoretical questions."[12] She complains, as well, about the instrumental use of novels in courses where they are "taught as if they appear to have something to contribute to the debate about 'women's writing' or 'feminism' or 'post-colonialism' or 'postmodernism.'" Byatt's objections to heavy-handed application of theory to texts are well taken; yet her narratives are by no means innocent of poststructuralist subtleties. Even as her most attractive protagonists yearn for simpler times and less ambiguous truths, they are well aware of the more complex intellectual context in which they pursue their scholarly endeavors.

Another fascinating case is that of Marilynne Robinson's *Housekeeping* (1980), which displays numerous effects familiar to readers of Derrida; yet, as I demonstrate in detail, these effects are probably the result of quite different literary precursors on whom Robinson draws in this novel. Certainly, her later fiction moves decisively away from deconstructive effects. By contrast, two novels that seem to mention theory only in passing (Thomas Pynchon's *Vineland* and David Foster Wallace's *Infinite Jest*) turn out to be intricately structured by poststructuralist thought. The kinds of relations the novels bear to theory are thus quite varied.

None of the novels discussed in *The Novel After Theory* hews to a single poststructuralist line of thought. If they did, they would hardly be interesting as works of fiction: they would be nothing more than mechanical translations of a theoretical model into the fictional mode. Frequently, the novels allude to several different theories, and in some instances I discuss them in more than one chapter. Even in the case of novels treated here under a single heading, it is almost always the case that they might also have found a place in another category. These novels do not simply incorporate theory, they reflect on it, complicate it, and sometimes go beyond it. They engage with problems that theory has adopted, but they do so in ways that replace stark abstraction by rich detail. Their authors would be distressed by the faintest of suggestion that they had written their works simply by treading in the footsteps of major theorists. When asked point-blank about their indebtedness to theory, many writers are understandably wary. Kathy Acker, for example, takes pains to explain that she hadn't read theorists like Foucault and Deleuze when she first began to write fiction, although she was later relieved to find that theory confirmed some of what she had imagined was wildly idiosyncratic thinking that had no counterpart anywhere else.[13] None of the novelists I discuss is entirely happy about theory. As one scholar formulates it, "postdeconstructive" writing is at once "aware of, and anxious about, deconstruction."[14] Making appropriate substitutions, we can say that the novel after theory is "aware of, and anxious about," theory.

Reception of Theory

To understand how theory extended its reach beyond the world of academia, we need to go back further than the campus novels of the 1980s. The date of reference is a 1966 colloquium at the Johns Hopkins University. On this occasion, Jacques Derrida gave a talk on Roland Barthes's essay, "To Write: Intransitive Verb?"[15] This talk set a long fuse that was eventually to explode in the late 1970s and early 1980s in the form of heated debates. In 1990, Mark Tansey created a poster depicting Derrida engaged in mortal combat with Paul de Man on the edge of a precipice beside a waterfall, an image modeled on a well-known illustration from *The Death of Sherlock Holmes* in which the detective does battle with Professor Moriarty. In Tansey's poster, the terrifying cliff face is made up entirely of typewritten words, none of them completely legible.[16] By that time, even the broader public knew that "theory" was reputed to consist of words signifying nothing, a tangled grab bag of incoherence. Derrida's own terminology, in particular the word "deconstruction," did not help endear him to the American public, which tended to take it, erroneously, as a synonym for destruction. The press took to making fun of theory, especially in reports on the annual convention of the Modern Language Association of America. Every year, reporters scoured the titles of papers given at the convention to identify the juiciest and cast doubts upon the trendiest. By 1991, the critic Camille Paglia had begun to launch a series of attacks on theory, which she saw as an imposture that had hoodwinked large numbers of malleable academics and led them to subscribe to irrational modes of thought.[17] The language of theory, she believed, was arrogant and unaesthetic.[18] This criticism was to become one of the broader public's principal objections to theory.

Those who had followed intellectual developments closely during the 1980s were well aware that "theory" in this sense was an American usage that did not correspond to the self-perceptions of Derrida, Barthes, and their French contemporaries. Nor did it correspond to what had previously been called "literary theory," though a proliferation of academic courses on "theory" in the English-speaking nations has tended to occlude this fact. Such courses pulled together a range of different ideas that also included reflections on the nature of literature and the workings of literary texts, as well as ideas derived from Marxism and the Frankfurt School of critical theory. Freudian psychology, which still plays a substantial role in academic thinking about literature, was to provide the basis for the new French theories developed by Jacques Lacan. As many scholars have pointed out, the English-speaking cultures liked to think of these "theories" as a variety of different "approaches" that could be called into service according to individual need. This view was in fact a holdover from the older dispute among biographical criticism, the New Criticism, and F. R. Leavis's idea of a "great tradition." One way of proceeding in this highly charged environment was to take a middle position, what Herman Rapaport describes as "synoptic historicism supported by formal analysis."[19] Another method was to regard the rival models as alternatives capable, to some minimal degree, of coexistence.[20]

"Theory" was really no more than an encompassing term for ideas presented by what in French are called *maîtres à penser* (intellectual guides). Some scholars and students became devoted to a particular thinker, seeing his or her ideas as the key to unlocking an otherwise divergent array of literary texts. At the same time, the notion of a body of thought that could be subsumed under the heading "theory" worked to reduce the threat of fragmentation in literary studies. "Theory" became a kind of lingua franca capable of bringing scholars together in a period when the canon was expanding so rapidly that knowledge of a particular text could not always be taken for granted. This conglomerative view of theory enabled a passage from a period when literary scholarship had been dominated by single "masters" such as F. R. Leavis (d. 1978) or Northrop Frye (d. 1991). The transmission of these two diametrically opposed sets of ideas was significantly aided by colleagues and former students, who themselves created further acolytes among a younger generation. This master-student model was only gradually replaced by a model that owed much more to the emergence of theory courses in which students read samples from the new (mainly French) theorists without regard to a specific hierarchical arrangement. The 1980s were the period when theory positioned itself most decisively in literary and related fields, and it held strong well through the 1990s.

More recently, the view has arisen that theory is "dead." If so, its death does not seem to have stemmed the tide of anthologies and introductions aimed at a largely student readership. A proliferation of introductory works in graphic form reinforces the notion that "theory" is virtually impossible to understand.[21] Whatever has happened to theory, these study guides are still in demand, even as new anthologies designed for introductory graduate courses emerge.[22] The "death of theory" may be little more than a way of registering that the high point of the theory vogue in the English-speaking countries has now passed; but it may also be an expression of theory's failure to attain some of its more idealistic goals. In April 2003, the editors of *Critical Inquiry* convened a public symposium on the future of theory, but as it turned out, they ended up spending more time discussing the war in Iraq than they did discussing theory. This was entirely understandable. Henry Louis Gates Jr. commented, for example, that as far as he could tell, theory had never directly liberated anyone.[23] Theory appeared to have been crushed under the pressure of world events.

As a matter of fact, theory had been declared dead many times already. Both Paul de Man and Stanley Fish, for example, declared it dead in 1982.[24] But theory refused to succumb so rapidly. One scholar, mounting a vigorous argument opposing deconstruction, wondered all the same whether those who were proclaiming the death of theory were engaging more in "wishful thinking than [in] accurate observation."[25] Another scholar, a distinguished proponent of deconstruction, argued that "rumors about [its] death have always already been exaggerated."[26] Indeed, the debate over the "death of theory" continued in a spate of books, most of them published between 2000 and 2004. Two separate groups addressed the topic "What's Left of Theory?"[27] Two "manifestos" appeared in the Blackwell series, the first sympathetic to theory, the second opposing it.[28] Terry Eagleton published a book-length essay called *After Theory*, but he claimed that "those to whom the title of this book suggests that 'theory' is now over, and that we can all relievedly return to an age of pre-theoretical innocence, are in for a disappointment." Still, he does think that theory should renew itself by taking more risks and breaking out of old patterns.[29] Several other books explore the "death of theory" or the problem of what comes "after theory" from a variety of different angles.[30]

Some scholars use the term "posttheory" to describe the age in which we live now. The term, however, has different meanings for different scholars. For David Bordwell, Noël Carroll, and the contributors to their collection of essays, *Post-Theory: Reconstructing Film Studies*,[31] the term indicates a dramatic shift in focus that leaves French theory behind in order to attend to matters more specific to film itself. By contrast, the contributors to *Post-Theory: New Directions in Criticism*, edited by Martin McQuillan, Graeme MacDonald, Robin Purves, and Stephen Thomson, employ the word "posttheory" to indicate a continuity that also involves difference.[32] Rather than discarding theory, these scholars argue that, "although we have entered a post-theoretical world, we are definitely not in an a-theoretical one."[33] In some ways, we might see the argument over "posttheory" as related to the questions raised in connection with the terms "postmodern" and "postcolonial."[34] "Posttheoretical" has not (or not yet) captured the imagination in quite the way the other two "post-" compounds have done.

The flurry of works on the purported death or surpassing of theory did not prevent the emergence of new introductions to theory and new anthologies of canonical texts in the field. Tried and true guides for use in courses appear in updated editions, even as new approaches to literature emerge. This continuing focus on theory, not just in academic monographs but also in the public sphere, cannot help but impact writers of fiction. Theory infiltrates recent novels in ways that are often specific to the linguistic and cultural context in which the books took shape. Writers from different backgrounds picked up on different aspects of theory at different moments and inflected it in different ways.

In America, theory entered the scene mainly by way of academic conferences, but also by other routes. One of the most important mediators was a little series called Foreign Agents, put out by *Semiotexte(s)*. The first of these small black volumes, in truly pocket-sized format, presented English translations of essays by French thinkers; there was something at once chic and subversive about these books that set themselves apart from the academic system of the time. Many readers discovered the Foreign Agents by themselves, and in so doing, felt that they were uncovering a secret science. To traverse New York with one of these books in hand was to become a sort of spy, able to see beneath the surface of social and cultural reality. Selections from Deleuze and Guattari were the first to be published as a little black book (in 1983), and these were rapidly followed by key essays from Baudrillard.[35] This move was well calculated. These first Foreign Agents volumes did not present theories about literature, but rather a new and different kind of thinking about modern social reality. This allowed the little black books to make themselves at home in places outside literature departments. Visual artists and authors of science fiction were the first to take up the alluring ideas that seemed to belong to a special undercover world, and although there were many mis-understandings between the theorists and their followers about how best to put the new modes of thought into practice, the effect of the Foreign Agents series was to support a kind of infiltration into American culture that might otherwise have been virtually unthinkable. By 1985, there was an entire cadre of creative people who had fallen in love with the new ideas.[36]

In a parallel movement, the journal *Critical Inquiry* began to devote sub-stantial attention to the Yale School, a group of literary scholars strongly influenced by Derrida.[37] In the early 1980s, *Critical Inquiry* published pieces by Derrida, Foucault, and Julia Kristeva, gradually expanding its scope in the later years of the decade and continuing to introduce important works of European theory well into the 1990s.[38] The journal *October* took a some-what different tack, highlighting such radically different theorists as Walter Benjamin and Jacques Lacan, and finally providing a medium for important essays by Slavoj Žižek[39] (probably a partial model for Malcolm Bradbury's character, Bazlo Criminale).

The rise of theory in Britain was intricately connected with its rise in Amer-ica, but with important differences. While I. A. Richards's *Practical Criticism* (1929) crossed the Atlantic to join the New Criticism as developed and prac-ticed by Cleanth Brooks, Wimsatt and Beardsley, and Robert Penn Warren, the tradition established by F. R. Leavis and Q. D. Leavis in the journal *Scru-tiny* (starting in 1932) was not precisely identical with the New Criticism—although it did demand close attention to texts. F. R. Leavis's book *The Great Tradition* (1948) moved decisively beyond analysis of form to questions of ethics. The long life of this strand of criticism, with its enlargement of the scope of critical writing to encompass what he called "moral intensity" gave a particular inflection to British literary studies.[40] In the period that primarily concerns us here, however, Marxist thought played an important role in Brit-ain. Raymond Williams, with his book *Culture and Society: 1970–1950* (1958) laid the groundwork for British cultural Marxism. As also in America, theo-rists such as Walter Benjamin and the cofounders of the Frankfurt Institute in 1955, Max Horkheimer and Theodor Adorno, received much attention within the framework of cultural studies in Britain. Despite differences in inflec-tion between Britain and America, poststructuralist theory joined Frankfurt School theory in the anthologies of "literary theory" intended for university study in the United Kingdom. Key figures in the acceptance of theory in Brit-ain were Terence Hawkes, Frank Kermode, and David Lodge.[41]The British resistance to theory, though overlapping in many ways with similar resistance in America, was also motivated by a feeling that it was heavy-handed and lacked the tact appropriate for treating literary texts.[42]

French poststructuralist thought had a different fate in Germany. In part, it was absorbed into the academic system by way of its reception in America. This meant that the debates about literary theory occurred somewhat later on the German scene than in America. In the 1970s, the word *Literaturtheorie* (literary theory) was still more closely attached to ideas about how literary texts functioned and how they might be classified; it was not attached to French thought.[43] Structuralist and poststructuralist ideas entered the German-speaking world in the late 1970s through translations of some of the major thinkers, followed by explications of their ideas by scholars whose work reached a wide public: Manfred Frank and Friedrich Kittler. These ideas were at first more frequently called *Diskurstheorien* (theories of discourse).[44] As in the English-speaking world, the German academy first showed resistance to the new ideas or treated them, at best, as a field apart rather than as a central component of students' induction into literary study. Not until the 1990s did the term *Literaturtheorie* begin to take firm hold as a designation for what had been termed "literary theory" in America for almost two decades.[45] An anthology of theoretical texts modeled on the many similar anthologies that emerged in Britain and America since 1986 appeared under the title *Texte zur Literaturtheorie der Gegenwart* in 1996,[46] and several English-language books about theory were translated into German around the same time.[47] In the past few years, handbooks and study guides have continued to appear in Germany.[48] Theory is now presented as something that students of literature need to know about. Nonetheless, one scholar suspects that the rapid assimilation of theory into the German academic system may have come at the price of suppressing its more playful element.[49] The theory boom in Germany toward the end of the 1990s was already accompanied by a sense of depletion caused by scholars' inability to bring the various theoretical discourses into a coherent system.[50]

France itself was an intriguing case. The term "theory" has never been accepted there in the broad sense that has become common in English. *Théorie littéraire* refers to attempts to systematize textual phenomena and to understand how they function, but it does not cover social and cultural theory. It includes some topics taught in the Anglo-American sphere under "theory," notably narrative theory, intertextuality, and reader reception, and also looks broadly at the nature of literature and its distinction from other types of writing. Literary theory in this sense is best represented in the writings of the structuralist Gérard Genette, whose work includes not only narratology but also poetics and aesthetics.[51] Insofar as they examine questions involving the author, narrator, and reader, poststructuralist theorists like Derrida and Foucault can also be seen as participating in this enterprise, although they are not to be found on the literature shelf in most bookstores. Nor should we expect to find all of them under philosophy: writers like Barthes and Kristeva are often classified as linguists. So remote is the American category "theory" from French usage that the author of a French history of the theory boom in America can find no more apposite title for his book than the English term, *French Theory*.[52] To use an English phrase in such an exposed position is almost unheard of: it indicates the extent to which French speakers find the notion foreign. The concept "French theory" has much more to do with American intellectual life than with something special to France. As Sylvère Lotringer explains, the transformation of French thought into theory "pertains to strange psychopolitical facts about America."[53]

Antoine Compagnon's *Le Démon de la théorie* (1998; The Imp of Theory) may help us understand what French speakers do mean by literary theory. The body of the book traces a course through such topics as the nature of literature, the concept of the author, the relation between literature and reality, the role of the reader, the question of style, the relation of literature to history, and the question of values. These chapters make only brief mention of thinkers like Michel Foucault, Roland Barthes, Jacques Derrida, and Julia Kristeva. In the introduction and conclusion, which take the form of personal essays, Compagnon writes nostalgically of what he calls the "hour of glory" when literary theory captured the imaginations of French students in the late 1960s and early 1970s.[54] Students found this literary theory attractive, he recalls, because it presented a "counterdiscourse" that questioned traditional assumptions of literary criticism. Compagnon does not examine so much the students' desire for new ways of thinking in a period of political and cultural unrest[55] as highlight the specifically literary emphasis of the ideas that so fascinated them. Compagnon's argument is that we need to reconsider once again our intuitive notions of literary phenomena in order to understand them more accurately. This is quite the opposite of the approach taken by most "French theory."

Resistance to Theory

Dismissive responses to French theory emerged early in its American reception. Paul de Man introduced the phrase "resistance to theory" to describe this effect. Yet de Man saw resistance as an inevitable accompaniment to theory, an accompaniment that was actually even, in some sense, part of theory itself.[56] After all, deconstruction, both in Derrida's version and in de Man's adaptation, was essentially a way of thinking two things at once.

Still, it took quite some time after the first appearance of theory in America before the French ideas generated serious conflict. For American scholars trained in the 1960s, "theory" still evoked Wellek and Warren's *Theory of Literature* (1942), an introduction to literary scholarship that remained dominant until the late 1970s and beyond.[57] Although Wellek and Warren treated both intrinsic and extrinsic approaches to literature in their book, the focus was firmly on the nature and function of literary texts. In 1982 and 1983, Walter Jackson Bate and René Wellek decried the infiltration of the new form of theory into the American university and the decline of literary studies to which they believed it contributed. In 1982, Steven Knapp and Walter Benn Michaels published an essay in *Critical Inquiry* titled "Against Theory," in which they focused on problems of intention and interpretation. In sum, they believed that "the whole enterprise of critical theory is misguided and should be abandoned."[58] This sweeping indictment of literary theory led to a rash of responses, also published in *Critical Inquiry* between 1982 and 1985.[59] John Ellis's *Against Deconstruction* (1989) continued the argument, focusing primarily on Derrida's reading of Saussure, in other words, the point of transition from structuralism to poststructuralism. He also examined arguments in texts by proponents of deconstruction such as Paul de Man and Barbara Johnson. From a broader perspective, he contrasted the position of deconstruction in France, where it represented a focused "revolt against an extremely narrow rationalist tradition,"[60] and its position in America, where it entered an already pluralist field that was hardly a "well-guarded citadel."[61] The debates about poststructuralism continued to rage in the early years of the twenty-first century. Herman Rapaport's *The Theory Mess* (2001) is a spirited and thoughtful reconsideration of deconstruction that argues for a more careful reading of key texts by Derrida and other deconstructionists. A few years later, a thick anthology of essays by distinguished scholars who reject the domination of theory in the university curriculum appeared under the title *Theory's Empire: An Anthology of Dissent*.[62] In spite of these debates, a series of theory anthologies emerged beginning in the 1980s and continuing until the early years of the twenty-first century. In certain literary fields, notably comparative literature, these anthologies were the basis for graduate students' induction into literary studies.

A "foreign" mode of expression that characterized much theoretical writing and was often exacerbated in available English translations had much to do with American resistance to theory. The journal *Philosophy and Literature* gave annual prizes for "bad writing" that were frequently won by literary theorists.[63] Such critiques of obscure, turgid, or prolix writing propelled the whole phenomenon of theory into public view, surrounding it with negative associations. The sinning sentences did not entirely deserve the castigation they received, yet readers unfamiliar with theory had trouble seeing how the sentences made sense. The ideas contained in them turned the familiar world upside down.

As long as theory remained at the center of highly publicized debates, it seemed paradoxical to proclaim its death. Instead, something much less dramatic has happened to theory. In a 2005 newspaper article, Hans Ulrich Gumbrecht described theory's "uncharacteristically soundless and almost hurried" departure from the stage.[64] Yet theory has not entirely disappeared. *Critical Inquiry* continues to publish reflections on theory and the history of theory.[65] A new scholarly periodical called the *Journal of Literary Theory*, founded in 2007, reclaims the term "literary theory" for systematic studies of "the foundations of literary study" rather than as a designation for a "proliferation of approaches and varieties of theory": the journal aims to foster broad explorations of how literature is understood, how it functions, and under what conditions it is produced and read.[66]

The October 2010 issue of *PMLA*, a special issue on "Literary Criticism for the Twenty-First Century" assembles an eclectic set of essays on this topic.[67] Only one of them takes an avowedly poststructuralist position: Robert Klein's manifesto-like article "The Future of Literary Criticism."[68] Opening with a gesture toward André Breton, Klein proclaims that "the future of literary criticism will be Derridean, or it will not be" (920).[69] His argument presents a sympathetic interpretation of Derrida that emphasizes those elements in his thought that demand closer analysis and reflection within literary scholarship. Klein highlights Derrida's recasting of the very concept of a text as one that at first conceals "the law of its composition and the rules of its game."[70] The texts studied in *The Novel After Theory* fall into precisely this category. We can read them without regard to their engagement with theory, but once we perceive this engagement, they acquire additional meaning.

Characteristic of the October 2010 issue of *PMLA* is its use of the term "literary criticism": does this imply a return to criticism from theory? That's far from clear. In his introduction to the issue, Jonathan Culler regards theory as intertwined with criticism. Asking whether new models may emerge for literary criticism, he writes: "If what we call 'theory' has been the deployment of discourses and analytic perspectives originating in other disciplines than one's own, are there new theoretical constructions available that may enrich literary studies in this new century?"[71]

Novels as Case Studies

The Novel After Theory looks at a series of case studies that track the conversation between poststructuralist thought and the fictions that respond to it. The project is a comparative one that draws on several languages and cultures. In the main, the novels I examine are by well-known authors writing in a range of different languages and from the vantage point of various cultures: Margaret Atwood, J. M. Coetzee, Don DeLillo, Marguerite Duras, Umberto Eco, Thomas Pynchon, and W. G. Sebald, among others. Given the general resistance to theory, especially in the English-speaking world, the success of these novels is testimony to the skill with which their authors engage with theory while still speaking to a wide range of readers. One might even see their novels as a response to the charge that theory is inevitably ponderous and jargon ridden.

My own approach to their responses is essentially an intertextual consideration. The novelists' reworking of poststructuralist theory is prompted by a desire to clarify elements that seem to defy conventional reason. By clothing theory in the details of material, social, and psychological life, they can often render it easier to understand. The difficulties of poststructuralist theory arise in the main from its attempts to escape the constraints of binary thinking. Real life can be understood in binary terms, but it is not intrinsically structured that way. The "reality effects" of fictional narration allow us to move more easily between binary and nonbinary thought. At the same time, theories of any sort are likely to have weaknesses and blind spots. In many cases, the novelists home in on these problems and try to overcome them. My discussion of the novels attempts to capture this complex intertextual relation between narrative fiction and poststructuralist ideas.

The Novel After Theory is divided into three main parts, focusing on theories of textuality, psychology, and society respectively. This sequence enables a progression from more text-oriented to contextual issues, illustrating not only various facets of poststructuralist theory but also the increasingly probing engagement of novelists with questions of the historical, political, and ethical implications of theory. At their best, the novels emerge as a proving ground for theory and its larger implications for society.

Part 1 consists of two chapters. The first of these takes as its starting point Roland Barthes's provocative concept of the "death of the author." Using two novels from 1984, Alain Robbe-Grillet's *Ghosts in the Mirror* and Marguerite Duras's *The Lover*, I stake out contrasting positions in the debate about Barthes's ideas. From there, I explore other novels that draw out the seemingly more scandalous implications of Barthes's theory. These include Margaret Atwood's *The Blind Assassin*, Helen Darville's *The Hand That Signed the Paper*, Michael Krüger's *Himmelfarb*, and John Banville's *Shroud*. Does the concept of an impersonal "scriptor" allow the real author to avoid grappling with the moral problems that arise in his or her fiction?

The second chapter moves to Derrida and deconstruction. It is easy to see why this theory might conflict with readers' desires for answers to questions about personal identity; it might also trouble those who are deeply invested in the reality of an outside world with which individuals interact. How far are novelists willing to go in the direction of uncertainty and indeterminacy? Marguerite Duras is again a key figure in this chapter, which looks at *The Lover* from a different angle. The chapter also examines two British novels, Graham Swift's *Waterland* and Marilynne Robinson's *Housekeeping*, exploring the tension between deconstructive tendencies and the desire for stable identities and clear answers. At the heart of this chapter lies the question whether deconstruction is a kind of game or a serious method suited to complex moral issues.

In part 2, the focus shifts to poststructuralist psychoanalytic theories. It opens with a chapter on Jacques Lacan. Often criticized by the psychoanalytic establishment, Lacan entered the literary domain through his important essay on Marguerite Duras's *The Ravishing of Lol V. Stein*. Not surprisingly, Duras herself subsequently engaged with his ideas in several of her works, most strikingly *The Vice-Consul*. Two other French writers, Julia Kristeva in her detective novels and Camille Laurens in exuberant spoofs on theory, have continued this dialogue with Lacan. Like Duras, Kristeva and Laurens ask whether Lacan's views of women are accurate and whether a man, be he a lover or a psychoanalyst, is capable of understanding female psychology. By means of subtle wordplay, furthermore, the three French novelists explore Lacan's view that the unconscious is structured like a language. They also expand Lacan's notions of the "mirror stage" in individual human development to make them apply to the specular society that has taken shape in recent decades. Coetzee's *Age of Iron*, the final work treated in this chapter, expands the Lacanian schema into a more specifically political arena, South Africa under apartheid, thus putting the theory to an even more severe ethical test.

The second chapter in this part studies Kristeva's notion of "women's time," a way of conceiving time outside the linear chronology that she identifies with male thinking. If women substitute their own forms of temporality for traditional ways of understanding time, how can they also insert themselves actively into history and the social power structure? This chapter looks at ways in which novelists have wrestled with this paradox. Two of the main witnesses are Christa Wolf, whose *Cassandra* imagines a female countersociety to the predominantly masculine political world of East Germany, and Monika Maron, whose *Animal Triste* examines the implications of German reunification for the female psyche and implicitly engages with Wolf's idea of a female utopia. The chapter concludes with a discussion of Kristeva's own recent novel *Murder in Byzantium*, which reexamines from today's perspective the concepts she developed in her famous essay of 1979.

Part 3 moves to theories of society. It begins with a chapter about Michel Foucault's work on the institutions that have shaped and controlled modern society since the Enlightenment: hospitals, insane asylums, prisons. It shows how his famous essay "What is an Author?" fits with this larger project and the influence it has had on such different writers as the former East German writer, Wolfgang Hilbig (in his novel *"Ich"*) and the Italian semiotician Umberto Eco (in *Foucault's Pendulum*, a novel ostensibly about a different Foucault). J. M. Coetzee's *Waiting for the Barbarians* and W. G. Sebald's *Austerlitz*, works deeply indebted to Foucault's theories, open up important moral questions. I argue that these last two writers spell out the consequences of Foucault's ideas for periods he falls short of treating in his books: the colonial era and the twentieth century.

The social focus continues with a chapter on Baudrillard's concept of simulation. Cybernetic fiction, an important point of entry for Baudrillard's ideas, is addressed by a brief discussion of Samuel Delany's *Stars in My Pocket Like Grains of Sand*. Central to the reflection of Baudrillardian ideas in recent novels is his observation that culture today has become a proliferation of imitations that seem designed to cover up an underlying emptiness at its heart. Don DeLillo's *White Noise*, with its focus on the way simulation functions as a pacifying device for an anxious public, is an obvious choice to illustrate this issue. Christoph Ransmayr's dystopian novel *The Dog King* (*Morbus Kitahara*) is another critical example. DeLillo's focus on a "toxic airborne event" and Ransmayr's presentation of an alternative post-Holocaust world bring out the darker underside of Baudrillard's "hyperreality."

The final chapter in part 3 turns to Deleuze and Guattari, in some ways the most challenging of the French theorists. Like Baudrillard's ideas on simulation, Deleuze and Guattari's early works on the man-machine interface attracted writers of cybernetic fiction. William Gibson's *Neuromancer*, best known for his introduction of the concept of the matrix, is a key example. Yet major novelists like Thomas Pynchon and David Foster Wallace soon took over the baton, engaging with psychological and social issues drawn from Deleuze and Guattari's *Anti-Oedipus* and *A Thousand Plateaus*. Pynchon's *Vineland* and Wallace's *Infinite Jest* explore the relation of enlightenment rationality to the modern world in which, according to Deleuze and Guattari, we can no longer move in straight lines or engage in logical thinking, but are perennially impelled to think and act in irregular "lines of flight." Finally, the very structure of W. G. Sebald's writing, as I show with respect to *The Rings of Saturn*, enacts these nonlinear thought patterns of Deleuzian theory. Sebald highlights the paranoia that results from the more sinister aspects of modern society into a constitutive feature of his narrative posture.

The overarching argument of *The Novel After Theory* concerns the moral implications of theory. The novelists' engagement with theory consists in part of an attempt to correct the erroneous impression that theory consists in a facile manipulation of unfamiliar terms. In narrative fiction, key ideas of poststructuralist theory emerge untrammeled by cumbersome technical terminology. Some of the most remarkable novelists of the last few decades have confronted ideas originating in French theory with fictional situations that call for moral response, such as the colonial era, the Holocaust and its repercussions, or the problem of apartheid in South Africa. Writers like Marguerite Duras, W. G. Sebald, and J. M. Coetzee, for example, are each deeply informed by theory while also challenging it in subtle and astute ways. Their novels not only put flesh on the bones of poststructuralist theory, they fill its gaps, complete it where it stops short, and argue with it when it appears too reductive. Much of the debate about theory has been motivated by its abstract nature; reading theory in conjunction with its responses in narrative fiction gives the entire discussion a much more vivid aspect.

I *Theories of Textuality*

1 *The Death of the Author*

Few concepts in literary theory have given rise to such agitation as Roland Barthes's notion of the "death of the author," first developed in his essay of the same title (1968). The essay recurred to ideas of Mallarmé and Proust, who argued in favor of a separation between the author of a text and its speaker. Mallarmé's position had largely to do with his conviction that in a literary text, the pronoun "I" is a function of language rather than the expression of a specific person. Proust, though influenced by Mallarmé on this point, was more concerned to shift the critical emphasis away from the author's biography. In opposition to the nineteenth-century critic Sainte-Beuve, who maintained that it was impossible to understand a literary work without detailed knowledge of its author's life and personality, Proust argued that "a book is a product of another self than the one that is revealed in our habits, our social life, and our vices."[1] Modern linguistics, Barthes argued, gave new support to this idea by developing a new conception of what a text is: recent linguistic theory no longer accepted a simple continuity between a writer and a text produced by that writer. Barthes had already made this point in his contribution to the conference at Johns Hopkins in 1966 when some key French thinkers of the time first presented their ideas to an American audience: "The 'I' of the person who writes," he said on that occasion, "is not the same as the 'I' who is read by 'you.'"[2] The 1968 essay, "The Death of the Author," elaborated on this point in a more radical way. "Writing is the destruction of every voice, of every point of origin," Barthes wrote.[3] The old notion of authorial originality is not justified, since every text is in fact nothing more than a web of language. Every writer builds on what has been written before. Multiple linguistic elements—familiar phrases, fragments from other texts, arguments with points made by others—come together to create an assemblage that cannot solely be ascribed to a single, unitary author. "Writing is that neuter, that composite, that obliquity into which our subject flees."[4] The text should not be understood as produced by an author, but rather by an anonymous "scriptor," a writing mechanism devoid of individuality, interiority, or intention. This meant that real-life authors no longer had exclusive authority to determine the meaning of their works. What held any given text together was not the author who had written it, but the reader in whose mind the various elements of the text came together. Thus, in what was to become a much-cited flourish, Barthes argued at the conclusion of his essay that the "death of the author" gave rise to the "birth of the reader."[5] Texts were constituted not by their authors, but by their readers; and meaning, consequently, was what the reader found in the text.

Barthes's argument in "Death of the Author" differs in crucial ways from the author-narrator distinction that has become a foundational element of literary criticism in English-speaking countries.[6] It is difficult to establish precisely when this distinction was first introduced. Wimsatt and Beardsley's essay "The Intentional Fallacy" (1946), did not specifically mention the author-narrator distinction, but a precursor of the idea might be seen in their argument against the use of extrinsic and in favor of intrinsic evidence in literary criticism.[7] The two Americans were concerned with critical judgment as well as with interpretation. They argued vigorously against the view that "in order to judge a poet's performance, we must know what *he intended*."[8] By the same token, they dismissed appeals to what they termed "author psychology,"[9] which, they claimed, amounted to preferring "private evidence to public, external to internal."[10] Following in their wake, but in a somewhat gentler way, Wayne Booth distinguished between the author and what he called the author's "second self."[11] In a subtle discussion of the degrees of distance that can obtain between the author and various kinds of narrators,

Booth pointed out that "in any reading experience there is an implied dialogue among author, narrator, the other characters, and the reader."[12] In his
discussion of these relations, Booth laid the groundwork for what we now
call the author-narrator distinction. Barthes's "Death of the Author" may
have seemed less shocking to some English-speaking readers who assimilated his ideas to those of Wayne Booth; but in fact, Barthes's essay was far
more radical. Where Booth leaves room for the author by calibrating degrees
of distance between author and narrator, Barthes does not even grant the
author as a point of origin for the text.[13] In arguing, further, that texts are
constituted not by their authors but by their readers, Barthes broke down
traditional ideas about the limits of interpretation. In this respect, his essay
went much further than either Wimsatt and Beardsley or Wayne Booth.

Against the Impersonal Style: Robbe-Grillet's *Ghosts in the Mirror* and Duras's *The Lover*

When Alain Robbe-Grillet first began the text that would eventually become
Le miroir qui revient (1984; translated as *Ghosts in the Mirror*), he believed he
could count on a readership that regarded the concept of the "author" as
outmoded and reactionary. By his own account, he started writing the book
"towards the end of 1976 or the beginning of 1977."[14] Looking back at this
period, Robbe-Grillet noted that the concept of the "death of the author"
had become so thoroughly assimilated that its impact had been substantially
weakened. "The moment a bold theory stated in the heat of battle has become
dogma," he wrote, "it instantly loses its attraction and violence and, by the
same token, its efficacy" (*Ghosts*, 16). *Ghosts in the Mirror*, he decided, would
challenge the formerly audacious concept by raising the older idea of the personal author. In one of many reflective passages in the book, he claims, "I've
never spoken of anything but myself" (*Ghosts*, 14). Robbe-Grillet was determined to question the rigid distinction between the author and the narrator
of the text. In addition to taking issue with the academy's unquestioning
acceptance of "the death of the author," however, he was not merely contest-
ing the concept of the impersonal scriptor. He was more specifically taking
up a debate between Jean-Paul Sartre and Roland Barthes during the 1950s
about the neutral style of writing introduced by Albert Camus.

In *Writing Degree Zero* (1953), Barthes described the style of Albert Camus'
novel *The Stranger* (1942) as a "transparent form of speech" that achieves "a

style of absence which is almost an absence of style."[15] The opening paragraph of *The Stranger* gives a good impression of Camus' manner: "Maman
died today. Or yesterday maybe, I don't know. I got a telegram from the
home: 'Mother deceased. Funeral tomorrow. Faithfully yours.' That doesn't
mean anything. Maybe it was yesterday."[16] This transparent style was, for
Barthes, the "degree zero" of writing: it is language stripped to its basics. In
the debate between Sartre and Barthes, the term used for this type of writing
was *écriture blanche* ("blank style" or "blanched white style"): for Sartre the
term was negative, for Barthes it was positive. The French word *blanc* means
both blank and white. Sartre regarded Camus' *écriture blanche* as an avoidance of political engagement. By contrast, Barthes believed that the neutral
mode was a way of frustrating the reader's expectation that meaning was to
be sought in the characters' inner life and the assumptions raised by the narrative about social reality. The new style, Barthes claimed, forced the reader
to work harder in order to make the novel meaningful. In this way, it functioned to undermine traditional assumptions and push the reader toward
a more radical understanding of reality. This type of novel interested him
because it shifted attention to writing as such.

The collection of essays by Robbe-Grillet titled *For a New Novel (Pour un
nouveau roman*; 1963) summed up the principles of what was becoming a distinctive literary movement. Michel Butor, Samuel Beckett, Nathalie Sarraute,
and Claude Simon were other important practitioners of the New Novel, in
which plot and character recede while minute details move to the forefront,
slowing down the reading process and hampering ready access to a sense of
narrative wholeness. Despite the movement's considerable international success, however, it had begun to run its course by the late 1970s. Robbe-Grillet
himself began to feel the need for a new approach.

Throughout *Ghosts in the Mirror*, he takes issue with the notion that the
narrative voice of his early works is a "blank" one. Given the support he
had received from Barthes from the mid-1950s on, this may seem somewhat
ungrateful; but by the 1970s and 1980s, the culture was more overtly politicized. Now Robbe-Grillet needed to show what a careful reader of his earlier
texts would have perceived: that he had in fact never failed to confront political
and moral issues.[17] *Ghosts in the Mirror* is certainly not written in Robbe-Grillet's earlier manner. Its style is complex and its structure multilayered: different
modes combine to create a text composed of many different ingredients.

The opening paragraph of *Ghosts in the Mirror* speaks from an autobiographical position: it tells how Robbe-Grillet first began working on the book.

But even as the book seems to set up an "autobiographical pact,"[18] it also comments on the problem of the personal versus the impersonal style. In this way, the opening defies the automatic reaction of contemporary literary criticism that calls for readers to distinguish between author and narrator. Early in the book, however, the autobiographical stance is interrupted by forms of writing less easy to identify. Gradually, we come to realize that *Ghosts in the Mirror* is an intercalation of three different literary genres: autobiography, literary essay, and romance. This mixture complicates our understanding of characters and events, of reality and fiction, and the often unclear lines between the component genres create challenging ambiguities for the reader.[19]

In a memoir-like passage, Robbe-Grillet tells us that his early novel *The Voyeur* (1955) received two important reviews. One, by Maurice Blanchot, focused primarily on the sexual crime at the invisible center of the novel, while the other, by Roland Barthes, did not notice at all the narrator's elision of this crime (*Ghosts*, 135). It seems odd that Barthes, the proponent of the blank style, did not look for what it might conceal. Did the blank style have the effect, at least on some readers, of obscuring moral issues? If so, that would appear to give Sartre the victory in the debate about stripped-down writing. In *Ghosts in the Mirror*, Robbe-Grillet claims that his own early style was in fact a coat of armor that concealed something quite other than the innocence it seems to project (*Ghosts*, 38). He goes on to suggest that there may be a connection between Barthes's insistence on the impersonal mode and his apparent inability to perceive ethical issues hidden beneath the surface of texts written in such a mode.[20]

Most of the autobiographical material in *Ghosts in the Mirror* has to do with historical and political reality. The mysterious Henri de Corinthe, who appears not only in the autobiographical parts of the book but also in those that imitate medieval romance, encapsulates the problem of the blanched white style. In the medieval romance plot, which recounts old Breton stories told by Robbe-Grillet's grandmother, Corinthe appears as a kind of white knight, swept up in an emotional search for his lost bride.[21] His actions in the autobiographical parts, however, stand in direct opposition to the white knight figure. Here, Henri de Corinthe is revealed to have been a neighbor of Robbe-Grillet's father, a political reactionary and Nazi sympathizer during the German occupation of France. We never discover exactly where Corinthe stands politically: we do not know if he is a collaborator or a member of the resistance.[22] This strand of the book reflects on the history of the German occupation of France by pointing out that, in addition to courageous men and women of the resistance, there were also people who collaborated with the Nazis. This raises tough questions about the "blanched white style." Barthes's use of the term to apply to *The Voyeur* is troubling precisely because the novel calls for its readers to recognize the unmentioned crime at its center. The emergence of the New Novel in the 1950s was solely an experiment in writing: it was also a way of probing blind spots, not just those in an individual field of vision, but those in our broader understanding of self and history. It is no accident that these novels began to appear in the fifties, a period when collaboration with the Nazis could scarcely be addressed outright, but when the immediate shock of the occupation was making a collected appraisal more possible. From this perspective, the "blanched white style" covers up the guilt of a narrator who refuses to confront directly crimes in which he himself may have been indirectly implicated. The apparently clean and innocent surface conceals something disturbing underneath. It is a cover that invites us to pull it away. To regard *The Voyeur* as merely a formal exercise would be to underestimate the moral scope of the novel.

What is the connection between the two versions of Henri de Corinthe? In the flamboyantly written medieval episodes, Corinthe is connected with a mirror that keeps on reappearing in the course of his wild ride. The mirror alludes to Stendhal's famous phrase about realism: "The novel is a mirror being carried along a road."[23] Through this allusion, Robbe-Grillet's text engages with the traditional problem of realism, yet it does so, paradoxically, in its more stylized rather than in its plainer sections. This also raises questions for the reader. Why does *Ghosts in the Mirror* make this link with realism? In order to answer this question, we need to recall that the New Novel was also realism of a sort. Stripping away the dense description that had characterized the nineteenth-century novel, the New Novel restricted itself to what could be seen from the vantage point of a single character. Yet its point of view was concerned not only with what the character saw, but also with the blind spot in the character's field of vision. Robbe-Grillet's *Ghosts in the Mirror* is a retrospective on his earlier novels, which reflected on French guilt during the German occupation even as they seemed to focus on quite different topics such as, in the case of *The Voyeur*, sexual jealousy. In this way, *Ghosts in the Mirror* argues against the notion that the blanched white style is one that avoids engagement with moral issues.

One year after the publication of Robbe-Grillet's *Ghosts in the Mirror*, Marguerite Duras presented her own challenge to Barthes in *L'Amant* (1984; *The Lover*).[24] The temporal closeness of the two works and the fact that both lack the genre definition "novel" beneath their titles suggests a new phase in these writers' understanding of the author function.[25] Like *Ghosts in the Mirror*, *The Lover* also depends on autobiographical material, while at the same time teasing the reader about the degree of fictionality with which it is cloaked. By using an unnamed narrator, Duras's narrative appears at first glance to support Barthes's contention that writing is a disembodied function that is neither the author as a person nor the author in the guise of a literary personage.[26] Yet although the narrator remains anonymous, the text ends with a precise indication of the time and place of composition: "Neauphle-le-Château—Paris. February–May, 1984" (*Lover*, 117). These were places where Duras actually lived at the time, as many French readers would have been aware.[27] In effect, *The Lover* challenges the reader to decide whether the book emanates from an empirical author, located in the real world, or a blank narrative mechanism cast in the Barthesian mold. Duras's spare style contrasts tellingly with the emotion that permeates her novel.

Duras's *The Lover* also explores questions of guilt and complicity. The mother's fits of madness and the older brother's violence are symptoms of a colonial situation in which white people, however badly off they may be, are nonetheless perceived as superior to the original inhabitants of Indochina. The novel turns on the paradoxical social consequences of its narrator's involvement with an older Chinese man who helps the family survive financially while bringing shame upon the adolescent girl. At the center of the book, however, the setting shifts from the narrator's childhood in Indochina to her adult years in Paris. World War II and the political complications of the German occupation briefly take over the narrative. Two mysterious foreign women, Marie-Claude Carpenter and Betty Fernandez, make a brief appearance, yet we find out little about them. Fernandez and her husband, Ramon, are explicitly described as collaborators (*Lover*, 68),[28] while the narrator reveals that she herself, by contrast, was a member of the Communist party. How is the war period connected with the narrator's childhood in Indochina? The reader is left to draw the lines between colonial violence and life under German occupation.

In the year after the publication of *The Lover*, Duras published a memoir of the war years under the title *La Douleur* (1985; the word means "pain," but the book was translated as *The War: A Memoir*). It consists of several narratives written mainly in 1944 and not finished until 1985. Here we see Duras working with François Mitterrand in the resistance movement, we see her fending off the amorous advances of a Gestapo officer, and we see her interrogating a collaborator. The most poignant of these pieces depicts the return of her husband, Robert Antelme, from the Nazi concentration camp Bergen-Belsen. Although most of the people in these stories are given full or partial pseudonyms, the text leaves little doubt that it reflects Duras's personal experience. This book is, as it were, the lower part of the iceberg whose tip we see in the Carpenter and Fernandez sections of *The Lover*. As such, it provides a key to the exploration of guilt and suffering in the 1984 book. The novel's stripped-down style does not depersonalize experience, but deals directly with its particular intensities. It does not evade moral issues, but profiles them more clearly and more poignantly.

One way to read *The Lover*, then, is to see it as a pointed debate with Barthes's theories about the impersonal style. Far from being the expression of a neutral instance, Duras's style is an expression of profound pain that cannot be adequately articulated. The reader must work to apprehend this difficulty and to supplement the narrative by filling the gaps left by traumatic experience. In this case, we need to ask whether the narrator could have done more to help her mentally disturbed mother and her violent elder brother, with whom she admits that she has something in common. Could she have rescued her younger brother whom she loves more than her other family members? Was she right to consort with the Chinese lover, whose patronage ensured that the family had food to eat but whose attitude to them demeaned her and brought shame on them? Why does the book end by alluding to cheap romance novels ("he had said that it was still as it had been, that he still loved her, that he could never stop loving her, that he would love her unto death"; *Lover*, 117)? The solution to these difficulties lies in the book's complicated time line. Only after the narrator's experience during the Nazi occupation does she begin to understand how much she had compromised herself in Indochina. She now sees how easy it is to go along with something wrong, even against one's own interests. Those who collaborated with the Germans during the occupation now appear in a new light. The blanched white style sets these complications more clearly into relief than would a more traditional narrative mode.

Playing Games with Roland Barthes: Laurens's *Index*

In contrast to Duras and Robbe-Grillet and separated from them by seven years, Camille Laurens presents a parody of the "death of the author" in her debut novel *Index* (1991). A French professor of literature, Laurens[29] has produced an entire series of novels that are also witty explorations of literary problems. Her novel, *Dans ces bras-là* (2000), with its Durassian title, won the Prix Femina and was subsequently translated into English as *In His Arms*.[30] Laurens is a virtuoso stylist with a gift for wordplay, a fine sense of irony, and a deft use of intertextual allusions. *Index* exemplifies Barthes's contention that writing always consists of "multiple writings, proceeding from several cultures and entering into dialogue, into parody, into contestation."[31] Still untranslated and possibly untranslatable, *Index* is an ingenious metafiction. Without the slightest heavy-handedness, the novel explores such issues as the relation of art and reality, readers' identification with fictional figures, the narrative presentation of consciousness, problems of ambiguity, and matters of literary genre and form.

Index revolves around a book that is also titled *Index* and whose author is also named Camille Laurens. This doubling of the title and the author's name creates a loop effect, ingeniously complicated by gender ambiguity (in French, Camille is both a male and a female name)[32]. The protagonist, Claire Desprez, buys the fictional novel *Index* at a railroad bookstore and is shocked to read in it an account of her own life—or so she thinks. In a grotesque parody of Barthes's theory, the novel presents what Claire experiences as a frustrating run-around as she attempts to identify the author of the railroad station novel. Similarly, the exterior (real) reader follows the interior (fictive) reader, Claire, as she as she goes on her frantic search for the author of the railroad station book. *Index* depends on a discrepancy between the sophisticated exterior reader and the naïve interior reader. In this way, the text engages in a long lineage of novels that reflect on the problematic nature of reading. Like such predecessor novels as *Madame Bovary*, *Index* explores the issue of empathy between reader and text, but Claire's relation to the railroad station novel goes beyond emotional identification. Whereas Emma Bovary is a romanticizing reader of books, Claire is a literalizing reader. From her perspective, someone has flagrantly exposed her personal life to the world; she is determined to find the scoundrel and take him to task. Naturally, Claire is ignorant of the theoretical debates about authorship. The novel suggests, however, that Claire's search for the author is destined to be a wild goose chase. The narrator tells us that Claire has never been a serious reader: Chateaubriand's *Memoirs from Beyond the Grave* props up a heavy armoire in her Paris apartment (*Index*, 90), while her everyday reading is limited to newspapers and magazines. In contrast, epigraphs to each of the novel's main sections alert the exterior reader of Laurens's *Index* to the novel's horizon of literary expectations. Quotations from Carlyle, Rimbaud, Borges, Hugo, Mallarmé, Barthes, and Beckett indicate a metalevel on which *Index* can be understood as a reflection not only on the theme of reading in the novel, but also on the fundamental nature of literary texts altogether.

Although the narrative presents Claire's outrage about the railroad station *Index* from outside, it nonetheless refrains from revealing the full reason for her distress until close to the end. Mundane as Claire's life seems to be, she turns out to have been keeping the secret of an unwanted baby that she had abandoned many years before. Retrospectively, this casts a new light on her correspondence with the publisher of the railroad station book. In response to her complaint that the author has made use of her life to create his fiction, the publisher explains that it is precisely the life-like aspect of literature that permits the reader to see it that way: "It is one of the miracles of genuine literature that it touches in its readers that which is most profound and authentic in the human being. Every individual who, like you, recognizes himself [the original uses the masculine] in one of the books we publish indicates that we were not mistaken [in deciding to publish the book]" (*Index*, 121).

This conception of good literature as universal is matched by a conversation between Claire and a student she notices reading *Index* on the train. Repairing to a café, they argue over the gender of the author and over the location of the narrated events. Claire justifies her view of the novel by arguing that it tells the story of a "childhood friend" of hers, albeit with a number of errors. The student is skeptical: "Are you certain," he asks, "that you recognize your . . . childhood friend? For after all, if you've noticed so many errors in the story, perhaps it's simply that it doesn't speak of you, or rather, of her" (*Index*, 223). Half-persuaded by this reasoning, Claire begins to think that she must put the old story behind her and "turn the page" (*Index*, 241): after all, the female protagonist of the novel is called Blanche, not Claire. "Do all the Irises, Roses, and Violets identify with the Marguerite of novels, did they exclaim in chorus in letters to the publisher, 'The Lady of the Camellias, c'est moi'?" (*Index,* 240).[33] In symmetry with the copy of Chateaubriand's memoirs that props up her armoire at home, she leaves her copy of the railroad station novel beneath one foot of a glass vitrine in the Mauresque Villa, the house of the writer Guy de Maupassant (*Index*, 241).

Throughout the better part of the novel, however, Claire is figured primarily as an unsophisticated reader who cannot believe that the events narrated in the railroad station novel are not derived from real-life events. Her attempt to locate Camille Laurens by consulting the Paris telephone directory results in a comedy of errors. A tango teacher of that name, energetically denying authorship of *Index*, forces her to take a lesson from him. Although the dancing teacher claims that "you live the tango, you don't narrate it" (*Index*, 142), the text in fact narrates this tango brilliantly. Closing the gap between text and body, textuality and sexuality, this episode conveys what Barthes called the "pleasure of the text."[34] "The text you write," Barthes wrote, "must prove to me *that it desires me*."[35] But although the dance teacher in *Index* demonstrates that the fulcrum of the tango is the male partner's sexual organs, Claire refuses to participate in the erotic game. Claire's belief that the railroad station *Index* is a scandalous exposé of her own life prevents her from responding with pleasure to either the dance or to the novel itself.

Claire's literal-mindedness prevents her from escaping the seductive effects that fiction sets for the reader. Still prey to unreflecting identification with the novel, Claire now suspects her former lover Alexandre Blache (coincidentally a professor of literature) has written the book under a pseudonym. Dropping in on one of his lectures, Claire is astonished to find that he is discoursing upon the same sort of narrative structure that characterizes the railroad station novel. Untutored in literary matters, she cannot differentiate among the many forms novels take. The reader, however, is well aware of the inadequacies in Claire's understanding of literary texts.

Shortly before the conclusion of *Index*, a report on a bizarre set of events reaches the editor of a literary magazine. Is the submitted text in fact a report? Could it be a short story? The typewritten text bears the title "Enquête" (Investigation), and is signed "Camille Laurens." Narrated by someone who appears to be a private detective, the text recounts how he was asked "to make a certain chick . . . read a certain book" (*Index*, 232). The method by which the narrator accomplishes this task bears resemblances to the circumstances under which Claire bought the book *Index* at the railroad station, and the woman for whom the book has been "planted" on the newsstand display leads a mundane life like Claire's. Yet neither her name nor the title of the book is mentioned. There is no way of telling whether this text provides the solution to the mystery of the railroad station novel or whether it is just a random piece of creative writing. The style mimics that of hard-boiled detective fiction like Michael Connelly's Harry Bosch novels. The journal editor, worn out from dealing with cases of possible plagiarism, cannot tell whether the story is original or not. The reader of *Index* might be inclined to assume that the magazine submission originates with the author of the railroad station novel. Yet the identity of Camille Laurens remains a mystery, in jocular accord, as it were, with Barthes's theory that texts do not originate with their authors.

The ambiguous ending of *Index*—in which Alexandre Blache seems to have gone mad in imitation of Guy de Maupassant, and Claire and the curator of the Guy de Maupassant house end up in a possibly fatal car crash—is reinforced by an incomplete and equally ambiguous index that pointedly runs from A to F, spanning the gamut from *abandon* (surrender) to *folie* (madness). By refraining from including a large portion of the alphabet, the index of *Index* suggests on one level that it might be well just to drop all this foolishness. Yet on another level, this index, like that of Nabokov's *Pale Fire*, can also be read with profit. In contrast to an index in a nonfiction work, the index highlights themes and motifs, places and objects that recur in the book. It alerts the reader to the careful construction of the novel as a literary text. At the same time, it teasingly suggests that further study of the text might yield the key (*clé* is one of the terms indexed) to the mystery.

When Laurens returns to the incomplete alphabet in two subsequent books, *Romance* (1992) and *Avenir* (1998), filling in first one part of the alphabet and then another, the reader might assume that these two novels are continuations of *Index*. They move in quite different directions from the first novel, however. Still, even her prize-winning *In His Arms* contains numerous allusions to Barthes, Lacan, and other theorists. Throughout her entire series of novels, Laurens continues to play with theories of textuality originally developed by Barthes and his contemporaries.

The Hand of the Scriptor: Atwood's *The Blind Assassin*

By the time Barthes's essay on "The Death of the Author" entered the canon of English-speaking universities around the world, the original presuppositions of his argument were no longer generally accepted—if they had ever fully been outside of France. The impersonal style (represented in English almost single handedly by the novels of Samuel Beckett) had not only become outmoded, it had become virtually unthinkable. Readers wanted the immediacy of authentic experience, and as a result, questions of authenticity came to the fore. Barthes's essay was not about authenticity, but its title now seemed to evoke new questions about authors who turned out not to be what they had seemed.

Margaret Atwood's *The Blind Assassin* (2000), a Booker Prize winner, is without doubt the most brilliant fictional enactment of the "death of the author" understood as a problem in authenticity. Presented with bravura and punctuated by knowing winks and allusions, the novel explores some of the major paradoxes of Barthes's claim that texts do not possess a specific point of origin located in an individual author. The novel's central conceit is that its narrator, Iris Chase Griffen, has published a book called *The Blind Assassin* under the name of her deceased sister, Laura Chase. By having one sister write the book in what masquerades as the voice of the other, Atwood exposes a troubling aspect of the "death of the author." Narrating as Laura permits Iris to present her own adulterous love affair with Alex Thomas as a genuine experience of her sister's. Women readers who believe it to be Laura's story feel it speaks directly to them: they respond to what they see as its authenticity. For these readers, the narrated experiences are all the more moving because their author is no longer alive. From Iris's point of view, in contrast, Laura's death is convenient. Atwood uses this clever intrigue to comment playfully on Barthes's "death of the author." What happens if we take the French thinker's concept literally?

If it is not the author's biographical self who is doing the writing, then all kinds of improprieties, transgressions, and even crimes can be recorded with impunity. Or so it might seem. The scriptor, in Barthes's exposition, is like the copyist of an earlier time: in contrast to the author, who let us believe that he was "transmitting his 'confidences'" to us,[36] the scriptor does not express himself, but rather "no longer contains passions, moods, sentiments, impressions," but is simply a product of "an immense dictionary."[37] Can such a scriptor bear any sense of moral responsibility? From Barthes's perspective, the scriptor comes into being with the text itself and has no existence before or after it. By the same token, Iris tells us that, while writing the book, she thought of herself as a "bodiless hand, scrawling across a wall." (*Assassin*, 512). Writing the story in the guise of someone else, Iris achieves something akin to Barthes's idea of writing as "the black-and-white where all identity is lost, beginning with the very identity of the body that writes."[38] Iris may believe that she is merely taking on her sister's persona, but in order to do so, she is also dipping into a vast reservoir of textual possibilities.

As if taking literally the notion of writing as a "negative," the novel employs a photograph as one its principal motifs. The snapshot shows Laura and Iris standing on either side of Alex Thomas at one of their father's annual firm picnics. There are two copies of the photo, one in which Laura's image has been cut away, the other in which Iris's image has been removed. When we first see the snapshot, we are not told which side has been cut away: "Over to one side—you wouldn't see it at first—there's a hand, cut by the margin, scissored off at the wrist, resting on the grass as if discarded. Left to its own devices" (*Assassin*, 5). At the second mention of the photo over five hundred pages later, we are informed that this time, at least, the copy is the one where the left-hand side is cut off. By this time, we also know that it was Iris who was standing to Alex's left when the photo was taken: "The photo has been cut; a third of it has been cut off. In the lower left corner there's a hand scissored off at the wrist, resting on the grass. It's the hand of the other one, the one who is always in the picture whether seen or not. The hand that will set things down" (*Assassin*, 517). Not until this fairly late point in the novel does Atwood resolve the question of which sister actually did the writing.

The cult of admiring readers who lay floral tributes on Laura's grave can be seen as a grotesquely literal version of Barthes's claim that the "the birth of the reader must be requited by the death of the Author."[39] Needless to say, Iris richly appreciates the ironic situation that makes it possible for her to watch her own fans placing flowers at the gravesite of the book's alleged author. She dryly comments that for them, she was merely "Laura's odd, extra hand, attached to no body—the hand that passed her on, to the world, to them" (*Assassin*, 287). According to Iris, the real-life Laura was not only verbally inept, conversing with her was "like talking to a sheet of white blotting paper" (*Assassin*, 200)—an example, in other words, of what Sartre and Barthes call the "blanched white style." Near the end of the novel, Iris writes: "Laura was my left hand, and I was hers. We wrote the book together. It's a left-handed book. That's why one of us is always out of sight, whichever way you look at it" (*Assassin*, 513). The ingenious *chassé-croisé* of Atwood's novel is a comic commentary on the bizarre effects that arise from Barthes's conception of the scriptor when it is taken literally.

The authorship problems that arise from Iris's forgery of her sister's memoir are complicated by a series of inset stories told by Alex Thomas. In the course of Iris's affair with Alex, the two invent an elaborate set of narratives that are also part of their love play. While Alex initiates the tales, Iris guesses ahead and proposes new variants for stories in progress. The tales function on two levels: on the one hand, they cement the lovers' relationship, but on the other hand, they serve as first drafts of science fiction comic books that Alex has been commissioned to write. This dual purpose means that the versions they create at their trysts cannot actually be the final versions. Accepting some of Iris's feminist suggestions during their times together, Alex is well aware that he cannot adopt them for his primarily male readership with their eagerness to read about "never-fail dead women, slavering for blood."[40] Still, when Iris comes across the first published comic book in a drugstore, she is aghast to see that Alex has omitted her contributions. Does this matter, though, if texts really have no point of origin, as Barthes claims in his essay? From an admittedly exaggerated theoretical standpoint, Iris might be said to have reverted to an unsophisticated position on the question of authorship.

The Blind Assassin involves yet another wrinkle: its frame narrative is written in a retrospective at considerable remove from the events it narrates. Iris, the narrator of this frame, is eighty-three years old. Her love affair with Alex, Laura's death, and Iris's writing of Laura's supposed memoir are now temporally distant. This permits Iris the luxury of another narrative convention: that telling a story brings new understanding. Rather than the victim she has always considered herself to be, she now recognizes that she has in fact been indirectly responsible for three suicides: those of her sister, her father, and her husband. The novel she attributes to her sister was published shortly after Laura's death in 1945; Iris is writing the new book in 1999. Copyright on "Laura's novel" has now lapsed, Iris notes, and thus "Laura's novel" passes prematurely out of its real author's control. But, as we discover toward the end of the book, Iris is writing all this shortly before her own death. The newspaper obituary about Iris Chase Griffen is inserted just before the final pages of Iris's text. Who put the announcement in this place? Is it the scriptor? We do not know.

The mysteries that remain unsolved until close to the end of the book, such as which sister actually had the affair with Alex Thomas, continually put the author's identity into question. In this way, Atwood's novel at once confirms and undermines the theory of the "death of the author."

The Scriptor After the Holocaust: Darville's *The Hand That Signed the Paper* and Krüger's *Himmelfarb*

The tension that emerged from the split between poststructuralist theory and readers' expectations is perhaps most clearly evident in the debates surrounding Helen Darville's *The Hand That Signed the Paper* (1994).[41] Educated in

Australia at the University of Queensland, Darville was introduced to post-structuralist theory in various English literature courses, but at the same time she was also exposed to a trenchant critique of the "death of the author" by her tutor, Con Castan, a scholar and translator of writing by recent immigrants to Australia. In a cultural situation where the ethnic identity of a writer is important, the concept of an impersonal scriptor is virtually unintelligible.

The status of Darville's novel is difficult to assess: is it a serious work of literature or a parody of recent theory? Darville published it under an assumed name, Helen Demidenko, and gave her female narrator the name Fiona Kovalenko (Fiona, as it happens, is Darville's own middle name). In the novel, Fiona is the daughter of Ukrainian immigrants to Australia. The story is Fiona's account of her family history, based on tapes her grandmother has sent at her request. This theme builds on wide recognition of the value of oral history, a form prominent in Australia at the time. Against this backdrop, it was not surprising that the public was outraged when it turned out that Helen Demidenko was not herself Ukrainian. From the point of view of literary theory, however, this public anger seemed scarcely justified, given that the narrator Fiona Kovalenko was, after all, a fictional figure.

To a large extent, the problem arose because Darville played the part of Helen Demidenko following the book's publication and, more disastrously for many readers, even after it had received several literary prizes. Posing as Helen Demidenko, Darville presented herself at public events in a rudimentary Ukrainian costume that apparently convinced a surprising number of people. A peasant blouse, high boots, and an elementary knowledge of Ukrainian folk-dancing were all she needed to complete the illusion.

What few readers saw at the time was the way in which *The Hand That Signed the Paper* engages with Barthes's famous argument that writing was an impersonal product. From this perspective, Barthes wrote, "his [the scriptor's] hand, detached from any voice, borne by a pure gesture of inscription (and not of expression), traces a field without origin—or at least, with no origin but language itself, i.e. the very thing which ceaselessly calls any origin into question."[42] The author's identity was thus totally irrelevant to her text. The title Darville chose for her novel, a quotation from a 1933 poem by Dylan Thomas, should have tipped readers off that she was playing with a grotesquely literal version of Barthesian ideas; but in the epigraph to her novel she cleverly omitted the most relevant stanzas of the poem. These stanzas raise precisely the moral issues that Barthes did not broach in "The Death of the Author":

The mighty hand leads to a sloping shoulder,
The finger joints are cramped with chalk;
A goose's quill has put an end to murder
That put an end to talk.[43]

Unlike the guilty hand of the tyrant in Thomas's poem, the "hand" that writes Helen Darville's novel is that of the scriptor—one that, according to Barthes's theory, cannot be connected to any real shoulder at all. From this point of view, it does not matter whether Helen's last name was Demidenko or Darville: she is simply enacting Barthes's theory of the "detached" hand of the author. Darville's concealment of her actual ethnic identity (Anglo-Australian) is probably best understood as a prank played by a student of contemporary literary theory.[44] But despite a few glitches, one of them an unlikely description of Fiona Kovalenko's Ukrainian immigrant father amusing her school friends by imitating the English actor John Cleese, she carried off the prank with remarkable sophistication.

The novel is full of knowing winks. In one passage, the narrator even invokes Martin Heidegger and his claim that "authenticity emerges out of a basic condition of inauthenticity." Within the historical context of the novel's thematic concerns, collaboration with the Nazis during the 1940s, Heidegger can hardly be seen as a completely untainted figure. Even the author's pen name, Demidenko, is drawn from another work of literature: Anatoli Kuznetsov's *Babi Yar: A Documentary in the Form of a Novel* (1967) mediated by D. M. Thomas's flamboyantly postmodern novel *The White Hotel* (1981).[45] The plagiarism charges that arose in connection with *The White Hotel* (precisely because of its use of material from Kusnetsov) had also raised questions of authenticity. Finally, the authorial posture of *The Hand That Signed the Paper* throws into sharp relief the puzzling contradiction in contemporary thinking about literary texts: how can we retain the concept of "the death of the author" while also valuing texts that wrestle with their author's personal experiences of class, ethnicity, or gender? In effect, Helen Darville exposed the incompatibility of these two coexisting approaches to literature.

The novel's central theme was Ukrainian collaboration with the Nazis during the period of World War II. More relevant to Australia of the 1990s was the way the book took up the topic of war crimes trials that were then taking place in Australia. The trials had unleashed passionate debate. Should one leave war criminals in peace because they are now elderly and frail—and also have descendents who are loyal Australian citizens? Or should one pursue them regardless of such scruples? The oral history taped by Fiona's grandmother, an account of her experiences in Ukraine under the Nazi regime, puts a personal face on what might otherwise have remained a remote abstraction for many Australians. The responses of other family members, friends, and Fiona herself represent the range of opinion about the war crimes trials that was current in Australia at the time. Although a substantial portion of the novel consisted of the grandmother's memories of Ukraine, the novel's link to Australian debates about war crime trials persuaded the Miles Franklin Prize committee that Darville deserved the award (the condition of the prize is that the winning entry have relevance for Australian culture).

Although Darville's publisher at first tried to make her remove some passages that might be thought anti-Semitic, she strongly resisted this suggestion. The novel's dual point of view—the grandmother's tapes embedded in the granddaughter's frame story—meant that racist views, where they appeared, could be attributed to a particular character rather than to the author herself. Concerns over this problem, not only in the publishing house but also among some members of the Miles Franklin Prize committee, were allayed to some extent by this argument. The real battle broke out after it was discovered that the voices in the novel were not those of "authentic" Ukrainians and their descendents. The novel had seemed more interesting—and more poignant—when it seemed to have been written by a Ukrainian-Australian washing her family's dirty laundry. The scandal of Darville's imposture changed public reaction dramatically. Attention to the guilt of Nazi collaborators suddenly shifted to her own fraudulent attempt to pass herself off as an ethnic author. By using the quotation from Dylan Thomas as the motto of her novel, Darville had indicated that she was well aware of the debates about the impersonal scriptor. By the same token, she was also aware that this notion brought with it a possible charge that the "death of the author" might in certain cases be an evasion of the author's moral responsibility. The text of her novel probes this issue in far-reaching ways. To be sure, the novel has manifest imperfections, not least its inability to sustain its tone evenly throughout and to get all of its historical facts straight. Still, if Helen Darville had refrained from her publicity-seeking antics, her book might have gained a more serious hearing, and the literary establishment might have explored more deeply the question of moral responsibility in the context of the "death of the author." Despite several book-length publications and a great deal of journalistic energy devoted to the matter, however, the implications of the Darville case remained inadequately thought through.

In particular, the novel took up several issues that were important to Australian culture at the time. First, the question of what it means to be Australian should not simply have been reduced to the ethnic heritage of Helen Darville and the conditions of the prize itself. The novel in fact probes the issue of Australian identity quite closely, and the John Cleese glitch is a telling indicator of its position on this point. Is an immigrant father more appealing if he comes from England rather than Ukraine? What is the role of the older immigrants, those who had come as refugees from World-War-II Europe, in the new context of a more multicultural society that includes immigrants from Vietnam and other Asian cultures? Second, naïve assumptions about the value of oral history needed to be reconsidered in more sophisticated ways. To what extent can oral histories stand alone? *The Hand that Signed the Paper* suggests that the younger generation needs much richer historical contextualization of oral memoirs in order to understand them fully. Further, the novel's allusions to theory cry out for more elaboration. Issues of memory and trauma hover on the edges of the novel, but do not receive the young narrator's full attention. In the end, the public furor over the author's ethnic identity drowned out major questions raised (at least implicitly) by the novel's narrator.

Michael Krüger's novel *Himmelfarb* (1993) hinges on the appropriation of a book manuscript by someone other than its actual author.[46] As head of the German publishing house Hanser, Michael Krüger is familiar with international trends in literature and literary theory. His own writing treats fashionable paradigms and catch phrases with a humorous touch. One obvious example is his novella *The End of the Novel* (1992), a farcical tale that plays on modish ideas like Fukiyama's "end of history." *The End of the Novel* tells the story of an author who is struggling to reduce an ungainly eight-hundred-page novel in progress to a more manageable shape and size. Making cut after cut in his manuscript, he tries to "kill off" his protagonist and ultimately the novel itself. With *The End of the Novel*, Krüger is only a step away from the problem of the "death of the author," a topic he addresses directly in *Himmelfarb*.

Set in the early 1940s, the novel explores a complicated relationship between a German and a Jew. The narrator, Richard, a doctoral candidate in ethnography who has received a grant from the German government to study native cultures in Brazil, needs an assistant with skills in native languages. In a stroke of ironic coincidence, the person he hires is a Jew, Leo Himmelfarb, an aspiring novelist whose first book was prohibited by the

Nazis. Leo has fled to Brazil in order to escape persecution. This situation—that Richard's work is financed by the very government that has expelled his assistant—is the primary motor of the novel. It means, among other things, that Richard knows from the outset that he will not be able to acknowledge Leo's contributions to his work in any reports he files with his university.

Like some of the other novels we have considered, *Himmelfarb* is premised on a playfully literal reading of Barthes's conceit about the "death of the author." Richard's status as an internationally renowned anthropologist rests on his publication of notes that Leo had dictated to him from his logbook while he was suffering from a serious illness. Assuming that Leo had died in the jungle, Richard publishes Leo's dictated text under his own name some years after his return to Germany. Obviously, a sophisticated author and editor like Krüger does not take Barthes's dead author metaphor as any less of an intellectual construction than Fukiyama's claims for the end of history. To take theory seriously does not mean, however, that one cannot have fun with it in fiction.

According to Barthes's theory, as we have seen, it is not the writer but the reader who constitutes the text. Yet in *Himmelfarb*, Leo and Richard are both writer and reader at different moments. Leo writes the logbook in his tiny indecipherable hand; he reads from it during his illness when he dictates the text of the book to Richard. Since Richard is merely an amanuensis, one might say that he is more truly a "scriptor" than most other authors. When Leo, now living in Israel, discovers a Hebrew translation of the book three decades after Richard's publication of the text under his own name, he sends an angry letter to Richard chastising him for stealing his work. One might expect that much would be lost in translation into another language, but the translator has managed to keep many of Leo's images and characteristic modes of expression. The fact that Leo's style comes across in the Hebrew translation of material that Leo had originally dictated in German only underscores the irony of the situation.

Himmelfarb is a witty reconfiguration of Barthesian ideas that underscores its awareness of literary theory by humorous allusions to the writing process throughout the narrative. The opening of the novel, for example, dwells insistently on Richard's hands, finger, and handwriting as he metaphorically shovels the grave of the friend whose text he has stolen. The death of the author gives rise to the birth of the imposter, we might say. In the depths of the Brazilian jungle, fueled by indigenous drugs, Leo recites poems by Mallarmé. In Mallarmé, Barthes had written, "language performs."[47] For Barthes,

Mallarmé's poetry is precisely the kind of writing in which the speaking subject is nothing other than a function of language itself. Leo's drug-inspired performance of the famous poems is a witty enactment of Barthes's claims.

An entire chapter of the novel focuses on Richard's attempts to evade inquiries from an old friend of Leo's about how he can get in touch with Leo. At first Richard writes that to the best of his knowledge, Leo has probably died. When Leo's friend persists, Richard continues his evasive posture, suggesting (contrary to Occam's razor) that the friend may be thinking of an entirely different person with the same name. On a visit to Germany, the friend continues to be frustrated by Richard's evasiveness. "Don't get me wrong, dear friend," the visitor remarks, "but sometimes I think you killed Leo" (*Himmelfarb*, 153). Subsequently, the old friend himself is "found murdered, without the circumstances that led to his death ever being cleared up" (*Himmelfarb*, 151). These allusions to death form an amusing commentary on Barthes's theory. With the suspicious friend no longer alive, who apart from Leo is left to challenge Richard's claim to authorship of the famous anthropological study?

In a final ironic twist, the novel ends with the presumptive death of the narrator, Richard. He and Leo have arranged to meet on the island of Corfu, and Richard anticipates this encounter with a mixture of wariness and resignation. Before leaving Germany, he makes elaborate preparations for his own death, giving away treasured possessions, selling his house, and removing the logbook from his bank deposit box where it had been safely hidden. It seems almost improbable that this fraudulent author is actually planning to take Leo's logbook with him. "Down with posthumous fame!" he thinks to himself, as he enters the bank to get the logbook (*Himmelfarb*, 151). In the future, he reflects, some other scholar may perhaps discover that the logbook is written in the hand of "a different writer, unfortunately not identifiable" (*Himmelfarb*, 177). At the end of the novel, Richard is sitting on the sand waiting for Leo and writing in a notebook the story we are reading. There is still space, he notes, for "one word." At this point, the text breaks off, leaving the reader to imagine what this word might be—a nice tip of the hat to Barthes's claim that the death of the author means the birth of the reader.[48]

Despite these playful elements, *Himmelfarb* is also a very serious novel. Like almost all of the novels we have examined in this chapter, *Himmelfarb* builds on Barthes's theory of the "death of author" in order to raise important questions. If writing is a mere mechanism of language, how can a literary text address the moral issues involved in reflection on National Socialism? Surely we cannot accept Richard's attempt to absolve himself from ethical responsibility toward Leo? By leaving blank the space in the notebook where Richard might have written a final word, *Himmelfarb* reminds us that sometimes a crucial apology remains unspoken. Readers who fill in the missing word are imaginatively enacting that apology. If the novel gives birth to such readers, its playful approach to the "death of the author" may have a moral function after all.

The Death of Paul de Man: Adair's *The Death of the Author* and Banville's *Shroud*

The question of ethics is broached rather differently in two British novels that bring the "death of the author" into relation with the Yale professor and literary scholar Paul de Man.[49] One of the main channels through which French poststructuralist thought entered the American university system was the Yale School, clustered around de Man. Upon the later discovery that de Man had written articles for a fascist newspaper in Belgium during the German occupation, a scandal broke out that led some critics to decry poststructuralism as a whole. Perhaps their distance from the American academic scene accounts for the fact that two British writers turned the de Man affair into fiction: Gilbert Adair in *The Death of the Author* (1992) and John Banville in *Shroud* (2002).

Adair's short book is an academic parody in the David Lodge mode: set at a university called New Harbor, its narrator is a professor and theorist named Leo Sfax. There is no pretense at subtlety in the construction of Sfax's ideas: his approach to literature is called "the Theory," and his most decisive work bears the title *Either/Either* (pronounced "eyether/eether"). The central premise of Sfax's book is "that literary meanings were generated not by their nominal author but from an accumulation of linguistic conventions and codes" (*Death of the Author*, 23). This is as good a paraphrase as any of the argument Barthes makes in "The Death of the Author" about the origin of texts. In a move that parodies popular notions of deconstruction, Sfax argues that every text can ultimately be found to say the opposite of what it may have been "meant" to say. Although Sfax hardly reaches the standards set by David Lodge's Morris Zapp, Adair's spoof of fashionable terminology ("aporia" is one of Sfax's favorite terms) testifies to the pervasiveness of poststructuralist theory in university departments of literature and the resistance it engendered.

Yet there is something more at work in Adair's *Death of the Author*. The plot culminates in a double murder, the first of which is merely a set-up to distract from the second. The real target is a feminist scholar named Astrid Hunneker, who, having recently embarked on a biography of Sfax, will inevitably uncover his collaboration with the Nazis. Ruminating about what he can do to prevent Astrid from finding out about his past, Sfax has an idea that directly alludes to Barthes's essay on the author: "What, I thought, was to prevent me from *truly* killing the Author, and along with Him one author in particular whom I despised above all others and whom I longed to liquidate, to use the picturesque military formula, with extreme prejudice?" (*Death*, 89)

The novel is deftly structured around several unresolved mysteries. The most prominent of these is Sfax's death. Is he the victim of a faked suicide or did he actually pull the trigger himself? Within Sfax's first-person narration, the statement "then he pulled the trigger" is a narratological enigma akin to the aporia or dead end that, according to Sfax's theory, is an inevitable element in any text. Who has written these words? Even more puzzling is the epilogue that states that "Ralph's [the possible murderer's] apprehension and arrest followed my death by no more than a matter of days" (*Death*, 131). Yet if it is true that all authors are "dead," there is no reason why Sfax cannot continue to write. Ultimately, the narrator concludes that "death *is* merely the displaced name for a linguistic predicament" (*Death*, 135). Folding strangely back on itself, this narrative experiment refuses to resolve paradoxes that, in Barthes's theory, must remain irresolvable.

In comparison to this academic satire, Banville's darker *Shroud* (2002) makes ampler use of facts about de Man's life and works. Networks of imagery in the novel, including that of light and darkness, absence and presence, invoke the deconstructive tradition that de Man had inherited from Derrida. An additional ingredient in the psychological makeup of the protagonist is drawn from the life of Althusser, who murdered his wife by strangulation.[50] A central theme of the novel, the ways in which the dead haunt the living, allows Banville to address the notion of the "death of the author" in a way that also suggests a possible dark side to theory.

Like several novels we have examined in this chapter, *Shroud* turns upon an identity theft, the details of which emerge in layers, as if the narrator were peeling an onion. Told from the point of view of the guilty party, the narrative is also traversed by other voices, many speaking from beyond the grave. By the time we reach the end of the novel, it is not clear how much of the narrative is a hallucination on the part of a narrator who has caused the death not only of his wife Magda, but also perhaps of his lover Cass Cleave, and, indirectly, his friend Axel Vander, whose name he appropriated during the German occupation of Belgium. References to literary and philosophical writers also abound, among them Coleridge, Shelley, and Nietzsche. Major incidents in the narrator's life are modeled on Paul de Man's early collaborationist writing and Louis Althusser's murder of his wife. As Lene Yding Pedersen comments in an astute essay on *Shroud*, "it is hard (fallacy or not) not to read these names in a kind of referential way. It is true that when we say that we hear the voice of de Man or Shelley in Banville, we think not so much about the 'persons' de Man, Shelley or Banville, but rather their writing. From this point of view 'personal identity' is textual identity."[51]

The narrator's relation to the Axel Vander of wartime Belgium is complex. Although he initially took his friend's name to avoid deportation by the Nazis, he had long envied Axel's talents. His impersonation of his dead friend enables him to attain an important academic position in the United States, yet also brings with it constant fear of exposure. Under this stress, he concocts a plan to absolve himself from the fraud if his imposture is ever revealed: he would claim that he himself had written the anti-Semitic articles and had simply persuaded Axel to "put his name to them" (*Shroud*, 151). Yet he resists the idea that he has drawn any benefit from Axel's name. Instead, he claims that "Axel Vander's reputation in the world is of my making. It was I who clawed my way to this high place. I wrote the books . . ." (*Shroud*, 150). In this way, the original Axel Vander, in fact the victim of the narrator's unwillingness to track him down after his departure from Belgium, is transformed into a beneficiary of the narrator's theft of his name. Intriguingly, even the impostor has never succeeded in writing the study of Coleridge's aesthetics that Axel had planned: "He did not live to write that book, and when, years later, I tried to write it instead—to write it for him, as it were—I could not do it either" (*Shroud*, 146). If the false Axel Vander is hampered by residual guilt toward his friend, it is strange that he was able to write the other books in the first place. What is it about Coleridge that throws up such a roadblock? On one level, the problem may be a kind of transference from Coleridge's own difficulties in finishing such works as "Kubla Khan" and "Christabel." On another level, Vander's difficulties may be connected with Coleridge's distinction between imagination and fancy. For all his ability to write other books in his predecessor's name, the narrator simply does not have the creative ability that Coleridge terms "imagination," a powerful faculty that can create an organic unity out of diverse ingredients. For this reason, Coleridge explains, imagination is "essentially vital," whereas fancy is a weaker faculty, associative rather than truly creative.[52] Vander the narrator is not "vital" in Coleridge's sense: he has, after all, taken over the persona of a dead person.

In addition, the false Axel Vander is obsessed with death. He believes that he can see and hear his late wife Magda, while the young Irish girl Cass Cleave, with whom he has become romantically involved, also believes that she can communicate with the dead. After her suicide (or has she been pushed from the church tower?), the narrator claims that the story we are reading is really being told by her. "Who speaks?" the novel begins. "It is her voice, in my head. It talks to me as I haul myself along these cobbled streets, telling me things I do not want to hear" (*Shroud*, 3).[53] This confusion about the origin of the narrative can be seen as an adaptation of Barthes's theory that a text has no single, definable point of origin.

Plagued by "the awful possibility that the mind might survive the body's death" (*Shroud*, 16), the narrator fears the possible fate of living death. Presumably this obsession derives from his recognition that the dead Axel Vander lives on in the books written by the false Vander. His fear that he might actually witness the final demise of his own bodily system alludes to an experiment recounted in Poe's tale "The Facts in the Case of M. Valdemar" (1845). This story about a man who dies while under hypnosis and thus can remark on his own death, was part of the discussion at the 1966 conference in Baltimore. When Roland Barthes adduced what he believed was an impossible utterance—the sentence "I am dead"—Jacques Derrida countered by citing Poe's story, where the hypnotized man utters precisely these words.[54] In a subsequent essay (1973), Barthes analyzed the story in further detail, using it to show how communication functions by means of identifiable linguistic codes. These, Barthes writes, function much as mesmerism was thought to do, by means of a fluid exchange in which "there is a passage of something from one subject to another."[55] Writing, Barthes explains, draws its strength from an excess of overlapping codes and voices, but most importantly, "writing occurs just at the moment when speech ceases, i.e. from the moment when we can no longer identify who is speaking and we can only establish that speaking has begun."[56] This statement is an elaboration of the views Barthes had already set forth in "The Death of the Author." In addition, Poe's

"Valdemar" also illustrated, for Barthes, the fundamental "undecidability" that constitutes "a structural condition of narration."[57]

Banville's *Shroud* takes to an extreme Barthes's idea of texts as a complex mixture of different voices. The labyrinth of speakers in the novel presents navigational difficulties for the reader. Not only do we hear Vander, Magda, and Cass, there is also a seemingly impersonal narrator: the text oscillates between first- and third-person presentation. The multiple voices that speak beyond death recall not only Barthes's "death of the author," but also Paul de Man's favorite figure of speech, apostrophe, which he understood as a kind of converse with the dead.[58] *Shroud* is punctuated by apostrophe, either to the narrator's deceased wife or to the dead Irish girl.

Shroud alludes in multiple ways to poststructuralist theories of difference, erasure, word play, and writing as defiguration.[59] More than academic allusions, these motifs are also connected with larger ethical issues. Franco Bartoli, the companion of the dying Kristina Kovacs, voices this fact with barely concealed malice when he explains that "Professor Vander . . . holds that every text conceals a shameful secret, the hidden understains left behind by the author in his necessarily bad faith, and which it is the critic's task to nose out" (*Shroud*, 222–223). Vander's own "shameful secret," of course, goes beyond the doubleness inherent in any text. He bears guilt for having escaped the Nazis when Axel did not succeed in doing so, and may in fact have been the "treacherous friend" (*Shroud*, 256) who denounced Axel and led to his death. In the last analysis, furthermore, Vander's guilt is also the result of his claim that the critic can perform his task without ideological commitment.[60] By introducing this idea, Banville evokes the debates about poststructuralist playfulness and its seeming avoidance of moral conviction.[61]

It is striking that so many novels that engage with "The Death of the Author" also wrestle with issues concerning the Holocaust. In different ways, collaboration with or sympathy for the Nazis is at issue in *Ghosts in the Mirror*, *The Lover*, *The Hand That Signed the Paper*, *Himmelfarb*, and *Shroud*. In some instances, as in Duras's *The Lover*, the reference to collaboration is brief, but it is tellingly placed at the very center of that novel, where it functions as a comment on the theme of French imperialism that takes up the larger part of the book.

The big question at issue in this sampling of "death of the author" novels is whether the notion of an "impersonal scriptor" lets real authors off the hook of moral duty. In *Ghosts in the Mirror*, Robbe-Grillet argues that a seemingly neutral style of writing is not necessarily a way of avoiding responsibility. The blanched white style demands, rather, a specific kind of reading that considers the historic context in which the New Novel was born—a context in which it was scarcely possible to admit that any French citizens had been at fault during the Nazi occupation of France. *Himmelfarb* and *Shroud* also hark back to the Nazi past. Theft of a manuscript and theft of a name are set against a historical backdrop that calls for moral judgment. These novels put Barthes's "Death of the Author" to the test of difficult realities and ask their readers to reflect on the moral burdens this conjunction brings with it.

In what may well be the last gasp of the novel's dialogue with the "death of the author," J. M. Coetzee's novels *Diary of a Bad Year* (2007) and *Summertime* (2009) also allude to the concept. Guilt about leaving South Africa, the country that motivated him to write some of his most remarkable fiction, is doubtless part of Coetzee's reason for picking up the theme. *Summertime* (2009), a partial autobiography organized around the conceit that a biographer, unable to interview Coetzee himself after his death, is reduced to talking with various friends and colleagues of his in order to find out the truth about Coetzee's life and character. In contrast to Coetzee's more straightforward autobiographical accounts of earlier parts of his life in *Boyhood* (1997) and *Youth* (2002), this sequel (covering the period 1972 through 1977) permits Coetzee to present himself from an ironic and self-deprecating perspective. The strategy of inventing interviews after his death enables him to probe the moral implications of his actions during an important period of his life in South Africa from a perspective that purports to lie outside the perimeters of his own subjectivity. In this respect, *Summertime* joins novels like *Himmelfarb* and *Shroud* that mobilize the "death of the author" as a way of exploring moral issues. By displacing the historical point of reference from the Holocaust to South African apartheid, Coetzee's novel testifies to the continuing usefulness of the "death of the author" as a literary trope to probe the issue of narrative responsibility.[62]

2 *Structure, Sign, and Play*

   The novelists closest to the scene in which theory emerged were also the most keenly aware that, despite its apparent formal abstraction, it was not really divorced from real life. Indeed, writers like Marguerite Duras and Alain Robbe-Grillet might be seen as bringing its latent historical and social underpinnings to the fore while also "writing back to it" from their own vantage points. Yet few scholars who heard Jacques Derrida's lecture, "Structure, Sign, and Play in the Discourse of the Human Sciences" in 1966,[1] realized that, in addition to speaking about the history of structuralism, the argument of the talk had hidden roots in circumstances specific to Derrida's life. Readers who encounter the text of the lecture in an anthology today are no more likely to be aware of this connection. If we look closely at this text, we can discern two intertwined strands: one concerned with disciplinary history, and another that derives from personal experience. Lee Morrissey has shown that, while writing on one level about Saussure's inauguration of a new academic method, Derrida was indirectly describing his own complex relation to his native country, Algeria, a French colony during the time of his childhood and adolescence.[2] With the advent of the Vichy government, the young Derrida was subject to its laws, which did not permit Jewish children to be educated in the French school system. His expulsion from high school in 1942 was a first exclusionary experience that was decisive for his later thought. In 1949, he left Algeria for France, where he spent several years in intense preparatory courses before being finally admitted to the prestigious *Ecole normale supérieure*. This personal journey from the colony to the metropolitan center and from exclusion to acceptance lies not too far beneath the surface of his 1966 talk in Baltimore.

The lecture begins by describing Ferdinand de Saussure's introduction of a structural approach to the study of linguistics as a decisive "event."[3] What interests Derrida about Saussure's method is that it was at once a break with older conceptions of sign systems and a reconfiguration of those ideas that brought their intrinsic ambiguities to the fore. Derrida's term for the advent of structuralism is "rupture"—though it is a rupture that is also a "redoubling," a reworking of familiar territory using new techniques. Thinking about structuralism allows Derrida also to reflect on the way in which any structure is supported and governed by a "center." Traditional thought about structure, he says, claims that "the center is, paradoxically, *within* the structure and *outside it*."[4] As Morrissey argues, Derrida's references to "the center," can be understood, among other things, as reflections on the circumstances under which Algeria was subjected to an overseas government but later managed to escape that government's purview.[5] The emphasis on "rupture" can be related not only to Derrida's expulsion from school, but also to the historical rupture of the Algerian War.[6] From this perspective, one can see why he claimed, many years later, that "in order to recast, if not rigorously refound a discourse on the 'subject' . . . one has to go through the experience of deconstruction."[7]

Deconstruction, as Derrida uses the term, means to think of opposites as coexisting tendencies that, reduced to their most basic denominator, function as a presence that is at the same time an absence. A vivid way of understanding this paradox is to think of the figure-ground illusion: if we focus on the white goblet in the center of the image, the goblet might be said to be "present"; if we focus on the black human profiles on either side of the goblet, the profiles are "present." Both the goblet and the profiles are there all the time, of course: it's simply a matter of which dominates in our perception at any given moment. In deconstruction, the idea of simultaneous presence and absence determines not only spatial but also temporal configurations:

language, for example, both makes things present and establishes distance (since it is not, after all, identical with what it presents through its system of signs). This two-faced aspect of language gives rise to a sense of "broken immediateness" and nostalgia for what thus appears to be an "absent origin." In order to uncover such ambiguities, we need to learn to perceive in new and different ways.

The aim of deconstruction is to show that texts not only say what they state on the surface, but also include opposing statements that lie below. To read a text from the deconstructive perspective is to read it both with and against the grain. Only when we have uncovered what at first remains hidden in the text, Derrida argues, can we begin to understand the tension between the evident and the less overt significance of the text. The first step in this kind of reading is to establish a binary system that pairs the key terms of the text's surface with their opposites. Deconstruction assumes that when one term of a binary pair is present in a text, its opposite is also implied: every positive also has its negative. Yet Derrida does not rest there. Instead, he attempts to overcome binary thinking by disturbing the traditional hierarchy in which what is present takes priority over what is not. Derrida does not simply over-turn the overt meaning of a text by substituting its opposite. Instead, he opts for what he terms "undecidability," in other words acceptance of the text's inescapable ambiguities. The paradoxes inherent in texts are irresolvable; undecidability is part of the intrinsic nature of texts. Derrida's close attention to language permitted those who had been trained in close reading or "expli-cation" (in the French usage) of literary texts to continue the exercise with a new twist. Instead of focusing on words, images, and motifs that constitute the aesthetic wholeness of the text, the deconstructive reader looks for con-flicts and contradictions. These apparent chinks in the argument are now key moments in the text, since they bring the reader straight to the ambiguities at the heart of linguistic expression. The French word *brisure*, with its dual meaning of "break" or "hinge," is a central concept in Derrida's understand-ing of language and how it functions.[8]

This characterization of language is not merely abstract, however. Der-rida's experience of xenophobia in Algeria subtends his description of writ-ing in *L'Ecriture et la différance* (1967; *Writing and Difference*), a book that includes the lecture "Structure, Sign, and Play." The French verb *différer* means simultaneously to differ and to defer. Language, the medium in which distinctions are made, is paradoxically an instrument that separates us from the world to which it claims to refer. This means that texts are both unified and divided within themselves, coherent and yet undermining their own assumptions. The underlying idea is that we cannot think sameness without also thinking difference, difference without also thinking sameness.

Barbara Johnson, the most significant mediator of Derrida to the English-speaking world,[9] was—pace Morrissey—hardly unaware of "the Francophone North African situation."[10] She not only recognized that *différance* also applied to social differences such as gender and race, but also set forth the consequences of this recognition.[11] In her discussion of Paul de Man's wartime writings, furthermore, she posited a political reading of a "rupture" addressed by deconstructive theory that also incorporates the major event of the twentieth century, the Holocaust.[12] Still, for some English-speakers who took up the practice of deconstruction, Derrida's strategy was closer to a "method" than a far-reaching philosophical position. In order to capture the elements that sometimes fell by the wayside in the English-language reception of Derrida, we need to look more closely at his 1966 lecture.

"Structure, Sign, and Play" sets forth a complex argument about the reductive nature of structuralism and its preference for working with binary opposites. As Derrida notes, the linguist Saussure was the initiator of structuralist method; but he does not use Saussure's work as his prime example. Instead, he shifts his focus to Claude Lévi-Strauss's approach to anthropology. On the one hand, this move allows Derrida to work with material that resists purely formal analysis. On the other, it enables him to focus on a discipline that had come into being at the high point of the imperialist venture:

> What is the relevance of this formal schema when we turn to what are called the "human sciences"? One of them perhaps occupies a privileged place—ethnology. In fact, one can assume that ethnology could have been born as a science only at the moment when a decentering had come about: at the moment when European culture—and, in consequence, the history of metaphysics and of its concepts—had been *dislocated*, driven from its locus, and forced to stop considering itself as the culture of reference.[13]

One of the key problems ethnology (anthropology) had to confront was that of studying another culture from the position of an outsider—an outsider, however, who had lived for a time within the target culture, to the degree that a stranger can do so. The anthropologist's intellectual movement between the familiar and the unfamiliar, self and other, is precisely the operation that, for Derrida, underpins all inquiries into sameness and difference. The process of looking back and forth between the two objects (in the case of Lévi-Strauss, cultures) in order to identify their similarities and dissimilarities is part of what Derrida understands by the concept of "play." Derrida opposes this method to the process of "totalization," which, instead of moving infinitely between the two objects of comparison, subsumes the unfamiliar object into the familiar system, judging it by the measure of the familiar alone. Alluding to the strong centralizing tendency of the French cultural system, Derrida observes that "play" is a term "whose scandalous signification is always obliterated in French" precisely because its existence depends on "the lack or absence of a center or origin."[14] To put it somewhat differently, play tends to work against hierarchical thinking.

Derrida places this new way of thinking about the relation between self and other against the backdrop of a revisionary concept of history. "History," he claims, "has always been conceived as the movement of a resumption of history, as a detour between two presences." [15] This extremely condensed statement needs to be understood as an expression of suspicion toward traditional history as a construct dependent on a specific cultural "center." It is no accident that the age of empire and the rise of nationalism are historically linked. These two powerful forces are implicated in what Derrida calls traditional history, and they are part of what he finds suspicious about it. Accordingly, Derrida argues that history and play are in tension with one another: "play is the disruption of presence," because play refuses to recognize positions of dominance.[16] Play, as he understands it, is tantamount to recognition of "irreducible difference."[17] The notion of irreducible difference is, of course, opposed to the totalizing imperialist view. Not for nothing is the typical gesture of the imperialist a panoramic mountaintop view that makes an explorer feel like the "monarch of all he surveys."[18] Several of the novels that engage with Derridean theory also take issue with the imperial past.

Colonialism and the Dislocation of Culture: Duras's *The Lover*

Marguerite Duras's personal experience bears some resemblance to that of Derrida. Both were born in French overseas colonies and did not move to France until they were ready to enter university. In this sense, they both participated in what has come to be called the process of decolonization—

although this process worked itself out rather differently in the two countries where they spent their respective childhoods.[19] Born and brought up in French Indochina (a federation of territories that included today's Vietnam, Cambodia, and Laos), Duras spent some childhood vacations in France, but Indochina was her home until she moved to France for good in late adolescence. As a French child living overseas young Marguerite had followed the same curriculum as all French schools; yet her mother's aspirations for her children could really only be fulfilled in France. As a girl, Duras thus experienced something closely akin to what Derrida describes as a system that has its center "paradoxically *within* the structure and *outside* it."[20] In the 1990s, Derrida explored this paradox more explicitly in *Monolingualism of the Other; or, The Prosthesis of Origin*,[21] which takes its starting-point in his complicated relation to the French language. This short book is a meditation on a claim he formulates on its opening page: "I have only one language; it is not mine" (*Monolingualism*, 1). Duras's *The Lover* (1984), built around similar paradoxes ("I have never written, though I thought I wrote, never loved, though I thought I loved," *Lover*, 25) probes with particular poignancy the connection between the colonial situation and the critique of structuralism.

Playing with the book's ambiguous status between autobiography and fiction, *The Lover* opens with a public reading by Duras, or more properly, a fictional stylization of her. A member of the audience comes up to the writer after the reading to tell her how much he prefers her lined, older face to the one he recalls from years ago. She herself believes, however, that her face was "laid waste" (*Lover*, 3) or "destroyed" (*Lover*, 4–5) at an early age: when she arrived in France from Indochina at the age of seventeen. Her departure from the colonies is interpreted here as a decisive rupture not only in her sense of self, but also in her personal appearance. Marked by wrinkles, her face has become a desert landscape that resembles a dried-up version of the watery delta of the Mekong where she spent her childhood. The incantatory voice of the narrator in *The Lover* seems to speak from beyond the barrier formed by the physical and psychological devastation caused by the girl's dislocation from margin to center.

The narrative proper begins with a description of the young (unnamed) narrator standing on a ferry about to cross the Mekong River on her way to the dormitory where she lives while attending high school in Saigon. In the memory of her later self, the image of the younger self endures; yet no photo was ever taken of the fifteen-and-a-half-year-old girl on the ferry.[22] Despite some regret over this lack of visual evidence, the narrator believes that she owes her power as an author precisely to its absence. If a photo existed, it would testify to her past; without it, she must testify to it through writing. The narrative's double opening—the scene of the literary reading and the reconstructed description of the young girl—depends on a rupture between past and present and enfolds that rupture into its structure. The girl's later departure from Indochina, her separation from her Chinese lover, and a series of losses that include the death of a brother and her mother's continuing failure to make a success of life, combine to create something akin to what Derrida terms "the absence of a center or origin."[23] As colonial culture, which posits Paris as its center, reveals its explanatory inadequacy, everything is thrown back on the individual subject, in this case, the young woman who decided early in life to become a writer.

Yet for precisely the same reason, it is impossible to be an author or "origin" in a world that no longer functions with respect to a clearly defined center. Looking back at a long literary career, the narrator is perturbed by the recognition that she has "never written" though she "always wrote" (*Lover*, 25). Circling incessantly around the problem of writing—writing that represents experience but that also reveals gaps in experience—the narrator despairs of ever resolving this paradox. But this is precisely the point. A photograph of her son with two friends, taken during a trip in California, seems to balance the nonexistent picture of herself on the ferry in Indochina. Unlike the real photo of her son, the imagined photo of herself is subject to constant metamorphoses. Details appear and disappear as she tries to recall her younger self, yet the snapshot of her son keeps superimposing itself on the image in her mind's eye. The poverty of the hand-me-down dress she wore on the ferry is overlaid by her son's casual clothing, which—in her view—deliberately mimics poverty. Pictured with two white Ugandan friends, her son seems to her like a "white Ugandan" himself. She is struck by his arrogant but also self-mocking smile, an expression she cannot imagine herself having adopted during her childhood in Indochina. Nonetheless, this photograph "comes closest to the one never taken of the girl on the ferry" (*Lover*, 13), a teenager whose cheap gold-lamé sandals and petulantly provocative look announce her as ready to step out of the bourgeois bounds set by her school-teacher mother. For the narrator, the real photo of her son and the imagined photo of herself form the positive and negative of a single image. The photo not taken sets in motion a series of substitutions that puts into narrative form the decentering that she has undergone. Her gaze, moving back and forth between the mental image and the real photo, enacts the process encapsulated in Derrida's term *différance*.

The Lover is structured around numerous paradoxes involving presence and absence. First in a series of critical absences is the girl's dead father: his absence denotes the lack of a patriarchal center that the girl's mother is unable to fill, even though as a school teacher, she stands in for the centralized French system. Psychologically damaged by her struggle in the colonies, her relation to her children alternates unpredictably between firmness and flexibility. In moments of apparent mental absence, she loses control over them, as when she allows her daughter to buy the rose-brown felt hat and the provocative gold lamé sandals. The girl's brothers cannot substitute for the absent father or provide a sane counterbalance to their mother's erratic behavior. The older of the two, a violent child and later a cruel young man, undermines their mother's efforts to reestablish herself in France by his uncontrollable violence, dissipated lifestyle, and addiction to gambling. In accord with the novel's theme of oppositions, the other son is the opposite: passive and ineffectual. The narrator says of him that he "couldn't speak, could scarcely read, scarcely write, sometimes you'd think he couldn't even suffer" (*Lover*, 106). Yet she adores him and may perhaps have had an incestuous relationship with him.[24] His death long after their departure from Indochina forms another rupture in the narrator's psyche.

Just as the photo of herself on the ferry does not exist, so, the narrator claims, "the story of my life doesn't exist" (*Lover*, 8).[25] She feels, furthermore, as if she herself were not really alive: "My younger brother gathered me to him, drew me to him, and I am dead" (*Lover*, 105).[26] This feeling is intensified by her partial identification with her school friend Hélène Lagonelle, a developmentally handicapped girl unable to manage even the most rudimentary schoolwork. Hélène's lack of self-awareness gives her an "almost illusory" quality (*Lover*, 73) that is belied by her sexually mature and exquisitely beautiful body. Hélène and the narrator's younger brother have much in common: they are at once her opposites and her doubles. As the text unfolds, the narrator appears in many ways more substantial than either of these two figures, yet she continues to assure us that her own life is illusory and inauthentic. One of the most striking features of this narrative is the way in which it succeeds in holding these two views of reality in suspension.

The girl's love affair with a Chinese man also enacts the theme of presence that is also absence. The "man from Cholon," an outsider to the local society, is tolerated only because his father has brought business to the area. And although the girl's affair with him is based on erotic attraction, it is partly motivated by economic necessity as well: the expensive Chinese meals to which he treats her family enable them survive their financial duress. Again, two views are held in suspension: the family's need for the dinners and their profound scorn for the man who is paying for them. By acting as if he were not there while eating the sumptuous meals, the family is locked in an irresolvable dilemma. The narrator's ambiguous feelings about him and the underlying Western bias they betray becomes evident when she observes his smooth, almost hairless body during their lovemaking. In her mind, he acquires an odd equivalence with Hélène, a paradox that aligns with other disruptions of traditional gender boundaries throughout the novel. The analogy between Hélène and man from Cholon is cemented, as it were, when both go away to enter arranged marriages. When the Chinese lover telephones the narrator many years later and tells her that he would "love her until death" (*Lover*, 117), his clichéd language is a poignant rendering of the dominance of discourse in a decolonized world.[27]

In addition to these paradoxes concerning authenticity and illusion, other motifs also contribute to a narrative structure determined by repeated reversals that nonetheless do not lead to the resolution of ambiguities. Earth and water form one set of motifs that represent these irresolvable tensions. The Mekong Delta, with its shifting boundaries, forms the backdrop of the narrative. There are joyous moments involving water, such as the periodic house cleanings in which the floors are thoroughly sluiced and water flows around the legs of furniture, even around the legs of the piano, and the children squeal with delight. Water is also pleasurable when the Chinese lover pours large jars of water over the girl's naked body. Yet the girl's mother remains trapped in a hopeless struggle to protect her land against the ravages of the ocean, a struggle that never comes to an end. Later, when the narrator leaves Indochina on a steam liner, the ocean tempts her with thoughts of suicide. In retrospect, she thinks that someone actually leaped over the railings to his death, but then she remembers that this was actually a story she had heard about a classmate of hers who had been on a different ship. Like the "photo never taken," this story represents an impulse not acted upon:

> And the girl started up as if to go and kill herself in her turn, throw herself in her turn into the sea, and afterwards she wept because she thought of the man from Cholon and suddenly she wasn't sure she hadn't loved him with a love she hadn't seen because it lost itself in the

affair like water in sand and she rediscovered it only now, through this moment of music flung across the sea. (*Lover*, 114)

This run-on passage deftly captures the paradoxical nature of the young girl's experience as she tries to cope with her departure from Indochina; at the same time, it also captures the ambiguities of the older narrator's struggle to give coherence to her memories.

The narrative is constituted as much by gaps as by what is presented. Forgetting, omitting, not knowing, not speaking: all these are structural elements in the novel, just as functional as remembering and communicating. The story is told in short sections that jump unpredictably from one time frame to another. Episodes are told and retold, often with significant differences and punctuated by questions about their truth status.

At the very center of the novel, the narrative leaps forward to World War II and its immediate aftermath; yet although this section of the book delves into issues of political agency, responsibility, and guilt that reflect indirectly on the colonial past in which the affair with the Chinese lover takes place, it is a center that at first appears to be a digression. In fact, however, it is a thumbnail sketch of resistance and collaboration in wartime France that forms an instructive foil to the story of the girl and her family in Indochina. Behind both stories lie questions about the mandate to prevent wrong and the difficulties of actual intervention in real events.

The narrator addresses the issue of colonial guilt in several ways. First, the story of the mother's ineffectual struggle to cultivate land on the flood-prone flats of the delta is a metaphor for the way in which Western attempts to domesticate the East are frustrated by the foreignness of these territories. Second, the actions of the cruel older brother reflect the repressive structures of the colonial system. Third, the erotic relationship between the young lovers is corrupted by the power of money. The Chinese man exploits for his pleasure a young white girl his family will never permit him to marry, and at the same time the French family exploits him for the financial support he brings even while he also ruins their daughter's reputation. In this way, *The Lover* not only rethinks an individual story, but also meditates on colonial power, oppression, and violence. This historical dimension is precisely what Derrida means when he points to the moment "when European culture . . . had been *dislocated*, driven from its locus, and forced to stop considering itself as the culture of reference."[28] The novel is a powerful reflection on the oppressive force of colonialism and the traces it has left behind.

At the same time as the narrator uncovers her own unwitting complicity in the imperialist project, she resists narrative forms that would impose a false wholeness on this history. *The Lover* proposes alternative stories that cannot be completely reconciled. From this perspective, Duras's reworking of the plot in her subsequent book *L'Amant de la Chine du nord* (1991; *The North China Lover*) can be seen as expression of the unsettled character of the story. Duras wrote this second version as a protest against the more linear form of Annaud's film version of *The Lover*. In particular, Duras was unhappy about Annaud's shift in focus to make the girl an object of observation rather than letting her be the one who recalls, observes, and imagines the experiences represented. A film version of *The Lover* would need to be, in certain respects, a companion film to *India Song* (1974), which also mobilizes competing stories that cannot be satisfactorily resolved. Whereas in *India Song*, the stories emanate from four different voices, in the book version of *The Lover* they originate in a single consciousness that understands itself as multilayered, dissociated, and internally contradictory. Despite its perspicacious reflections on the problems of cinematic representation, *The North China Lover* is less successful than the first version in doing justice to the fundamentally unsettled nature of consciousness and memory. By contrast, *The Lover* succeeds in using narrative to express postcolonial consciousness in terms of recurrent gaps and slippages. By linking the problem of language with the problem of colonialism, Duras's *The Lover* gives life to the seemingly abstract argument of Derrida's "Structure, Sign, and Play": it renders brilliantly the "broken immediateness" characteristic of decentered experience. In its constant oscillation between apparent opposites, the text enacts what Derrida calls the "tension between play and history."[29]

The American Idyll and the Loss of Center: Robinson's *Housekeeping*

Like Duras's *The Lover*, Marilynne Robinson's *Housekeeping* (1980) depends heavily on the oscillation of presence and absence, oppositions and their dissolution.[30] Yet it presents something of a problem case for the "novel after theory." In her book of essays, *The Death of Adam* (1998), Robinson does adopt several positions that derive from recent theory: the notion that history may be "constructed," the question "what fiction is" and "where its boundaries are, if they exist at all," and the notion that "collective fictions matter."[31]

In the main, however, she seems antipathetical to theory in its poststructural forms: she expresses concern, for example, over the extent to which thinking is predetermined in academic courses "by a filter of specialists who can tell us what we must see"[32] and argues for "humanism" against the increasingly hermetic nature of university and college education.[33] The question arises, then, why *Housekeeping* seems so uncannily close to deconstruction.

Part of the answer lies in the way in which several literary models and philosophical systems interact in this novel to create a single luminous text. Robinson reaches back to canonical European works like Rousseau's *Emile* (1762), Wordsworth's *Prelude* (1850), and Nerval's *Sylvie* (1854), as well as to the American Trancendentalists Emerson and Thoreau. A commitment to nature continues in her later publications: the environmentalist exposé *Mother Country* (1989), her essays in *The Death of Adam* (1998), and her two subsequent novels *Gilead* (2004) and *Home* (2008). At issue in all of these works is the question how humane concern for our social and natural environment is to survive in the modern world. History and religion, present only on the margins of *Housekeeping*, take center stage in the two essays on Calvin in *The Death of Adam*, as also in *Gilead*, whose protagonist is an elderly Calvinist minister, and *Home*, which takes place in the home of another minister in the same town.

Shortly before the publication of *Gilead*, an interviewer asked Marilynne Robinson whether *Housekeeping* could legitimately be described as a postmodern novel. Robinson replied that much of what is termed postmodern is not substantially different from the structures and issues at work in a novel like *Moby Dick*. Nineteenth-century writers, she went on to explain, "just knew a great deal about the problem of knowledge."[34] Indeed, she emphasized that these writers confronted the paradoxes inherent in consciousness and experience in a spirit of intellectual exhilaration rather than despair as many people might today. These earlier thinkers are the key, I believe, to the puzzling mixture of deconstruction and old-fashioned common sense in Robinson's first novel.

Several scholars have shown how deeply indebted *Housekeeping* is to nineteenth-century thought, specifically that of the Transcendentalists.[35] Tace Hedrick demonstrates in detail that *Housekeeping* derives its central imagery and characteristic mode of thought from Emerson's essays.[36] His analysis reveals the striking presence in *Housekeeping* of Emerson's ideas about "shifting and sliding borders," "breaches and cracks in one's perception and experience of the world," and the impossibility of finding a "principle of fixity."[37]

The pervasive sense of "loss, erasure, and fragmentation" in Emerson's melancholic essays is imitated, Hedrick shows, in the textual accumulation of related images in *Housekeeping*.[38] Emerson's argument that "the surface upon which we stand is not fixed, but sliding,"[39] and that things in nature "cannot be moored"[40] is echoed in the dominant imagery of *Housekeeping*, and his contention that "the way of life is wonderful: it is by abandonment"[41] underlies the ending, but also much else, in the novel. These images are very close to certain aspects of deconstruction.

Indeed, some scholars have wondered whether Emerson's notion of how thought proceeds might be seen as an anticipation of Derrida.[42] Several of Emerson's essays show affinities with deconstruction: "Illusions," "Nature," "Experience," and "Circles." In his book *Emerson*, Lawrence Buell describes how the new literary theory of the 1970s contributed to a view of "Emerson's fragmentary, self-reflexive prose as an anticipation of deconstructive thinking."[43] In a nuanced discussion of those who have made the case that Emerson might have been "a harbinger of Postmodernism," Lawrence Buell argues that one must balance the advantages of seeing Emerson as a kind of Nietzschean thinker against those of seeing him as a Pragmatist.[44]

Marilynne Robinson's debt to Emerson—she has claimed to be "an Emersonian"[45]—doubtless accounts in part for the seemingly Derridean elements in *Housekeeping*. Tellingly, the balance tilts more toward stable presence in *Gilead* and *Home*, a difference that is not merely thematic, but connected with her choice of narrators in the these novels as opposed to the less "anchored" narrator, Ruth, in *Housekeeping*. When *Housekeeping* appeared in 1980, its success was largely due to its ability to project the idea that something troubling lay beneath a seemingly calm surface. While some readers found its lyrical prose and finely nuanced descriptions mesmerizing, others had initial difficulty with the slow reading it demanded. Yet by inviting the reader to linger and explore the complexities of the narrative, *Housekeeping* held a special appeal for readers trained in close textual analysis. In fact, it illustrates nicely the ways in which deconstruction can be seen as an inversion of the New Criticism. While a New Critical approach permitted readers to bring together the unity that held together what seemed to be slipping away, deconstructive strategies were better suited to understanding the novel's emphasis on ambiguities and contradictions. The notion of rupture, problems of center and margin, and the idea of complicated border-crossings had acquired special resonance in literary discourse, although their provenance in deconstruction was not always openly acknowledged. Robinson's genius was to transform these ideas into what she calls the "extended metaphors"[46] that subtend the novel. Beyond the novel's poetic style and its sensitive treatment of outsiders in a society that would prefer to ignore them, *Housekeeping* struck a chord with readers who were ready to question accepted categories and reconsider familiar cultural expectations.

Housekeeping begins with an opening event that is also a rupture: an accident in which a train slides off a bridge into an ice-covered lake below. In Emerson's terms, the train crash illustrates the notion that "this surface on which we stand is not fixed but sliding."[47] The submerged existence of the train and its dead passengers beneath the surface of the water creates a subtle interplay of absence and presence. Among the dead train passengers is Edmund Foster, the grandfather of the narrator and her sister Lucille. The girls' lives are marked by a similar rupture in which their mother commits suicide by driving her car into a lake. Just as the story of the train's plunge into the water forms a secret pivot for the history of the lakeside town, Fingerbone, the girls' dead mother becomes a defining presence in their imagination, a constant reminder of loss at the very heart of their existence. The two ruptures are thus, on the one hand, what Derrida would term the "absent origin" of mythopoetic activity, and on the other hand, ghostly presences that continue to inhabit cultural and personal imagination. The two stories are at once losses and reminders of a past that never ceases to determine the present.

From the outset, Ruth observes that Fingerbone contains "a number of puzzling margins" (*Housekeeping*, 4). The arrival of the girls' aunt Sylvie, an erstwhile transient who has spent many years riding on freight trains and sleeping under bridges, exacerbates this problem. Even after she comes to take care of the girls, she cannot completely abandon her old life: she likes to join the group of drifters who gather on the edge of the town or to leave housework undone while she wanders in the woods. In her resistance to the middle-class lifestyle, she embodies a key argument of Emerson's "Circles": "People wish to be settled: only as far as they are unsettled is there any hope for them."[48] The novel at once confirms and questions the conventional view of the transients who gather by the tracks and hop aboard the freight trains to experience random adventures.[49] While her sister Lucille opts in the end for the settled life, Ruth stands by Sylvie even when the authority figures in the town condemn her. Sylvie takes, in effect, an Emersonian position toward transience and fixity: when circumstances force her to look after her orphaned nieces, she splits the difference by living in the house as if she were still a hobo. Ruth formulates Sylvie's unspoken idea: "if she could remain a transient here [in the house], she would not have to leave" (*Housekeeping*, 103). Ruth, too, tries to have it both ways. When the house is flooded, she imagines a manner in which a seemingly stable home can also be on the move: "if the house were not to founder, it must soon begin to float" (*Housekeeping*, 125).[50] A house can still be home even when it is transformed into a boat. In this way, the novel develops a network of alternatives that are never fully separable: land and water, light and darkness, sanity and insanity, culture and nature, housekeeping and transience. Events are at once posited and revoked; home is established while it is also allowed to disintegrate.

Robinson's decision to have Ruth narrate the story is akin to Emerson's construction of the speaker in "Circles." By giving Ruth a sister who is in part her opposite, however, Robinson completes the dialectic between shifting and stable views that Emerson develops in his essay. Emerson builds this opposition into his argument by having his speaker imagine the reproaches some readers will lodge against it. In *Housekeeping*, similarly, Lucille gradually emerges from her original companionship with Ruth as a more clearly defined opposite of her sister. Yet, as is inevitably the case with such dialectical movements, Ruth and Lucille are not completely cut off from one another. Under Sylvie's influence, both girls enter her fantasy world for a while: "We were now in Sylvie's dream with her" (*Housekeeping*, 110). Ruth and Lucille each contain aspects of the other, despite the radically different paths they ultimately take. The novel's conclusion suggests that they are not even fully separable, since the one lives on in the imagination of the other.

The narrative is punctuated throughout by competing stories. Personal recollections, town gossip, newspaper reports, and imaginary constructs jostle one another. These versions of reality are not completely reconcilable: Ruth and Lucille argue about the color of their mother's hair, and together with Sylvie, they speculate about what really happened in the train accident in which their grandfather died. Sylvie's eccentric attitude removes events from temporality: she tells stories derived from old newspaper articles as if they told of events that had just occurred. Her tenuous links with the world of middle-class housekeeping is undercut by these fragments of newspaper that she keeps pinned to the inside of her coat lapel. Ruth understands the multiple stories of Fingerbone and Sylvie's newspaper clippings as a fluid set of alternatives that cannot be forced into a logical structure. Sylvie's fancy that the woods contain fairy children eager to communicate with human beings is an adaptation of Emerson's notion of the "spirit that lurks each form within" and "beckons to spirit of its kin."[51] It is, of course, also a reflection of her name (etymologically linked to "sylvan") and an allusion to the title character in Nerval's *Sylvie* (1854). Altogether, the world of nature to which Sylvie introduces the girls owes much to Romanticism more broadly speaking: her theft of a rowboat recalls a well-known episode in Wordsworth's *Prelude,* and her delight when the water-logged sofa must be taken outside to dry echoes Thoreau's argument that our houses are too cluttered and we would do better to sit in the open air.[52]

Still, there are several aspects of *Housekeeping* that seem to burst the bounds of Romanticism and bring the narrative closer to Derrida. A case in point is Lévi-Strauss's concept of bricolage as a mythopoeic activity, which Derrida discusses in "Structure, Sign, and Play." While the term "bricolage" does not occur in *Housekeeping,* makeshift constructions are dominant motifs. When Ruth's grandfather built the house with no prior knowledge of carpentry, the result was an amateurish dwelling with off-kilter walls and floors and home-made furniture adjusted to fit bizarre angles. The story of the house becomes a foundational myth in the family, as well as in the town of Fingerbone itself. Sylvie is a different kind of bricoleur, one who is also a hoarder. In a misbegotten attempt to establish order, she washes, dries, and neatly arranges empty cans to form an irregular construction that is part child's play, part intuitive design. When Ruth and Lucille spend an entire night in the woods, they create a hut for themselves out of materials at hand: using a big stone to form one wall, they add driftwood and torn-down fir branches to make the other walls, the floor, and the roof. "It was a low and slovenly structure, to all appearances random and accidental" (*Housekeeping,* 114). In creating this structure, they recreate the American myth of survival in the wilderness, but they also join the family lineage of bricoleurs who are creators of myths and stories. In the last part of the novel, after Lucille has moved out of the house, Ruth and Sylvie collaborate on the construction of a new myth.

Derrida's presentation of the relation between structure and play resonates with a central motif of *Housekeeping.* On one level, play is taken literally: under Sylvie's care, Ruth and Lucille play card games and engage in fantasies. For Sylvie, an adult who should be supervising the children's education and social development, play is synonymous with freedom. When the proper, regulated world of Fingerbone encroaches too much, she escapes into her imagination or else into the outdoor world of undomesticated nature. *Housekeeping* both idealizes this concept of play and reveals the costs at which it is purchased. In the Wordsworthian scene where Sylvie steals the rowboat, she is impervious to the angry cries of its owner: "He might just be some sort of lunatic," she says, telling herself a story quite at odds with the actual situation. For her, play becomes a substitute world in which she no longer has to consider property and the rights of others.

In place of an absent authority figure, a chain of caretakers—Derrida would call it "a series of substitutions of center for center"—emerges to give temporary structure to the girls' life. Following their mother's suicide, the girls live in turn with their grandmother, with two spinster great-aunts, and finally with their aunt Sylvie. Later, when Lucille is virtually adopted by her home economics teacher, Ruth chooses to remain with Sylvie. Through this relay of mother-figures, the novel sets up an intricate chain of substitutions that shapes the girls' upbringing. Each attempt to establish structure is undermined, however, by something that escapes structure. A continual interplay between system and the disruption of system underpins the novel. After the flood, the town library shows "vast gaps in the Dewey decimal system" (*Housekeeping*, 62). When the girls find old photographs in a shoe box, they cannot tell if they have been stored there rather than being stuck into an album "because they were especially significant or because they were not especially significant" (*Housekeeping*, 90). Yet the sense of loss connected to these gaps and conundrums is not entirely negative. It is also part of a passage toward something new. In this way, the novel not only looks backward, but also continues to look forward by imagining new trajectories.[53]

The loss of center and the infinite series of substitutions that succeed it, the establishment of system and its repeated breaching, appear in *Housekeeping* as a set of continuing reversals. The visible and hidden sides of Sylvie's coat lapels serve as a miniature version of this reversibility. Toward the end of the novel, Sylvie and Ruth make a huge bonfire that ultimately threatens to burn down the house. Along with other items of household clutter, they throw the old photographs into the fire. As the photos are touched by the flames, they gradually turn a silvery black, reverting almost to the state of negatives. To speak of reversal here would be inaccurate, however, since the photographs do not actually revert to negatives: rather, they are destroyed. The scene comments implicitly on the problem of reversibility. Whereas Sylvie's habit of pinning news items to the inside of her lapels merely hides these items from public view, the burning of the photos recognizes that it may not be possible to hang onto both "sides" of recorded experience equally.

At the end of the novel, Ruth and Sylvie leave the fire and make their way along the railroad tracks. Two possible outcomes are suggested: either the two of them are killed by a train as they attempt to cross the bridge over the lake, or they miraculously escape to live a vagrant life by traversing the country on freight trains. The novel does not let us opt for one or the other of these possible conclusions—the two are held in suspension. To be sure, if Ruth has been killed in a train accident, she must be dead throughout the entire extent of her narration. Perhaps she is telling her story from beyond the tomb. Yet the novel allows us to think of this as an entirely sustainable paradox.

In the final lines, Ruth imagines that Lucille may have moved to Boston. Conjuring up a vivid image of Lucille sitting in a restaurant waiting for a friend, Ruth nonetheless admits that she has no direct knowledge of Lucille's present whereabouts; furthermore, she and Sylvie are "nowhere in Boston" and thus are not in a position to track Lucille (*Housekeeping*, 218). The novel concludes with a remarkable claim: Ruth's belief that Lucille "does not watch, does not listen, does not hope, and always for me and Sylvie" (*Housekeeping*, 219). What are we to make of this extraordinary sentence? Combining a series of negatives with the adverb "always," the statement defies reason while also suggesting a way of thinking beyond the reach of ordinary syntax. Unlike real events, texts are always present for their readers. Whatever else it means, this sentence is a vivid representation of the paradoxical coexistence of presence and absence in *Housekeeping*.

In this remarkable novel, a seemingly dualistic world formed of earth and water, housekeeping and vagrancy, return and departure, loss and recovery, past and present, gives way in the end to an infinite series of possible reversals. However much its final lines reclaim a kind of positive presence, it is one that only thinly conceals the psychological trauma of accident, suicide, and social ostracism.[54] In this respect, like Duras's *The Lover*, Robinson's *Housekeeping* understands rupture and reversal as the result of social and historical power structures. It is not surprising that much of the scholarship on *Housekeeping* has employed poststructuralist frameworks, particularly the feminist theories of Julia Kristeva or Hélène Cixous.[55] The success of the novel no doubt has much to do with its ability to attract different kinds of readers with overlapping but not identical interests.

Amphibious Life: Swift's *Waterland*

Graham Swift's novel *Waterland* (1983) operates by means of similar sets of irresolvable oppositions. Its narrator, Tom Crick, finds a metaphor for history in the landscape where the novel is set: the English Fens, a large flat area formed from the silt that accumulates to the east of the river Ouse. He defines silt as a function of simultaneous, but contradictory movements: "Silt: a word which when you utter it, letting the air slip thinly between your teeth, invokes a slow, sly, insinuating agency. Silt: which shapes and undermines continents; which demolishes as it builds; which is simultaneous accretion and erosion; neither progress nor decay."[56]

In large measure a novel about the problem of origins, *Waterland* plays with metaphors that allude to deconstruction. At the same time, the deconstructive elements of the novel are mediated through engagement with Hayden White's theories about the role of narrative in the writing of history. White's *Metahistory* (1973) was one of several contributions to the reflections on historiography that emerged in the 1970s.[57] The underlying paradigm of *Metahistory* was drawn from a structuralist text, Northrop Frye's *Anatomy of Criticism* (1957). An opening toward deconstruction may be seen, perhaps, in White's distinction between "manifest" and "latent" levels of historical narrative. The "manifest" level, he explains, is the place "where the theoretical concepts that have been used to explain the data are deployed," whereas the "latent" level is "the linguistic ground on which these concepts are precritically constituted" (*Metahistory*, 431). He regards the nineteenth-century "crisis of historicism" as "little more than the perception of the impossibility of choosing, on adequate theoretical grounds, among the different ways of viewing history" promulgated by different philosophical visions of the subject during that period (*Metahistory*, 429–430).

Linda Hutcheon reconfigures White's central concept in her foundational study, *A Poetics of Postmodernism* (1988), where she introduces the term "historiographic metafiction" to describe key characteristics of postmodern fiction.[58] As she observes, historiographic metafiction questions simplistic models of "reality" as opposed to "fiction," focusing rather on the ways in which social meaning is constituted by historical discourses (*Poetics*, 15). "Historiographic metafiction clearly acknowledges that it is a complex institutional and discursive network of élite, mass, popular cultures that postmodernism operates in" (*Poetics*, 21). Although she gives no extended reading of *Waterland*, she refers to the novel repeatedly and in various stages of her argument. Particularly relevant to *Waterland* here is her observation that postmodern fiction "substitutes for History the value of histories, revealing how it is we who give meaning to the past, how it is we who make histories into History" (*Poetics*, 214).

Waterland prefaces its narrative with two epigraphs: the first of these is a dictionary definition of the Latin word "historia":[59]

Historia, -ae, f. **1.** Inquiry, investigation, learning. **2.** a) a narrative of past events, history. b) any kind of narrative: account, tale, story.

The narrator of *Waterland,* the history teacher Tom Crick, is acutely aware of the shifting character of language and its inbuilt tendency toward proliferation of meaning: he knows that words are slippery and hard to pin down. Even in older languages like Latin, words already had multiple meanings. Extending this understanding of language as inherently polysemantic, Crick tells his class that the Latin motto of his grandfather's brewery, "Ex Aqua Fermentum," can be translated in several ways: in addition to "Out of Water, Ale," it can be read as "Out of Water, Activity," or even as "Out of Water, Perturbation" (*Waterland,* 86). Language itself, he maintains, is a vehicle that determines to some extent our conceptions of things. Speaking of the first inhabitants of the Fens, he wonders how they regarded the river Ouse, to which they had given a name derived from the Sanskrit word for water. He speculates that they may have thought of the river "as a God, a sentient Being" (*Waterland,* 143). This notion corresponds to the early phase in the history of metaphysics that Derrida sketches in "Structure, Sign, and Play": the period when Being is still conceived as "*presence* in all senses of this word."[60] By imagining the center of their own world as a divine being, the Fen peoples were also setting out on a long journey that would end with loss of the divine. "By daring to transmute things into sound," Crick says, the primitive Fen peoples "were unconsciously forging the phenomenon known as History" (*Waterland,* 143). With this analysis, Tom Crick moves away from the solid ground of straightforward interpretation.

Crick's rambling personal narrative, which he substitutes for the set history curriculum, testifies to his loss of faith in the explanatory ability of history as a discipline. Significantly, his shift to his own life story occurs at a point in the official school syllabus that requires him to treat one of the most prominent "ruptures" in traditional history, the French Revolution (the very term "revolution" is another of the novel's ambiguities: does it refer to a one-time reversal or to the continuous revolving of a wheel?). His personal narrative provokes the students' curiosity about origins and causes much more intensely than textbook history, but the rationale behind his interpolation of private history into his lessons has little to do with appealing to recalcitrant students. Rather, the personal story is an attempt on Crick's part to understand his own life. It tests, in other words, the power of narrative to bring coherence and meaning to subjective experience.

Just as historical studies aim to recover lost facts in order to arrive at a coherent account of "what really happened" (to paraphrase Leopold von Ranke's famous phrase[61]), so Crick sees his narrative as something akin to the "land reclamation" that made the Fens habitable (*Waterland*, 9), a perpetual dredging action, an "endless and stationary war against mud" (*Waterland*, 346). Traditional history is not entirely absent from the personal narrative, however. Moving forward together, the two stories also work at cross-purposes. Crick sees his life as "amphibious," always shifting between fiction and reality (*Waterland*, 207). Much as he longs to believe in facts, he also knows that history is a construct. In his hesitation to privilege one view over the other, Crick represents much the same kind of turning point that Derrida identifies in the movement from structuralism to poststructuralism.

The difficult relationship between language and meaning is revealed most acutely in the attempts of Tom's handicapped brother, Dick, to understand the word "love." A young man past puberty but still mentally a child, Dick is unable to reconcile family love, his father's way of explaining the word, with the biological information about sex that his brother has given him. The devastating consequences of Dick's confusion form one of the central strands in the novel, highlighting the problem of origins by reference to human generation. Who was the father of Mary's aborted child, Dick or Tom? Many years later, when Mary, now Tom's wife, claims that God is going to give her the baby she has longed for but cannot bear as a result of that early abortion, Tom is the one who becomes confused. "But God does not talk any more," he thinks. "Didn't you know that, Mary? He stopped talking long ago" (*Waterland*, 268). Resisting the idea that Mary is psychologically disturbed and preferring to attribute her strange behavior to menopause, Tom fails to understand her condition until he is confronted with her theft of another woman's child. In this episode, even what appears at first to be a realistic reference, the name of the supermarket Safeways where Mary's theft takes place acquires an additional, ironic meaning. Mary's state of mind here extends the exploration of insanity that has begun in the retrospective parts of the novel that tell the story of the nineteenth-century Sarah Atkinson, mentally incapacitated by a blow to the head in 1820 and confined to an upper room of the family mansion. Is she "stark mad" (*Waterland*, 83) or has she turned into some kind of visionary in those moments when she utters her only words, "Smoke! Fire!

Burning!" (*Waterland*, 84)? When Tom goes for help in the final moments of Dick's life, he takes a shortcut by explaining why his brother is operating the dredger on a Sunday: "He's gone barmy. He got himself drunk and rode off on his bike. We d-don't know what he might do" (*Waterland*, 351). The American airmen who take a boat to bring Tom and his father out to the dredger are naturally puzzled by the British slang word "barmy." A glance at the OED reveals two meanings:

1. Of, full of, covered with barm, frothing.
2. Full of ferment, excitedly active, flighty.[62]

The dictionary definitions are perhaps a little too dignified: in colloquial use, the word means crazy. Nonetheless, the origin of the word in "barm" or froth returns us to the earlier parts of the novel where Tom Crick defined the Atkinson brewery motto "ex aqua fermentum."

Tom's reluctance to state certain things outright, his frequent recourse to periphrasis, ellipsis, and allusion, is characteristic of his mode of expression. Together with all too evident blind spots in Tom's perspective on reality, these occlusions demand that the reader work to fill in what is missing from his narrative. Registering Tom's skepticism about fixed chains of cause and effect, his gaps and indirections also alert us to the multiplicity of possible explanations that he shrinks from articulating (except, on some occasions, by means of questions). Repeatedly, Tom pushes himself to move from story to "fact": "But let us keep to the facts" (87), "But facts, facts" (88). He cites dates, gives information, and is clearly well informed about nineteenth-century history. Within the conceptual framework of the novel, such facts stand in contrast to the fictions embodied by the Fenmen's love of stories and fairy tales. And yet Tom is ultimately more sophisticated than this opposition suggests: he knows that what appear as facts are really part of accepted historical discourses, themselves subject to questioning.

Contradictory assumptions of realism and modernism pull the novel in opposite directions. To use Derrida's formulation, "we have no language—no syntax and no lexicon—which is foreign to this history; we can pronounce not a single destructive proposition which has not had already to slip into the form, the logic, the implicit postulations of precisely what it seeks to contest."[63] This is the double-bind that Tom struggles to unravel in his lengthy soliloquy.

In the imagery of the novel's final scene, where Dick's beloved motorcycle is surrounded by gathering darkness, the paradox of realism becomes overt.

The solidity of the cycle is played off against the indeterminacy of the dusk, just as fact and story, objects and language have formed the larger tissue of play within the novel. The cycle appears "abandoned, but vigilant," against the "will-o'-the-wisp" backdrop of descending night (*Waterland*, 358). In the last analysis, however, the two become little more than signs that yield up only some of their meaning while they also remain opaque. The "amphibious life" is reinterpreted in this scene as the tension between the modern world of machines and the ancient world of nature.

Waterland is full of endings that are also ruptures—among others, Dick's fatal plunge into the Ouse, Tom's dismissal from his teaching position, and Mary's placement in a mental hospital. Yet in a fundamental sense, the narrative remains open-ended, suspended between traditional and poststructuralist understandings of meaning and purpose. It stands on slippery ground from which no satisfactory leverage can be obtained. This, too, is part of the amphibious character of the text, which depends on precisely the kind of indeterminacies that interested Derrida. Various figures in the novel—notably Tom and his student Price—try to identify a secure position from which judgments can be made, but their attempts repeatedly fail. Tom examines but finds wanting such conceptions of history as the progressive view (embodied in the theme of industrial England), regressive history (in the theme of decline and fall), and circular history (in Johannes Schmidt's discovery of the eel's migrations patterns). What Hayden White calls "mechanistic" history (in other words, the rationalist history of the Enlightenment[64]) is ingeniously suggested in the motif of Dick's fascination with machines, his constant tinkering with his motorcycle, and his work on the dredger. The novel ends with an allusion to Dick's mechanistic bent by invoking his "abandoned but vigilant" motorcycle on the bank "in the thickening dusk" (*Waterland*, 358). Dick loves machines, but cannot understand rational argument. In the final analysis, *Waterland* demonstrates the difficulty of reflecting on either history or fiction in an age when the notion of an authoritative vantage point has lost credibility.[65]

The novel's engagement with theories of history and text moves beyond Hayden White's position in *Metahistory*, however. A crucial difference is that White's argument in *Metahistory* uses structuralist concepts as its springboard. This is apparent on the one hand in White's use of Northrop Frye's four major categories for literary texts—romance, tragedy, comedy, and satire—and on the other hand his interest in Roman Jakobson's and Levi-Strauss's four basic tropes—metaphor, metonymy, synecdoche, and irony

(*Metahistory*, 31).[66] *Waterland*, while including elements of all four of Frye's types and deploying (as any good writing does) all four of the major tropes, ultimately resists classification in such terms. Perhaps the closest to the position *Waterland* takes is irony, which, as White notes, "represents a stage of consciousness in which the problematic nature of language itself has become recognized" (*Metahistory*, 37). For White, irony characterizes modernist historiography; he does not refer to poststructuralism. Still, one might consider deconstruction as a special form of irony. The ambiguities apparent in Tom's narrative description of the Fens, his understanding of history, and his exploration of subjectivity clearly goes beyond modernism. Freddie Parr's "half-slipping, half-suspended body" in the river functions as an emblem of the narrative's deconstructive position (*Waterland*, 34).

Although ethics is at issue everywhere in *Waterland*, the novel does not settle on an identifiable ideological position. The gaps in Tom's narrative and the open ending of the novel summon the reader to think the ethical questions further than Tom himself is able to do. In many respects, Tom handles deftly the parallels between nineteenth- and twentieth-century history, private and textbook history, subjective and documented history. From his apparent rambling a carefully woven texture emerges. Some elements of the larger picture are partially subordinated, however; World War II, the historical backdrop to his and Mary's adolescence, makes only sporadic appearances. As the French Revolution was a defining moment for the nineteenth century, so—with much vaster moral implications—was the Holocaust for the twentieth.

While Tom ends his story ends in "obscurity" (*Waterland*, 358), we ourselves must read "beyond the ending."[67] In this respect, the novel parts ways with the apocalyptic fears evoked not only by the schoolboy Price with his fear of nuclear war, but also by Sarah Atkinson's invocations of smoke, fire, and burning. As Frank Kermode writes in *The Sense of an Ending* (1966): "Fictions are for finding things out, and they change as the needs of sense-making change. Myths are the agents of stability, fictions the agents of change."[68] The tension between history and fairy tale and the narrative that results from it in *Waterland* makes the novel into a sense-making enterprise of the sort Kermode has in mind. Instead of an apocalyptic ending, *Waterland* concludes with the flashback to Dick's death, an episode from Tom's childhood that precedes his career as a school teacher. In the context of the novel, Dick's fishlike nature (his underwater prowess)[69] and his mother's determination that he should become the "savior of the world" allude to Jesus's death and resurrection; but Dick's fatal plunge into the water does not lead Tom into clarity. The end of Mary's story, where she is placed in a psychiatric hospital originally built as an asylum to house the insane Sarah Atkinson, shifts from first-person to third-person narration on the second page as Tom, having imbibed an entire bottle of whisky, scrawls drunken comments on students' essays (*Waterland*, 329). At the official ceremony for his (forced) retirement at the school, he is unable to say anything, even in response to Price's final shout of protest (*Waterland*, 335).

Ethics is dependent on the construction of meaning. Yet for Tom Crick, meaning is elusive. He knows, of course, that his role in the lives of Dick and Mary has led him to incur guilt. Yet in one of his classroom debates with Price, he argues that "we're all free to interpret" history (*Waterland*, 140). This is essentially a poststructuralist position, of course. But Tom's thoughts on the question of whether we can "find whatever meaning we want in history" (as Price rephrases his statement) are less clearly poststructuralist: "But actually I do believe that. I believe it more and more. History: a lucky dip of meanings. Events elude meaning, but we look for meanings. Another definition of Man: the animal who craves meaning—but knows—" (*Waterland*, 140).

"A lucky dip of meanings" is not at all what poststructuralists claim when they emphasize the slipperiness of language. In Derrida's scheme, deconstruction makes use of existing polysemy (though it also calls on homophony, a pervasive feature of the French language). One accusation leveled at Derrida during the culture wars depended too heavily on the erroneous notion that deconstruction was a method in which practitioners merely juggled with words. Yet deconstruction was not merely a technique of turning texts inside out, nor did it exist in a political or moral vacuum. As we saw at the beginning of this chapter, the "rupture" that Derrida identifies as the decisive moment in his intellectual development was the Algerian War; as a result, he claimed, he attempted to reconfigure discourse about subjectivity by going "through the experience of deconstruction."[70] In *Waterland*, Tom Crick goes through his own "experience of deconstruction," but without ending up on one side or another of the discussion about history.

Against the backdrop of intense debates about deconstruction, the three novels we have considered in this chapter pay close attention to questions of guilt and responsibility in recent history. They spell out more clearly moral issues that were somewhat submerged in Derrida's early writing. *The Lover*, *Housekeeping*, and *Waterland* all work with notions of rupture, reversal, loss of center, absence, erasure, and indeterminacy in ways that go beyond the merely fashionable. The explorations these novels undertake find their starting points in complex historical events like war and imperialism, as well as social structures like patriarchy and bourgeois morality. These topics, the novels suggest, require substantial rethinking in today's world. They have ramifications for individual and national identity that cannot be avoided as we attempt to come to terms with a past that has begun to change its face as we gain increasing distance from it. Above all, these texts are informed by a deep-seated belief in the ability of narrative to rise above its limitations to become an agent of change.

II *Psychological Theories*

3 *The Mirror Stage*

The divergence between novelists working in French and the Anglo-American tradition is even sharper in their response to Jacques Lacan than to other French poststructuralists. One reason for this is doubtless that outside of France, Lacan's psychoanalytic theories are known primarily to academics, whereas in Paris, he was a celebrity during the late 1950s and throughout the 1960s. During that time, many French intellectuals thought it a privilege to undergo analysis with him. Lacan's public seminars, couched in often obscure language and accompanied by quasi-algebraic blackboard notations, attracted a substantial audience that included many interested laypeople. For some of those who attended, the point was the performance; they knew they wouldn't fully understand the content. Shoshana Felman recounts an amusing anecdote in which the French bookseller from whom she bought her first copy of a work by Lacan warned her against buying this "unreadable, totally incomprehensible" book.[1] Initially, Lacan claimed that he was elaborating on the writings of Freud, not overturning them; but later, as his own ideas came to appear increasingly heretical and his behavior more eccentric, he became the focus of intense controversy. Eventually, Lacan was repudiated by the International Psychoanalytic Association, and many professional French psychoanalysts remain troubled by his ideas. In 1980, he dissolved his "École freudienne de Paris," shortly before succumbing to illness in 1981.

Few English-language novels allude overtly to Lacan. We do encounter direct mentions of Lacan, of course, in academic novels like those of David Lodge and Malcolm Bradbury, which mock the way in which French theorists have become names to conjure with at scholarly conferences. In Bradbury's *Doctor Criminale* (1992), for example, the fictive Bazlo Criminale gives a lecture in which "he dismissed Lacan," and "told Foucault just where to go."[2] References to Lacan in David Lodge's *Nice Work* (1988) serve mainly to suggest the sheer impenetrability of his theoretical jargon.[3] Although much more than an "academic novel," A. S. Byatt's *Possession* (1990) employs citations and near-citations from Lacan to characterize one of its more theoretically minded figures, Fergus Wolff. In one of the letters Fergus writes to Maud, he asks whether she has "read Lacan on flying fish and vesicle persecution."[4] A few pages later, Maud has tracked down this reference, in which Lacan describes a patient's dream:

> I remember the dream of one of my patients, whose aggressive drives took the form of obsessive phantasies; in the dream he saw himself driving a car, accompanied by a woman with whom he was having a rather difficult affair, pursued by a flying fish, whose skin was so transparent that one could see the horizontal liquid level through the body, an image of vesicle persecution of great anatomical clarity . . . [5]

By including this direct quotation from Lacan, Byatt shows what Maud finds so exasperating about his thought: even if we know that a "vesicle" is a small, bladder-like pouch or blister, it is still not exactly clear what "vesicle persecution" might mean.

Since the publication of Anthony Wilden's translation of Lacan, accompanied by over sixty pages of "translator's notes" and a substantial essay on "Lacan and the Discourse of the Other," Lacan's ideas had become increasingly accessible to an English-speaking readership.[6] Between 1982 and 1987, important explications of Lacan were published in English.[7] Soon key essays by Lacan began to appear in anthologies of theory for use in English-speaking classrooms. This chapter begins with a series of French novels that put Lacan's ideas to the test, and concludes with a discussion of J. M. Coetzee's

The Age of Iron, which transports Lacanian thought to a strikingly different political environment: South Africa in the late 1980s.

Lacan and the French Novel

In order to present Lacan's complex relation to literature more clearly, I will begin with a flashback to the mid-1960s, when he was at the peak of his professional success. The novels by Marguerite Duras, Julia Kristeva, and Camille Laurens that we will explore in this chapter form a cohesive group, not least because all three authors spent considerable time reading, thinking about, and responding to Lacan. Their fictions take up not only the broad scheme of his ideas, but also engage intelligently with small details.

Duras's novel *Le ravissement de Lol V. Stein* (1964; *The Ravishing of Lol Stein*[8]) impressed Lacan so much that he was moved to write an eloquent essay in its praise.[9] His enthusiasm derived from his sense that Duras appeared to "know" his ideas without any prior acquaintance with his work. Lacan's essay opens with reflections on the title of Duras's novel. Two sets of alternative readings offer themselves, he explains: first, the word *ravissement* means both "rapture" and "rape"; second, the word "of" can be read as both an objective and a subjective genitive. Is Lol raped or enraptured? Does she prey on (meta-phorically: rape) the other characters, or is she swept away in the course of her involvement with them? Lacan's decision to begin with the ambiguity of the novel's title permits him to examine a number of other dualities that structure *Lol V. Stein*. Lol is part of an amorous triangle composed of herself, her lover Jacques Hold, and another woman named Tatiana Karl, with whom Hold is also involved. Although we do not realize it at first, Jacques Hold turns out to be the narrator. Lol's voyeurism as she watches Jacques and Tatiana make love places her, as Lacan explains, into a "doubled space" in which she is both herself and—by a kind of empathetic imagination—Tatiana. In addition to this "doubled space," Lacan identifies another doubling in the novel caused by the remembered scene of a ball that Lol attended when she was eighteen and where a woman named Anne-Marie Stretter seduced Lol's then fiancé Michael Richardson. This ball that haunts Lol's memory is itself doubled in the narra-tion, as Jacques Hold tries to reconstruct the scene. Following the story from Jacques Hold's point of view places the reader—again, through imaginative empathy—in a triangular situation with respect to the two women characters. Lacan comments on his position as a reader of the novel: "and here I am, the third to create a rapture, in this case a decidedly subjective one [i.e., he is enraptured]."[10] A new triangle emerges, consisting of Lacan as reader, Duras as author, and the narrative itself.

Several critics have pointed to weaknesses in Lacan's account of *Lol V. Stein*. In the first instance, Lacan is not fully aware of the problematic status of Jacques Hold's narrative, in which fact-finding and quasi-objective analysis is joined with identification and sheer invention. Jacques Hold, a doctor at the State Hospital, is in part a stand-in for "the figure of a psychologist or psychoanalyst."[11] At the same time, however, Hold is romantically involved with Lol and thus "caught in a full-blown case of transference."[12] Even in those portions of the story where he claims to report objectively on what others have told him, he admits that he has left out information he regards as irrelevant. As readers, we cannot judge how significant these omissions may be. This places us in a difficult position: we know that Jacques Hold's version is not complete, but we also lack information necessary to identify precisely the deficiencies of his narrative.[13] His determination to uncover the hidden springs of Lol's psychological disturbance is at the very least obsessive, and thus not solely the work of a disinterested observer.[14] For the first third of the novel, furthermore, Jacques Hold conceals his own identity, thus increasing our sense that his narration is not trustworthy. Susan Rubin Suleiman has demonstrated the close relationship between *Lol V. Stein* and Freud's case study of Dora, noting in particular that both texts have a "self-conscious male narrator" and a "mentally ill woman as main character."[15] Like Freud, Jacques Hold manipulates the facts of the woman's story in order to reconstruct it in his own fashion.[16]

In addition, the novel's insistence on point of view suggests the inherent limitations of a single individual perspective. The field of rye from which Lol observes Jacques Hold and Tatiana Karl making love in the disreputable Hôtel des Bois becomes literally a field of vision. From this vantage point, Lol can see the lovers only through a lighted window that shows them intermittently in different stages of dress or undress. Lol's position and her angle of vision are precisely described; yet the scene is filtered through Jacques Hold's narration. Hold gives different versions of his own relation to the scene: did he actually exchange glances with Lol from the hotel window, did he see someone who looks like Lol entering the field, or is he simply imagining Lol watching from the rye field? In the course of his narration, the reader becomes increasingly uncertain about his reliability. Even Hold himself becomes unsure about what, if anything, he has discovered about Lol. Is

Lol's madness simply a construction on the part of Jacques Hold?[17] As one critic comments, "the novel is a story of epistemological disappointment, a deferral of knowledge that loses its way amidst its own uncertainty."[18] In this respect, *Lol V. Stein* is a critique of narrative manipulation undertaken by a male psychoanalyst. One would have loved to have been the proverbial fly on the wall of the café on rue Bernard-Palissy where Lacan, the male psycho-analyst, met with Marguerite Duras and informed her of the parallels he had found between his work and her novel. Flattering though Lacan's admiration may have been, Duras was acutely aware of the crucial difference between their respective positions.

Responding to Lacan: Duras's *The Vice Consul* and *L'Amante anglaise*

Almost immediately, Duras's writing registered the effects of Lacan's hom-age in the form of a prolonged argument with him through the vehicle of literature. Her next novel, *Le vice-consul* (1966; *The Vice Consul*), is structured around two interwoven stories: the first, the mental breakdown of the vice consul of Lahore, Jean-Marc de H.; the second, a text being composed by a young English writer, Peter Morgan, about a beggar women in Calcutta. Both strands explore the problem of madness, one about a man, one narrated by a man. The first place to look for traces of Duras's engagement with Lacan is in this second narrative strand.

Peter Morgan's technique is to place himself into the consciousness of his main character, the beggar woman he has observed in Calcutta. Building on an episode he has heard from another character in the novel, he imagines that the woman came to Calcutta from Battambang (Cambodia), giving away a sickly infant at an early point in her travels. Though fully aware that he can-not actually see into the woman's mind, Morgan does not hesitate to recon-struct the woman's life through what he imagines to be her own point of view: "How to avoid going back. Get lost. I don't know how. You'll learn. I need some signpost to lead me astray. Make your mind a blank. Refuse to recognize familiar landmarks. Turn your steps towards the most hostile point on the horizon . . ." (*Vice Consul*, 1).

There is less to go on in Peter Morgan's narrative in *The Vice Consul* than in the case of Jacques Hold's narrative in *Lol V. Stein*. The life of the madwoman from Battambang is in fact so thoroughly unknowable that all

Morgan can do is make it up. Even the episode of the sick infant, culled from the childhood experience of the ambassador's wife, Anne-Marie Stretter, most likely has no connection at all with the beggar woman. Morgan's "reconstruction" of the beggar's adolescence is based solely on his own ideas about the psychological origins of abjection. Peter Morgan thinks of himself as taking "imaginary notes" on the woman.[19] He freely admits that he is including "fragments stored in his own memory" to fill what he regards as gaps in the story (*Vice Consul*, 54). Is fiction writing—"inventing"—a better kind of analysis? It might be tempting to take this position, but the novel does not encourage it: rather, it insists throughout on the purely imaginary status of Morgan's narrative.

The other main plot strand recounts the story of Jean-Marc de H., former French vice consul of Lahore, now dismissed from his post after a scandal and waiting in Calcutta for word on his professional fate. In its disconnected and conjectural nature, the story of the vice consul resembles more closely the uncertain narrative of *The Ravishing of Lol V. Stein*.[20] In order to follow— more accurately, to reconstruct—the tale of the vice consul, we need to attend not just to what is said, but also to hints, allusions, and gestures. Much of what we come to "know" about Jean-Marc de H. we glean from conversations among other people at the embassy in Calcutta, conversations that are often speculative or based on partial knowledge. Certainly, he has suffered some kind of mental collapse. The reason given for his dismissal is that he shot and killed lepers in the gardens of Shalimar, perhaps in a deranged reaction to the harsh conditions of life in India. But this does not completely explain another bizarre episode, reported by various characters, in which he shot at images of himself in the mirrors of the official residence in Lahore. Here we can identify a direct allusion to Lacan's concept of the "mirror stage" in human development.

Lacan's psychological theory presupposes that in babyhood we have no consciousness of separate identity. Rather, an infant is attached to objects of desire, such as the mother's breast, which remain disconnected from any sense of wholeness. Only during what Lacan terms the "mirror stage" does the child see him- or herself from outside, reflected in the responses of others. At that moment, a unified sense of self is first established. In later life, Lacan says, the "mirror stage" can sometimes return in dreams. During psychoanalysis, for example, dreams of the body in pieces tend to occur at the moment when the patient begins to reflect on his or her "most archaic fixations."[21]

Pieces of information about Jean-Marc de H.'s childhood and adolescence begin to surface, and we can see how these might arise from such "archaic obsessions." He is haunted, for example, by a melody called "Indiana's Song" that he used to play on the piano in his childhood home. (In Duras's later cinematic reworking of the material of *The Vice Consul* in her 1973 film *India Song*, the name of the tune is identical with the title of the film.[22]) We also discover that he has been expelled from two boarding schools, first for tasteless pranks against the teachers and then for petty theft from a local shop. Six months after the second expulsion, Jean-Marc's father died. Did the father die of shame over his son's expulsion, or did Jean-Marc kill him in some more literal way? We never find out. Although people at the embassy suggest that his adolescent history may provide an explanation of sorts for his strange actions in Lahore, the official inquiry rapidly drops this psychoanalytic approach. It is left to the reader to follow up the many indications of Jean-Marc's mental instability.

He manifests symptoms, for example, that suggest he may not have fully established a clear sense of self. He has a "blank voice," and his gaze seems somehow not to emanate from his own body; his speech and even his laughter seem to belong to somebody else. One of the people at the embassy comments that his voice creates an effect like "the sound track of a dubbed film" (*Vice Consul*, 87). When the authorities question him about the reasons for his peculiar behavior in Lahore, the vice consul cannot explain himself. From a Lacanian position, the vice consul's inability to put his experience into words would result from a disconnection between the "imaginary" (in Lacan's usage, the ego and its identifications[23]) and the "symbolic" (in Lacan's usage, language). From this vantage point, we can see why so much emphasis is placed on Jean-Marc's unmarried state and his apparent sexual abstinence. Remaining in a presexual condition, he retains a permeable psyche, empathizing with the suffering people of India in a way that his fellow Europeans find excessive. Confronted with the mirrors of his house in Lahore, he refuses to accept his own image, like the infant who has not yet passed through the "mirror stage."

Duras's entire "India cycle" can be understood as an undoing of the fiction of stable identity. In these works (*The Ravishing of Lol V. Stein*, *The Woman of the Ganges*, *India Song*, *The Vice Consul*), outlines that have almost begun to coalesce are repeatedly shattered into multiple versions. Repeatedly, these texts reverse the Lacanian mirror stage by showing identity in a process of dissolution.

In *L'Amante anglaise* (1967),[24] Duras's posture toward Lacan becomes more precise. Significantly, the novel focuses on a crime whose motivation is not understood by its perpetrator. Revisiting her earlier two-act play *Les Viaducs de la Seine-et-Oise* (1960), Duras inserts elements from Lacan's theory into an intrigue already susceptible to Lacanian interpretation. The play had been inspired by an actual crime in which an elderly couple committed a murder, cut the victim's body into pieces, and threw the parts onto various different trains as they passed under a viaduct.[25] The murder was solved when the police identified the specific bridge from which the body parts had been dispersed by establishing the point at which the various train lines crossed. In her 1967 novel, Duras transforms the original couple into a single perpetrator. Although the murderer in the novel bears the first name Claire ("clear"), her motivation remains obscure. Her full name, Claire Lannes, is actually an anagram composed of "Lacan" and "sirène" (siren). The Lacanian connection is almost literally spelled out, introducing a new substratum that had not been present in Duras's play of 1960.

In *L'amante anglaise*, a man who remains nameless conducts three interviews in which he attempts to find out more about why Claire murdered her deaf-mute cousin, Marie-Thérèse Bousquet. The third interview is with Claire herself. According to her statements, Claire seems to have carried out the murder on an impulse upon catching sight of a dark birthmark on Marie-Thérèse's sleeping body. In Claire's mind, the mark is not only a stain on her cousin's body, but a spot that calls for her to stab Marie-Thérèse to death. With respect to the dispersal of the body parts from a viaduct onto passing trains, the novel follows the original incident and the version presented in Duras's stage-play. In a new twist, however, the head is never found and Claire refuses to be more specific about what she has done with it (although she does eventually admit that she buried it somewhere). The location of Marie-Thérèse's head is never found, and more importantly, Claire's motivation for the murder is never revealed.

Is Claire insane? Her husband and other people who know her suggest that she is. She spends most of her time daydreaming on a bench outdoors, unconcerned about household chores. Unlike other housewives who might immerse themselves in a cheap novel, Claire has trouble understanding fiction, with the exception of children's picture books, which she steals from the school where she works as a cleaning lady. This interest suggests that she may be trapped in an early developmental phase. Due to her lack of education, she misspells words: sometimes she writes *la menthe anglaise* (English mint) as *l'amante anglaise* (the English woman lover), at other times as *l'amante en glaise* (the woman lover in clay, i.e., the dead and buried woman lover). The many homonyms in the French language provide rich material here. Like Freudian slips, these misspellings reveal aspects of her unconscious. Because of her misapprehension of *la menthe* (mint) as *l'amante* (the lover), she leaps to the perverse conclusion that Marie-Thérèse may have entertained sexual relations with her own lover. In Lacanian terms, Claire's problems with language suggest that she has not fully entered the "symbolic order." Further, although she cannot explain her behavior during and after the murder, she refuses to think of herself as actually insane: "Perhaps I'm very close to being mad. Or dead. Or alive. Who knows?"(*L'Amante anglaise*, 117). Lacan says of obsessional neurosis that those who suffer from it do not know whether they are dead or alive. Claire appears to fit this paradigm. Obsession and aggressivity go hand in hand in Lacan, and this may be another explanation for Claire's murder of her cousin.

Within the frame of the novel, Claire and Marie-Thérèse form an antithetical pair in which the former stands for the imagination, the latter for the body. The deaf-mute Marie-Thérèse has no access to spoken language; like Claire, she lacks full knowledge of the "symbolic order." She also appears to have no access to what Lacan terms "the imaginary." Claire, by contrast, is constituted by little other than the imaginary. According to her husband, "it must have occupied the most important place in her life" (*L'Amante anglaise*, 54). She clings to memories of an old love affair that she repeatedly attempts to relive in other amorous relationships. In Lacanian theory, the imaginary cannot be articulated in the bodily realm: the two spheres are distinct and cannot communicate with each other. Claire thus experiences a primary split that Lacan describes as a divergence, in women, between sexuality and language. Her murder of Marie-Thérèse, motivated on an unconscious level by the sheer physicality of the woman, fails to heal this rupture. This may explain, in part, Claire's odd response to Marie-Thérèse's severed head. Something Claire cannot articulate prevents her from throwing this part of her cousin's body onto the trains, as she does with the other parts of the corpse. Indeed, in a bizarre identification with the dead woman, Claire feels that she herself should be beheaded for having committed the murder: "They ought to cut my head off too for what I've done" (*L'Amante anglaise*, 115).

The fact that the investigation into Claire's case fails to resolve its mysteries continues the suggestion first raised in *Lol V. Stein*: that a male analyst may not be able to understand the psyche of a woman. Susan Suleiman's comparison with the case of Freud's Dora is pertinent here. In *L'Amante anglaise*, however, the male investigator does recognize some limitations that hedge in his research: his knowledge derives solely from what others tell him, and these other points of view are themselves limited. Accordingly, the book he plans to write will need to reconstitute a story available only in pieces. At one point, Claire claims that no one has asked the right question of her; yet she cannot disclose the question because she does not know it herself. That is, of course, the problem with the unconscious. Tantalizingly, the novel concludes with Claire's suggestion to the investigator: "If I were you, I'd listen. Listen." (*L'Amante anglaise*, 122). The investigator's inability to gain access to Claire's psyche accords with Duras's views about the problematic nature of work by a male psychoanalyst with a female patient.

Duras continued to be haunted by her exchange with Lacan long after her series of complex novels during the 1960s. Even late in her career, Duras spoke rather scornfully about Lacan's essay on *Lol V. Stein*. In an interview following the appearance of *L'Amant* (1984; *The Lover*), Duras remarked indignantly: "When Lacan found some of his own theories applied in *Lol V. Stein*, I lay low. I didn't say: Ah, Lacan thinks I'm brilliant. Not at all. I don't need critics to know that I'm brilliant."[26] Yet her fictions continued to do battle with Lacan's psychoanalytical ideas.

In *The Lover*, Duras makes considerable use of the Lacanian "mirror stage." Repeatedly, the narrator of *The Lover* sees herself either in the eyes of others or as a reflection of others. Her opening encounter with a reader who prefers her mature face to her younger one is just one indicator of this theme. In the Hélène Lagonelle sections, the presence of Lacan is almost too evident. The girl's name, containing both an allusion to the face that launched a thousand ships and the component *elle* (she), designates her from the outset as an allegory of woman. Yet, according to Lacan's famous phrase, "the woman does not exist." Hélène's mental retardation reduces her to little more than her beautiful body. Despite her chronological age, Hélène is has no consciousness of herself as a separate person: like an infant, all she wants is to return to her mother. To use Lacan's scheme, she has not undergone the normal mirror stage. In contrast, the narrator is engaged in a rite of passage that will ultimately lead her out of the mirror stage into adult existence. Hélène's blankness allows her to become a place-holder for the narrator's adolescent fantasies: the narrator would like to watch her own lover make love to Hélène; she would like to eat Hélène's beautiful breasts as if they were ripe fruit; she would like to murder Hélène's heavy, innocent, soft-skinned body. In contrast to Claire's murder of Marie-Thérèse in *L'Amante anglaise*, apparently motivated by the spot that disfigures her neck, the narrator's fantasies about Hélène Lagonelle in *The Lover* arise from the purity of her body and her total lack of self-awareness. These fantasies, coming from a young woman with high academic potential, suggest that there may be two aspects to the passage into adulthood. While Hélène will eventually return to her family and be married off to an eligible man, the narrator bears a burden that consciousness imposes. While she longs for the unselfconscious beauty of Hélène, she feels trapped in the ambiguities of self-awareness. In *The Lover*, Duras seems to ask whether women's selves can truly be as readily unified as Lacan's theory suggests.

Language and the Unconscious: Kristeva's *Possessions*

To the French filiation of novels that engage with Lacan we can add novels by Julia Kristeva, whose own theoretical work is indebted to his thought. Kristeva's mystery novel *Possessions* (1996) begins with a beheading. Gloria Harrison appears in the novel's first sentence as a dead body lying decapitated in a pool of blood. Her head is nowhere to be seen. The headless body gives rise to a long riff on Stephanie's part about headless figures in the history of art. While no allusion is made anywhere in the novel to decapitated women in literature, we can read *Possessions* as a reversal of *L'Amante anglaise*. Here, not only is the dead woman's head eventually found, but the discovery is made by a woman rather than a man.

The title of *Possessions*, like that of Duras's *The Ravishing of Lol V. Stein*, can be understood in both the active and the passive senses: as what people possess and what they are possessed by.[27] As a psychoanalyst herself, Kristeva pays special attention to the function of language in the constitution of the psyche.[28] The main narrator of *Possessions*, the journalist Stephanie Delacour, illustrates this issue in her detailed reflections on language and on the ways in which selfhood is both enriched and endangered by knowledge of two languages. Like Stephanie, Gloria Harrison, a professional translator, is also bilingual. With this motif, Kristeva complicates Lacan's notion that we enter into the "symbolic order" when we acquire our mother tongue in infancy. What happens, this novel asks, if we acquire a second language later in life? Wouldn't we then be entering a new symbolic order, and if so, how would that modify Lacan's account of human psychological development?

Gloria's deaf child, Jerry, and his speech therapist, Pauline, illustrate two versions of this problem. Through Pauline's lessons in phonetics and with the use of powerful hearing aids, Jerry acquires spoken language at a stage that, for a hearing child, would be quite belated. He is more at home with computers, mastering their arcane aspects more easily than he does the complex and ambiguous languages of human beings.

His speech therapist has herself undergone a belated induction into a second language. Pauline is marked by a traumatic experience that occurred when she was twenty-two: the death by drowning of her younger brother, Aimeric, while she was taking care of him. According to the official version of the incident, Pauline was taking a nap while her brother was swimming in the ocean, yet the narrative also suggests that Pauline may not have been asleep for the entire time: she may in fact have pulled Aimeric underwater while swimming alongside him. At this point, the reader attuned to linguistic slippage will have noticed that Aimeric drowns, not in some river or in the family swimming pool, but in the ocean: his death is caused by *la mer* (the sea), a word that is conveniently a homonym for *la mère* (the mother). The multiply homonymic nature of the French language allows for such overdetermined puns. Indeed, we are led to believe that the neglect of Aimeric's mother for her son may be the underlying cause of his death. Aimeric's first name suggests the verb *aimer*, to love. We are told that Pauline and Aimeric resemble each other physically, despite their seven-year age difference: "two bodies separate but together." "In the sunlight of our twin solitudes, steeped in it, clasped together, the space between us abolished, swallowed up. One sea, one heart."[29] Perhaps this intense love tipped over into sibling rivalry. Whatever may be the case, language seems in some way to be at the root of these complex family relationships.

Following Aimeric's death, Pauline is unable to speak for many months; even once her speech has returned, she contemplates suicide and undergoes several years of psychotherapy. In Lacanian terms, Pauline's loss of the brother who was her mirror-image throws her back into an earlier stage of psychological existence. Her solution is to switch to a new language. This decision enables her to restart her psyche, as it were, in a different mode, repeating her primary socialization by reinserting herself in a second language. Her move to Santa Varvara (in the French, "Santa Barbara") necessitates the acquisition of a language this text calls "Santavarvarian" ("Santabarbarois"). As if to underline the emphasis on language, this place is where Pauline earns her qualifications in speech therapy. Unfortunately, the English translation of the place name removes the ambiguity of what the French text calls "Santa Barbara": in Kristeva's novel, the place is located somewhere in Eastern Europe, but the echo of the Californian town Santa Barbara is surely part of a complex associative structure that subtends *Possessions*.[30] Similarly, the name of Pauline's brother, "Aimeric," is itself a near-homonym of "Amérique" (America). As Pauline takes charge of Jerry's speech therapy, she becomes a second mother to him, just as she had been a substitute mother to her younger sibling. In a grotesque displacement of Pauline's rivalry with her own mother, she ultimately decapitates Jerry's mother.

As in Duras, violence is associated with Lacanian theory. Santa Varvara is a violent place, situated in a run-down former communist country and controlled by international criminals. The French journalist Stephanie Delacour, the main narrator of *Possessions*, has traveled to Santa Varvara to investigate two different stories: the first, an intrigue involving deceptive real estate deals and illegal drug trafficking; the second, the interception of smuggled plutonium, coupled with rumors about increased black market sales of the radioactive material. In a few paragraphs, police commissioner Northrop Rilsky (a splendid name that is a cross between the literary theorist Northrop Frye and the poet Rainer Maria Rilke) gives an account of the global dangers that might accrue from such trafficking and the fluid nature of the groups involved, whom he describes with obvious bias as both "bearded Islamists" and "former red soldiers" (*Possessions*, 185). By introducing the motif of international terrorism, Kristeva shows—as Duras had done through the theme of colonialism in *The Lover*—that Lacanian theory is not merely a psychoanalytical instrument in the narrow sense, but more importantly a way of understanding larger social problems.

Stephanie sees her own position with clear eyes, while also understanding the psychology of the other women characters, Gloria and Pauline. Nonetheless, she cannot immediately unlock the secret connections between the murder case and the global intrigues for which Santa Varvara has become a hub. Yet the small community surrounding Gloria Harrison and her family is not sealed off from the outside world, which has increasingly become globally connected. Rilsky, whose perspective is larger than that of many inhabitants of Santa Varvara, perceives that the personal conflict between Pauline and Gloria is really a symptom of more insidious troubles that infect society as a whole. Still, although Rilsky comprehends the larger power structures that link the Eastern European country with global realities, it is Stephanie who, with her understanding of female psychology, is ultimately able to crack the case. So much, Kristeva seems to say, for Lacan's ideas about the talents of male psychoanalysts.

The Structure of Love: Laurens's *Romance*

Camille Laurens's prize-winning work *In Those Arms* (*Dans ces bras-là*, 2000), the presentation of one woman in her many different relations to men, quotes Lacan's statement: "There is no love, there are only proofs of love."[31] This quotation might well be the ironic motto of almost any of Laurens's novels. Her second novel, *Romance* (1992), is explicitly Lacanian. Its final section, titled "Kaleidoscope," opens with a parody of Lacan: "Thus, human space has at its origin a geometric, to be understood as 'kal-eido-scopic' structure: the 'fine form' of the other's domain [*champ*] fascinates me, as does also the structure of my own domain which subsequently returns from it and projects itself into the other's domain, in comparison, in competition, and in warlike conquest of the other's space."[32]

Within the framework of the novel, this passage occurs in a book on psychology being read by a minor character. In the text, the word "kal-eido-scopic" is accompanied by a footnote that refers the reader to "J. Lacan, *Ecrits*, 122" (*Romance*, 273). The reference is to the French edition of Lacan's *Ecrits,* but no discussion of the "kaleidoscopic" occurs there. Rather, the fictive quotation is modeled on a passage in Lacan's 1948 essay about aggressiveness in psychoanalysis. There, he writes:

> The notion of the role of spatial symmetry in a person's narcissistic structure is essential for laying the foundation of a psychological analysis of space, whose place I can merely indicate here. Animal psychology has shown us that the individual's relation to a particular spatial field [*champ*] is socially mapped in certain species in a way that raises it to the category of subjective membership. I would say that it is the subjective possibility of the mirror projection of such a field into the other's field that gives human space its originally "geometric" structure, a structure I would like to characterize as kaleidoscopic.[33]

As we have seen, a key element of Lacan's thought concerns the young child's concept of self. The child's actual reflection in a mirror is only one part of this process, which is augmented by what the child sees reflected by others. When parents suggest connections between the child and other family members, these suggestions can enter the child's self-image and reinforce such connections. Camille Laurens makes amusing use of this insight in the excessive and exaggerated repetitions across generations that inform the structure of *Romance*.

One of the novel's most striking features is its use of puns and wordplay. In accord with Lacan's idea that "the unconscious is structured like a language," the characters in *Romance* constantly glide through word sequences related by sounds and syllables they have in common. As Lacan formulates it in his lecture "The Insistence of the Letter in the Unconscious" (1957), "there is an incessant sliding of the signified under the signifier."[34] In Laurens's novel, verbal slippage occurs at moments where the narrative allows us to glimpse the figures' subconscious thoughts. The effects are brilliant and often very funny, although obviously, little of this sophisticated wordplay can be rendered in English. Not all of the linguistic slippage is deliberate wordplay on the part of the characters: sometimes they make revealing slips of the tongue, a phenomenon that Freud had explored in his *Psychopathology of Everyday* Life (1901). When the psychoanalyst Yves Morand first meets the female protagonist, Lise Imbert (later to become his girlfriend), he asks for her telephone number, but instead of saying "how can I reach you?" he says "how can I touch you?" (Où puis-je vous toucher?). Lise is surprised to discover from this lapse that "even psychiatrists have an unconscious" (*Romance*, 110). Soon afterward, however, she finds herself on the brink of similar slips. The French word *chemise* means both "shirt" and "file folder," but to prevent her reference to the folder from sounding too intimate, she hastily substitutes the word *dossier* (*Romance*, 111). Linguistic slippage of this kind forms a current through the entire novel.

We first see Yves Morand through the eyes of Martine Gras, who "knows him" from a television program in which he explained why certain woman cannot succeed in losing weight. Later, she catches sight of him in a Paris café, the Rostand, where he is deep in conversation with his colleague Gérard Tuyer (the person we later see reading about Lacan's ideas on personal space). Watching the two men say good-bye on the sidewalk outside, Martine notices that Gérard is clasping a thick book to his chest. It isn't the Bible, Martine thinks, as she slowly deciphers the lettering on the spine: "Sé-mi-nai-re" (*Romance*, 38). The volume is clearly part of an edition of Lacan's famous series of seminars on psychoanalysis.[35] In these seminars, Lacan developed his concept of the "little object a" (*petit objet a*), the thing that motivates desire and also becomes its object. This "little object" contrasts with a "big object," encapsulated in and identical with language. Subjective desire is not just aimed at the other, but also defined by the nature of that other. Similarly, it is couched in language that is not just subjective, but also the product of interaction with others, in the first instance in the child's relation with his or her mother. This is why Lacan claims that "man's desire finds its meaning in the desire of the other, not so much because the other holds the key to the object desired, as because the first object of desire is to be recognized by the other."[36] For the infant, this other person is the mother. Although the adult may have left behind this stage of desire for maternal recognition, something of it remains in the psyche at the level of what Lacan calls the Imaginary, the intersubjective backdrop against which the self is formed.

In Lise Imbert's relationship with Yves Morand, she gives him the pet name *petit a*. It is possible that Lise's affectionate term is simply an abbreviation of *petit ami* (boyfriend): indeed, at one point Lise turns the letter "a" of *petit a* into the initial of *ami, amour*, and *amant* (friend, love, lover; *Romance*, 111). She is, after all, a part-time translator who enjoys playing with words. From his more informed vantage point, Yves wonders if Lise actually knows about Jacques Lacan's concept of the *petit a* (*Romance*, 166). Could he have explained the term to Lise at some point? As he reflects on this question, Yves mentally summarizes Lacan's usage: "'The object small a,' the Master says somewhere, 'is the lost object, the cause of desire; its irreparable absence gives rise to the eternal nature of desire.'" (*Romance*, 167). Who or what is the lost object in *Romance*?

Yves's rival for Lise's affections is Max Grangier, a writer of film scenarios with whom she also collaborates from time to time. As the narrator comments, Max's parents named him Maxime; but everyone calls him Max. In this short form, the name seems appropriate for this large, heavyset man (we need to think of the Latin *maximus*, biggest or greatest). Lise, who has known him since childhood, occasionally calls him "*mon petit Max*" (e.g., *Romance*, 27), as if to play down the relation between his name and his size. Lise, Max, and Yves form a complex chain of desire constituted by tensions and ambiguities: these, the novel makes clear, derive from the mixture of identification and alienation that Lacan describes as characteristic of ego formation.

In this respect, the novel is a humorous adaptation of Lacan's formulation of aggressiveness in psychoanalysis, a phenomenon that has its origin in the relation of self and other created during the mirror stage. Aggressiveness,

Lacan argues, is often connected with corporal dislocation.[37] In the relation between Lise and Yves, this first emerges in the form of Yves's trip to Buenos Aires. Although the trip is not, as Lise at first thinks, a cover for something else, Lise is not wrong when she characterizes Yves as undependable. When her grandmother dies, for example, Yves refuses to attend the funeral, claiming not to be a close relative or friend ("je ne suis pas un proche," *Romance*, 72). Lise finds Yves's indifference to her loss distressing; it is also humiliating, since her family expects to see her boyfriend at the service. In contrast, Max does return for the funeral, thus showing up Yves's inadequacies. While Lise attends the service and the reading of her grandmother's will, Yves stays in her family house in Viorne. At the end of the day when she plans to return, he goes to a country fair, enjoys the amusements, ends up making love to another young woman, and sets off for Paris without waiting for Lise to get back to the house. In a callous note, he writes that he has been called away on urgent duties. His repeated departures at the very moments when Lise most needs his support are a sign of his unconscious aggression toward her.

For Lise, Yves' absences are also signs of what she regards as a male tendency to tell lies. "To lie, mentir. To die, mourir," she thinks at one point (*Romance*, 279). The sound she hears in the background of his phone call from Buenos Aires reminds her of the sound of a trumpet used to call people to order when they break a rule in the Luxembourg Garden in Paris. She leaps to the conclusion that he is not in Buenos Aires, but in Paris. In one of her characteristic plays on words, she identifies the verb "to deceive" (*tromper*) with the verb "to trumpet" (*trompeter*). Slipping from one word to the other, she thinks of elephants because they *trompent énormément* ("trumpet a huge lot" or "are tremendously deceitful"; *Romance*, 42). Telephone calls and telephone booths are associated in her mind with telling lies. When she observes a stranger using a telephone, she thinks right away that the man must be "telling lies" (*Romance*, 44). As her mind shifts to her suspicions about Yves, she longs to phone her mother and wail, "Mama, it's all over, he lied to me" (*Romance*, 43). But once she succeeds in reaching Yves in Buenos Aires, she realizes that she has made a mistake (*elle s'était trompée*, 48): he had not deceived her at all. The wordplay associated with the theme of lying and deception heightens the novel's unspoken critique of romantic clichés while also parodying Lacan's interest in linguistic slippage.

A related idea of Lacan's is that of the *chaîne signifiante* (signifying chain).[38] Through the motif of a white silk dress in a navy-blue boat print, the narrative shows how Lise identifies unwittingly with her female forbears. Originally, the dress had belonged to Lise's grandmother, Marcelle, who lends it to her daughter, Simone, to wear to a dance. Following the dance, she makes love to a young man; when her mother discovers her on the bidet, she is incensed and attacks Simone with such fury that a pearl button falls off the dress. Years later, Lise borrows the dress, which she finds when looking for nightwear to take to her grandmother in hospital. From Lacan's perspective, the recurrence of the dress reveals the way in which grandmother, mother, and granddaughter create a matrilineal heritage with respect to erotic desire.[39] In Freudian terms, the continual reemergence of the dress represents the "return of the repressed," in other words, the women's desire for sexual pleasure that is not socially sanctioned. When Lise inherits the family perfume shop from her grandmother, the relevance of several allusions to the perfume *Je reviens* ("I Return") becomes apparent. In a final twist characteristic of Camille Laurens's ironic handling of elements from psychoanalytic theory, the motif of the lost button returns in the form of a rose-shaped button lost by the young woman with whom Yves makes love at the fair. On one level, the lost button is a concrete piece of evidence against Yves; but on another level, it is also a humorous reference to the lost object of Lacanian theory.

Male and female fantasies about love are equally parodied in *Romance*. Just as Lise dreams of buying a flower-printed summer dress in which she will suddenly find herself marrying Yves, Max falls into a reverie at the grandmother's funeral in which he disrupts Lise's wedding to Yves by carrying her off on his shoulder. He imagines this daydream as a movie, complete with musical accompaniment (the wedding march that he seems to hear so vividly in his fantasy is actually the funeral music at the service for the grandmother). Yves's lovemaking with the young woman at the fairground is a repetition of the novel's opening scene, in which a male driver has a car accident and rolls off into a field with a female hitchhiker. There, the two make love before the astonished eyes of a farmer. But that scene is simply a scenario from Max's new film project. At a further remove, it also alludes to Lacan's account of his patient's dream in which "he saw himself driving a car, accompanied by a woman with whom he was having a rather difficult affair"—the dream about "flying fish and vesicle persecution" that A. S. Byatt's character cites with such bewilderment. As fantasy and reality intertwine in increasingly intricate ways, the novel repeatedly breaks through the wall between what Lacan terms the "symbolic" (i.e., the system of language) and the "imaginary" (the elements that constitute the self-identification of the individual).

Fantasy is repeatedly set off against violence in *Romance*. In his 1948 essay on aggressiveness, Lacan argues that aggressive tendencies originate in the mirror stage: "Aggressiveness is the tendency correlated with a mode of identification that I call narcissistic."[40] Although Lise puns on Yves's name by linking it with the words "offens-ive" and "aggress-ive," in fact all the characters in *Romance* show aggresssivity to one degree or another. Lise's confrontation with Yves about his fair-ground lovemaking is more than just verbally aggressive: she picks up an object from the table, "a letter-opener, a book press, a fire-poker, a garden tool" (*Romance*, 279), and batters her boyfriend until he falls to the floor, unconscious and bleeding.

One of Yves's patients tells him of recurrent dreams in which he "tries to strangle Simone" (*Romance*, 59). Simone is, of course, Lise's mother, who had divorced her Lise's father because he had threatened to kill her. Yves's patient is clearly Lise's father, Gilles. Yet the psychoanalytic process does not dispel his aggressive thoughts. Gilles' experience seems to argue against Lacan's view that psychoanalytic dialogue can sometimes substitute for the aggressive act. Lacan does point out in his essay, however, that an actual aggressive act frequently serves to "dissolve the delusional construction."[41] Gilles does not actually commit such an act, but Lise's act of battering Yves with a hard object suggests that her father's aggressivity has somehow been passed on to her.

Given Lacan's view that aggressive tendencies can be traced back to failure to pass through the mirror stage, it is not surprising that *Romance* abounds in mirrors. One "mirror" in the novel is not a reflecting glass, but simply a figure of speech. In French, the idiom *armoire à glace* (literally, a wardrobe with a mirror) refers to a chunky, heavy-set person. At the country fair, Yves notices such a person observing him. It is, of course, Max, with his square shoulders and hefty physique. Later, this "mirrored armoire" has moved to a different place—something unlikely to happen with a real piece of heavy furniture.

At the beginning and end of the novel, characters in an automobile watch the road unfold behind them like a ribbon (*Romance*, 17, 285). The first episode is part of the scenario Max is filming; the second depicts Lise's return to Paris after her attack on Yves. But whereas the scene in the film presents the road as a black ribbon (reminiscent of a mourning ribbon), the "real" scene at the end of the novel depicts the ribbon as pale. Perhaps the change has occurred because Lise has now enacted her aggression toward Yves and thus "resolved" this problem. That would certainly explain why she seems so unconcerned about the possibility that Yves may have died at her hands. In addition to this psychological explanation, the change in the road from dark to light can be connected with the photographic medium. Yet although the photographic process includes two reversals, one into a negative and the other into a positive image, a real act of violence like Lise's attack on Yves cannot be so easily reversed. This episode of the novel pointedly questions Lacan's argument that an act of aggression can "resolve" the problems caused by fantasies of aggression.

With this motif, *Romance* brings Lacanian theory into dialogue with traditional theories about literary realism. Nineteenth-century realism believed that individual development could be seen as a linear process; Lacan, following Freud, understands it as a constant "return." Where Stendhal had compared the realist novel with a "mirror carried along a roadway," Camille Laurens introduces the rearview mirror of an automobile. Camille Laurens gives a new twist to the much-quoted dictum. For traditional literary realism, the world can be represented by mirroring it in language; for Lacan, "the real" is precisely that which cannot be expressed in language. In a virtuoso manner, *Romance* ingeniously bridges the gap between the two modes of representation.

Beyond the French Tradition

J. M. Coetzee, whose many years of teaching literature in South Africa and the United States (notably the six years he spent affiliated with the Program on Social Thought at the University of Chicago) brought him into close contact with poststructuralist thought, engages less overtly with Lacan than the French writers we have been examining. Lacanian terminology makes no appearance in his novels, as it does in those of Duras, Kristeva, and Laurens. Rather, Lacanian theory is one strand among many drawn from his extensive reading in philosophy, psychology, and literature; it is this special mixture that gives his novels their rich texture, psychological depth, and political reach. Teresa Dovey's study of Lacanian allegories in Coetzee understands this aspect of his work when she explains that Coetzee's novels "may, for the most part, be located within the broad context of post-structuralism."[42] Coetzee not only "adopts and adapts" these theories,[43] his fiction "problematises rather than simply appropriates [Lacanian] theory."[44] This is an astute perception, and Dovey backs it up by sophisticated readings of individual texts.

She regards Coetzee's fiction as "not simply criticism-as-fiction, but as (Lacanian) psychoanalytic criticism-as-fiction."[45] Because her book appeared quite early, it covers only five major novels: *Dusklands, In the Heart of the Country, Waiting for the Barbarians, Life and Times of Michael K,* and *Foe.* Still, it is an important guide for later novels as well. Dovey's main argument concerns the ways in which Coetzee negotiates Lacan's understanding of the subject.

I will focus here on Coetzee's *The Age of Iron* (1990), where Lacanian ideas also inform the narrative.[46] Narrated from the perspective of a white woman, Mrs. Curren, this novel is concerned with difficult issues of complicity. Two decisive experiences confront the narrator with the complex way in which her own identity is linked with that of her country. Personal illness (her doctor's diagnosis of terminal cancer) and political violence (unrest in South African townships in 1986)[47] are the twin instigators of Mrs. Curren's lengthy exploration of her own position within the apartheid system of South Africa. It is, of course, a literary convention that writing can be a way of finding things out; here, however, it is not writing alone, but an enforced mirror stage that totally reconfigures Mrs. Curren's sense of self. In "Analysis and Truth or the Closure of the Unconscious," Lacan explains how the subject relates to the "Other" in psychoanalysis:

> It is in the space of the Other that he [the analysand] sees himself and the point from which he looks at himself is also in that space. Now, this is also the point from which he speaks, since in so far as he speaks, it is in the locus of the Other that he begins to constitute that truthful lie by which is initiated that which participates in desire at the level of the unconscious.[48]

In *The Age of Iron*, we find two "others" in this sense of the term: the old vagrant whom Mrs. Curren finds in her garage on her return from the doctor after her diagnosis, and her housekeeper, Florence, a woman from the townships whose struggle to keep her teenage son in check confronts Mrs. Curren with the terrors that have invaded the lives of black people on the outskirts of the city. These figures constitute the separate space in which the narrator sees herself and from which she increasingly comes to speak. At the same time, the novel is constructed as an almost two-hundred-page letter to Mrs. Curren's daughter in America who has left South Africa with the express intention of never coming back. By writing to her daughter, the mother inverts the desiring relationship that had begun in the daughter's infancy. In Lacan's theory, the mother's breast is the initial "object little a" or object of desire; for Mrs. Curren, that process is now reversed as she approaches her death from incurable breast cancer. Within the fiction, the letter is designed not to be sent to the daughter until after Mrs. Curren's death, a decision that has in part to do with the daughter's absolute break with South Africa, marked by her marriage to an American man and her consequent move to the United States. Yet although the letter employs some formulas proper to its genre, such as a reminder about information given in an earlier missive (*Iron*, 27), it also has a distinctly literary aspect. Still, Mrs. Curren is a former lecturer in the Classics, and thus a highly educated woman. Quoting Shakespeare's *Merchant of Venice*, she expresses her anguish by quoting Shylock's "Do I not bleed?" speech. Addressing her daughter, Mrs. Curren goes on, "I would cry my cry to you if you were here. But you are not" (*Iron*, 40). When she urges her daughter to read the letter "with a cold eye," she alludes to the epitaph that W. B. Yeats wrote for himself.[49] The literary aspect of the letter is not merely an aspect of its style: Derek Attridge comments that the letter functions "more like literature than most letters, since the work of literature, too, casts itself off from its author [by the "author" of the letter that is *The Age of Iron* Attridge means Mrs. Curren] and renders interrogation problematic."[50] Parts of the letter read like monologue: "And I? Where is my heart in all of this? My only child is thousands of miles away, safe; soon I will be smoke and ash . . ." (*Iron*, 50). Other parts take the form of a novel, with descriptive passages punctuated by conversations. Mrs. Curren asks the vagrant man if he will take it to the post office after her death, and despite initial reluctance, he agrees to do so. Yet Mrs. Curren knows she cannot trust the man she calls her "messenger." "To me this letter will forever be words committed to the waves: a message in a bottle with the stamps of the Republic of South Africa on it, and your [the daughter's] name" (*Iron*, 32).

The man who is at once a vagrant and a potential messenger provides an alternate other for Mrs. Curren. Repelled by his unkempt and foul-smelling body, she is also strangely drawn to him, in part because his condition anticipates the state to which her illness will ultimately reduce her. Still, it is odd that she writes at such length about him in her letters to her married daughter in America. "Why do I write about him?" Mrs. Curren asks. "Because he is and is not I. Because in the look he gives me I see myself in a way that can be written" (*Iron*, 9). Yet her absent daughter performs a similar function: "To whom is this writing then? The answer: to you but not to you; to me; to you in me" (*Iron*, 6). Vagrant and daughter become a symmetrical set of alter egos for Mrs. Curren: the one has imposed himself upon her, the other, upon whom she does not wish to impose herself, is held at a distance by the letters she writes but does not send. Making a kind of peace with the old man, Mrs. Curren gives him odd jobs and uses him as a make-do mechanic for her ancient car with its almost defunct battery. Although she recognizes that he exists outside the norms of civilized relationships,[51] she always addresses him as "Mr. Vercueil" as a sign of her refusal to treat him as riffraff. The old man's appearance in her garage just after she has received the verdict of incurable cancer is reinforced by his last name, which not accidentally reminds one of the French word for coffin, *cercueil*.

Another mirror is her black servant, Florence, a counterpart in her insistence on dignity, respect, and politeness, but an opponent in the violent struggle between the races. In a telling scene in which Florence does the ironing while Mrs. Curren looks on, Florence argues that the violence of young black people is a direct function of white repression. Florence envies the ability of the young black activists to express through action what she herself can only suggest indirectly. "These are good children," she says of some youngsters who poured more gasoline on a woman who had been set on fire in one of the townships, "they are like iron, we are proud of them" (*Iron*, 50). The clothes-pressing iron—another form of the word "iron"—allows Florence to express more than she can say explicitly: "The hand that held the iron pressed down hard. She glared at me. Lightly I touched her hand. She raised the iron. On the sheet was the beginning of a brown scorch mark" (*Iron*, 49).

The scorch mark, an objective correlative of the rash of fires in the black townships, is Florence's silent expression of resistance against her white employer. The antagonistic gesture also highlights Mrs. Curren's complicity in the white attitude toward blacks, at least insofar as she has never actively fought against the apartheid system. When Florence calls Vercueil "rubbish," Mrs. Curren responds sternly: "He is not a rubbish person. . . . There are no rubbish people. We are all people together" (*Iron*, 47). Florence is dismissive of this idealistic claim. Only later, after Mrs. Curren has experienced the violence in the townships and viewed the dead bodies of victims, including Florence's son Bheki, does she begin to see how she appears to others: as a "mad old do-gooder" (*Iron*, 105).

In addition to the strange symmetry between Vercueil and the daughter, a paradoxical mirroring is suggested by the contrast between Mrs. Curren's two grandsons in America, on the one hand, and Florence's son Bheki and his friend Johannes, on the other. In a seemingly counterintuitive reaction,

Mrs. Curren even identifies with the gun-toting Johannes whom she had at first found impossible to love: "He is with me or I am with him: him or the trace of him. . . . I am here in my bed but I am there in Florence's room too, with its one window and one door and no other way out" (*Iron*, 175). Her recognition resonates with her comment about her daughter as "you in me." This split in emotional allegiance—to her daughter's children and to the "rising generation" in the South African townships—causes a doubling of her identity that forms part of her learning curve in this last phase of her life. In comparison with Bheki and Johannes, hardened by their experience in South Africa, Mrs. Curren's American grandsons seem to her to be "two poor underprivileged boys" (*Iron*, 195)—underprivileged because they are protected from the moral issues South Africans must confront. The dead boys from the township become surrogates for the American grandsons, who seem too distant to be truly related to her.

Language creates a symbolic system in this novel as it does in Lacanian theory. The black families resist white language by concealing their real names and replacing them by seemingly acceptable substitutes. Bheki's friend bears an English name, John, which is translated into Johannes by the police; but his African name is not revealed. Similarly, although we learn that Bheki's name in the white world is Digby, the narrator never discovers the "black" names of his two sisters, Hope and Beauty. The girls' white names make Mrs. Curren think that she is "living in an allegory" (*Iron*, 90), but it is not at all clear that these names indicate any optimism on the part of the black family. Their true names might well have quite different meanings.

Mrs. Curren's own relation to language is similarly paradoxical. Despite her ready ability to lecture others such as Florence and Vercueil, she finds herself unable to articulate her response to her observation of police action in the townships: "I come to speak," she says, "but have nothing to say" (*Iron*, 105). By the same token, when she finally decides to engage in active protest, she can no longer articulate her position in words: "I have no voice, and that is that" (*Iron*, 164). Her repeated fantasy of setting herself on fire outside Government House—a design she does not, in fact, carry out—situates her as a mirror image of the woman immolated by fire in the township. In the letter to her daughter, however, Mrs. Curren focalizes profound reflections on vicarious experience and its function in narrative. Recounting the story of her nighttime drive to the township, the old woman is well aware that she summons her daughter's sympathy. "To me your sympathies flow; your heart beats with mine" (*Iron*, 103). As readers, we are inclined to include ourselves in this second-person address. Yet at the same time as Mrs. Curren solicits sympathy, she also begs her daughter to distance herself from the fact of her dying: "I am the one writing: I, I, I. So I ask you: attend to the writing, not to me" (*Iron*, 103–104); and further, contradicting the call for sympathy: "Do not read in sympathy with me. Let your heart not beat with mine" (*Iron*, 104). These instructions ward off and attempt to neutralize the appeal traditionally mobilized by letters in the epistolary novel.[52]

Coetzee's engagement with Lacanian theory takes place in the context of postcolonialism and is enriched by a climate of intense interest in this topic, as indicated by the emergence of postcolonial studies during the 1980s. In the case of *The Age of Iron*, among other novels by Coetzee, it might be more accurate to speak of the complex and lengthy process of decolonization.[53] In such situations, the symbolic order comes into acute conflict with the imaginary. The fantasies that underlie the psychology of individuals cannot find clear articulation: their complexities elude conventional language. As David Attwell puts it in his discussion of this novel, this is complicated in *The Age of Iron* by a "conflict of limits" in which Mrs. Curren speaks both against a historical other with whom she "has not made peace, exactly" but also against a more abstract limit, the "final horizon" of death.[54] Samantha Vice argues that this novel, with its "stringent ethics," "reminds us of neglected possibilities in the debate about partiality and impartiality."[55] At the center of what Mrs. Curren terms her "wager . . . with Vercueil, on Vercueil" is her insistence that she is "trying to keep a soul alive in times not hospitable to the soul" (*Iron*, 130). In Vice's perceptive analysis, the wager on Vercueil "is a wager on the possibility of ethics itself."[56] Yet, as she rightly notes, Coetzee is "seldom explicit about the content of the truths sought in the ethical realm."[57] In an age of iron, Vice suggests, a one-way conversation that also imagines the responses of its addressee is a compromise solution that "may be the best we can get."[58]

When Mrs. Curren, former teacher of classical languages, uses the phrase *amor matris* (*Iron*, 57), she is well aware that its second term can be understood as both a subjective and an objective genitive: mother-love and love of one's mother. The act of writing the letter to her daughter, an act of writing at once urgent and cautious, selfish and self-critical, brings out some of the complexities in Lacan's understanding of otherness. We are constituted not only by subjectivity, but also by the unconscious, which, though part of us, is also other to us. Coetzee complicates this idea by constructing a set of overlapping but different "others" in *The Age of Iron*: the daughter, Vercueil, Florence, her son Bheki, and his friend John. In this respect, the novel moves away from the triangular constructions of Duras and Kristeva to a more multidimensional understanding of the workings of desire in the postcolonial period.

4 *Women's Time*

Julia Kristeva's response to Lacan places the debate about female psychology into a framework defined not simply by the struggle between the sexes, but also by global power networks such as colonialism and terrorism. On a theoretical level, this position was heralded in her essay "Women's Time" (1979). In a period when feminists were asking major questions about the nature of femininity and the existence or otherwise of a characteristically female mode of writing, Kristeva looked for methods of extending and building on women's recent attempts to escape their historically subordinate position within social power structures. In particular, she explored the possibilities offered by new aesthetic practices as a way of counterbalancing traditional conceptions of history and economics. She had already published an important essay, "The Ethics of Linguistics" (1974), in which she went beyond the structuralist modes of thought that had been set forth by Saussure. This essay formed a significant part of the transition from structuralism, which worked in terms of binary oppositions, to a more fluid way of thinking characteristic of poststructuralism. Above all, however, it also highlighted moral and political questions. "Should a linguist, today, ever happen to pause and query the ethics of his own discourse," Kristeva wrote in her essay, "he might well respond by doing something else, e.g. engaging in political activity."[1] Her essay "Women's Time" continued this effort to address moral issues. Here, her desire to find a solution to problems of war and violence led her to conceive difference in terms of subversion and dissidence. Her belief that writing would provide the most appropriate instrument for creating a new social model made her theory especially attractive to women authors, especially those with an idealistic bent.

In "Women's Time," Kristeva describes the social basis of her theory in terms of two important historical changes: first, the new understandings of women's relationship to violence and nationhood that emerged during and in the wake of World War II; and second, the emergence in the 1970s of terrorist groups that included women (the Red Army Faction in Germany was a good example). Describing the history of feminist movements in the post-1945 period, she distinguished between a phase when women aspired to gain a place for themselves in history as it had traditionally been conceived by men, and a subsequent phase in which women attempted to revive mythic conceptions of history that might express female subjectivity without filtering it through male thought-structures. As Alice Jardine explained in a 1981 introduction to "Women's Time" in the journal *Signs*, the essay posed particular problems for American feminist readers for whom the "theoretical time and space" in which Kristeva's argument was located was bound to be "totally alien."[2] For one thing, as Jardine pointed out, the French concept of "history" did not accord with the American understanding of the word: it needed to be seen, rather, in the context of a sweeping change in the philosophical positions taken by French thinkers. Dialectical conceptions of history such as those espoused by Hegel had been replaced by a new posture of "suspicion" modeled on the views of Marx, Nietzsche, Freud, and Foucault. Traditional ideas of historical teleology were no longer in tune with this more skeptical position.[3] American readers were also puzzled by French feminism and its exploration of the ambiguous nature of the "feminine" in traditional thought (the French word *féminine* includes the sense "female" as well as "feminine"). When French feminists wrote about literature, they were not primarily concerned to reveal the existence of strong women characters or forgotten women's voices, as were members of the first wave of American feminist scholarship. In the case of Kristeva, this difference was compounded by her position within the French social and academic system: born and educated in Bulgaria until her early twenties, Kristeva was and still remains something of a foreigner in France, and she likes to stylize herself as an observer watching from the margins. Kristeva turns this apparent handicap into a strength, since it allows her to stand, in certain ways, outside traditional thinking about women in society. In "Women's Time," she shows how "various forms of marginalism" have enabled women to envisage new social organisms that could function as a kind of "countersociety" to traditional, patriarchal structures.[4] She takes pains to exclude one type of marginal figure, the terrorist, from this positive effect, arguing that the structures terrorism aim to put into place are "even more oppressive, more sacrificial than those it combats" (28). For American readers of "Women's Time" when it first appeared in translation in 1981, the idea of women terrorists must have seemed somewhat remote; but Kristeva was thinking of the Baader-Meinhof gang in Germany, which included women as well as men.

Parts of Kristeva's analysis did seem familiar, however: for example, the idea of two generations of feminism. By 1980, it was common to distinguish the politically activist phase initiated by Betty Friedan's *The Feminine Mystique* (1963) from the theoretically more complex ideas developed by Kate Millett in *Sexual Politics* (1970). Yet in fact, the two waves of American feminism were different from the two stages that Kristeva identifies in "Women's Time." In her analysis, the first generation was more concerned with women's position in national societies, while the second was more trans-European in focus.

Rethinking Nietzsche's ideas on temporality, Kristeva postulated three different ways of conceptualizing history: first, in terms of linear time and sequentially arranged language; second, as cyclical time defined by figures of repetition; and third, as monumental time, static and eternal. Linear time, in her view, belongs to the male order. This is history as we have traditionally studied it: conceived sequentially as a series of dated events. The first French feminists, she explains, "aspired to gain a place in linear time as the time of project and history" ("Women's Time," 18). "Cyclical time" and "monumental time" break with this traditional concept of history. "Cyclical time," a heightened consciousness of historical recurrence, seemed to Kristeva more in tune with women's biological rhythms and female sensibilities. In her analysis, the second generation of European feminists are influenced by aesthetic or psychoanalytic experience: they "seek to give a language to the intra-subjective and corporeal experiences left mute by culture in the past" ("Women's Time,"

19). Their self-understanding is more multiple and more fluid. "Monumental time," finally, is an apprehension for which "the very word 'temporality' hardly fits" ("Women's Time," 16). Kristeva finds it in mythic or mystical thinking, for example maternal cults where "the body of the Virgin Mother does not die but moves from one spatiality to another within the same time" ("Women's Time," 17). This conversion of time into space holds a certain appeal, Kristeva notes, but it also runs the risk of reviving archaic ideas unsuited to the modern world. For this reason, Kristeva argues, women need to go beyond these conceptions of history by interweaving all three approaches to temporality ("Women's Time," 33).

One crucial factor in Kristeva's theory is her personal experience of Eastern Europe. In "Women's Time," she writes about women in socialist countries who, having been promoted to positions of social, economic, or political power, suddenly became "the most zealous protectors of the established order" ("Women's Time," 26). Even in Western countries, she notes, women's rise to power does not inevitably guarantee liberation from tradition, but often leads to "the consolidation of conformism" ("Women's Time," 27). Her detective novels are set in a space where precisely such problems can be played out.[5] As we have seen, this location is the fictional city of "Santa Barbara" ("Santa Varvara" in English translations), situated in an Eastern European country.[6] Not until her third detective novel, *Murder in Byzantium* (*Meurtre à Byzance,* 2004), does Kristeva give any sense of the ways in which the space of her fictions might map onto real geographical space; but even there, we do not have a full picture. Her native country, Bulgaria, is certainly one possible, but by no means exclusive, model for this space. In Kristeva's first detective novel, *The Old Man and the Wolves* (1991; *Le vieil homme et les loups*), Santa Varvara combines vestiges of communism with the beginnings of a new, liberal society. In a 2006 interview, Kristeva explained that the idea for *The Old Man and the Wolves* came to her after her father's death as the result of medical error in a Bulgarian hospital shortly before the fall of the Berlin Wall in 1989.[7] The central figure of the novel, an elderly professor, dies when his heart-lung machine is turned off by unknown perpetrators, presumably the "wolves" of the novel's title. In contrast to France, presented as a place of light and reason, Santa Varvara is characterized by a violent undercurrent and its language is—from the French perspective—a kind of barbarian tongue. Nonetheless, the novels suggest that the Eastern and Western worlds overlap in peculiar ways that often resist common sense and rationality.

Suspended Time: Kristeva's *Possessions*

Kristeva's second detective novel, *Possessions* (1996), is not only an engagement with Lacan, as we saw in chapter 3, but also an attempt to negotiate
theories about feminism and "women's time." The opening scene contrasts
male and female ways of thinking in a conversation between the detective
Northrop Rilsky and the journalist Stephanie Delacour. Stephanie regards
investigative journalism as essentially another version of detective work.
Instead of focusing on the problem at hand—who could have killed Gloria Harrison, her previous evening's hostess?—Stephanie's mind wanders
through an entire list of headless figures in painting, sculpture, and history, including John the Baptist, Holofernes, Rodin's *Walking Man*, the
Winged Victory of Samothrace, and various victims of the guillotine. This
virtuoso meditation shows Stephanie as not only a person of intelligence
and cultural knowledge, but also of grim humor and a complete lack of
squeamishness. "Amid all the hassle that follows a crime, a sensitive soul
like me likes to pause for thought," she says. "For two thousand years the
gory neck of St. John the Baptist, the Forerunner, has been advancing
toward us from the shores of the Dead Sea." (*Possessions*, 5) She gives an
entire list of severed heads in Caravaggio: "To say he loves severed heads is
putting it mildly; he adores them, worships them." (*Possessions*, 7). Rodin's
Walking Man, "with both hands over his sex organs, is a supreme example
of how to lose one's head," she quips (*Possessions*, 8). While Stephanie's
mind bounds through large tracts of cultural history, time seems to stand
still as she confronts the dead body of Gloria Harrison. If Gloria's dead
body is merely another example in a long lineage of decapitation, as Stephanie's five-page riff on headless bodies suggests, we can understand this
scene as a parody of the cyclic vision Kristeva attributes to women's consciousness in her famous essay. Yes, Kristeva can parody herself, or at least
engage in a little mischievous self-critique. In Kristeva's subsequent novel,
Murder in Byzantium, Stephanie recalls having heard "Kristeva speaking
at the Arab World Institute" and later comments on "the theorizing of a
few Parisian psychiatrists along with Julia Kristeva, but it's far from the
dominant view."[8] Stephanie's rambling reflections create a strong retard-
ing moment, breaking the forward movement we expect at the opening
of a detective novel. Rilsky and his second-in-command are inspecting
the body and exchanging thoughts about the situation, but their conversation impinges very little on Stephanie's consciousness. When they do

interrupt her art-historical meditations, his observations about the crime scene appear mundane and to her, at least, superfluous. This is only natural, since they return her to the realm of male thought.

A flashback to the dinner party of the previous evening reproduces a provocative conversation about the differences between men and women, full of jocular references to psychological concepts of gender and to the "feminization" of modern society via the media. Stephanie and Rilsky, we discover, have differing cultural interests: while she loves painting and sculpture, he finds them too static; he prefers music, the art most obviously connected with time.

Stephanie is not the only woman in the novel for whom time stands still at critical junctures. Additional flashbacks reveal that Gloria Harrison had virtually suspended time in her devotion to her deaf son, Jerry. Ignoring her mother's suggestions that she devote herself to activist causes ("move with the times, get a breath of fresh air, take up a cause, be a feminist—*do* something or other!" her mother advises her)[9], she works at home as a translator in order to supervise Jerry's upbringing and make the handicapped child as much like other children as possible. Time had stood still for Pauline as well after the death by drowning of her brother Aimeric.

Still, the male-female division is not so simple. Stephanie is, after all, a journalist, professionally occupied with events as they occur day by day. In France she feels comfortably supported by Cartesian logic: "no more opacities, dramas, or mysteries," she remarks; "Everything obvious, transparent, in the open. Clarity in the language and in the unsullied sky." (*Possessions*, 162). Indeed, it is precisely during a return trip to Paris that Stephanie learns about the previous history of Pauline and her brother when she overhears another jetsetter talking about them at a bar. In a sort of empathetic reverie, Stephanie reconstructs the events of Aimeric's death in Brittany in a "close third-person" form, as if she were partially merging with the younger Pauline during the holiday on the beach. One of the women at the bar speaks in a rather catty way about Pauline's suicide attempts following her brother's drowning, implying that the young woman's wrist- and throat-slashing was merely a cover for her guilt. This new information allows Stephanie to intuit that it was actually Pauline who had decapitated Gloria. "Thinking about it later, Stephanie couldn't really tell why or how she came to suspect Pauline" (*Possessions*, 179). The text strongly suggests that Pauline's role in Gloria's murder can only be discovered by another woman, one who has the imagination to identify with this otherwise inexplicable act.

Passing from French clarity to the murkier atmosphere of Santa Varvara a year and a half later, Stephanie suddenly fits the story of Pauline's past into the story of Gloria Harrison's murder. Picking up on Jerry's account of his and Pauline's departure on vacation on the night of the murder, Stephanie imagines what must have happened: returning to the house to fetch some computer games Jerry has forgotten, Pauline finds the corpse of Gloria Harrison, which she decapitates using a scalpel she has kept from the time of her medical studies. Stephanie's intuitions about Pauline's state of mind result from her female ability to "take possession" of another by a process akin to transference.[10] She surmises that Pauline's feelings at the sight of Gloria's murdered body must have brought back memories of her depression after Aimeric's death, when Pauline herself felt like a corpse. In a sudden conflation of past and present, Pauline must have severed Gloria's head in a repetition of her psychological severance of herself from her mother. The "sleepwalking" state into which Stephanie falls in her "Santavarvarian" mode permits her to imagine Pauline as another sleepwalker, committing an act that she is unable to comprehend with her conscious mind. Through these somewhat overdetermined motifs, the text suggests that only a woman can identify in this way with another woman's psyche. By contrast, the male detective Northrop Rilky solves only those parts of the murder that are perpetrated by men: Gloria's strangulation by her lover and her subsequent stabbing by a random male serial killer.

If, as Lacan had stated, the unconscious is structured like a language, it is structured in this novel more like Santavarvarian. Indeed, as Colin Davis observes, Santavarvarian can be viewed as "the other scene" of the unconscious.[11] Tapping into that reserve is a crucial element in detective work, which thus reveals its kinship to psychoanalysis. In this respect, Stephanie differs from the two other women in the story, Gloria and Pauline, both of whom succumb to what Kristeva calls "the belief in the omnipotence of an archaic, full, total, englobing mother with no frustration, no separation, no break-producing symbolism." As Kristeva argues, women must "challenge precisely this myth of the archaic mother" ("Women's Time," 29). Stephanie is able to do so because she has come to terms with the loss of her still-born child and is no longer fixated on the myth of the archaic mother. Precisely because she maintains a degree of separation from Jerry, Stephanie is able to take on official responsibility for him at the end of the novel. "The ability to succeed in this path without masochism and without annihilating one's affective, intellectual, and professional personality—such would seem to be the

stakes to be won through guiltless maternity" ("Women's Time," 31). Kristeva
admits in her essay that this ideal perhaps remains utopian, but she argues
that it will be a central question for a third generation of feminists.

A Female Counterculture: Wolf's *Cassandra*

In late 1970s West Germany, French feminist theory was rapidly incorpo-
rated into the highly politicized debates about feminism. In East Germany,
by contrast, French feminism posed a challenge because its origins in psychoanalysis made it unacceptable to the official regime. Christa Wolf's *Kassandra*
(1983; Cassandra) is one of the most probing East German attempts to put
French feminist theory to the test. *Cassandra* is much more than a novel: it is
a cluster of texts in multiple genres including a "travel report," a "work diary,"
a personal letter to a woman writer, and a fictional reworking of the Cassandra myth narrated by Cassandra. Wolf had first presented these five parts
in West Germany as her Frankfurt Lectures on Aesthetics (a distinguished
series in which, each year, a different author is invited to develop his or her
ideas about writing). In Germany, the fictional narrative *Cassandra* was published separately from the other four parts, which appeared under the title
Conditions of a Narrative. In America, the narrative and the other texts were
published together in a single volume.[12] In contrast to the Frankfurt lectures,
which ended with the fictional text, the American edition places it first and
adds the other materials as a kind of appendix. In order to follow the argument Christa Wolf presents in *Cassandra*, however, it is essential to read the
texts in the original order of presentation. *Cassandra* is not a literary text
accompanied by a cluster of appendices or spin-offs. Understood correctly,
the entire project is a piece of experimental writing that explores questions of
history, temporality, and gender through the multiple lenses of genres with
varying relations to reality.

Oddly, Christa Wolf does not include any titles by Kristeva in the ambitious bibliography appended to the German edition of her work diary. Nonetheless, the list ranges broadly over works in different languages and from
different periods, among them Virginia Woolf's *A Room of One's Own* (1929),
Silvia Bovenschen's *Imagined Womanhood* (1979), Robert Graves's *The White
Goddess* (1948), and Klaus Theweleit's *Male Fantasies* (1977). A list of book
titles noted in the personal letter that immediately preceded the fictional text
in the Frankfurt lectures includes Johann Jakob Bachofen's *Mother Right*

(1861) and Luce Irigaray's *This Sex Which Is Not One* (1977). Wolf clearly cast her net very widely in her preliminary reading for the *Cassandra* project.

The absence of specific reference to Kristeva may be an oversight,[13] but its omission certainly tips the scale toward Irigaray. Kristeva did not entirely share Irigaray's belief in an essential female nature that gives rise to "feminine writing" or writing by women authors.[14] Wolf takes up this issue in the "Work Diary": "To what extent is there really such a thing as 'women's writing'? To the extent that women, for historical and biological reasons, experience a different reality than men. . . . To the extent that women belong not to the rulers, but to the ruled . . ." (*Cassandra*, 259). In this passage, Wolf accepts history and biology as determinants in the position of women in modern social structures. She also believes that women have special creative capabilities that need to be deployed in the struggle for women's rights. Other parts of the text make it clear that she agrees with Irigaray's idea that femininity is multiple and fluid, and that these attributes can be helpful to women as they attempt to escape their subordinate social roles. In the fictional narrative, however, Wolf draws a contrast between male and female conceptions of time and explores the idea of creating a feminist countersociety. These elements of *Cassandra* seem closer to Kristeva than to Irigaray. The theme of a women's countersociety picks up one of Kristeva's key ideas, but the narrative form—Cassandra's thoughts as she approaches death—allows for a more mobile kind of language.

The "Travel Report" that opened the Frankfurt lecture series tells of a trip to Greece that Wolf made with her husband. Reading Euripides while waiting to board a delayed plane flight, the speaker wonders if she could somehow strip away the surface of the text to uncover the archaic Cassandra beneath. Digging more deeply into the myth means replacing notions of Cassandra constructed by nineteenth- and early twentieth-century archaeologists and creating a different version more closely representative of ancient Minoan culture. The travel narrative becomes increasingly interwoven with reflections on the ancient world. On her way to view famous archaeological sites, the narrator encounters an American woman scholar with whom she has had previous professional contact: "Helen, from Columbus, Ohio," traveling with her friend Sue, from Los Angeles (*Cassandra*, 182). The two Americans are looking for evidence of strong female traditions in archaic culture in the hope of confirming their belief "that women called the tune on Crete and that the Minoans were the better for it" (*Cassandra*, 183). The narrator views the two women sympathetically, but also with a grain of skepticism. She herself takes a different route. Feeling her way imaginatively into early Minoan culture, she tries to reconstruct Cassandra as a figure in transition between matriarchal and patriarchal systems.

On the surface, the "Travel Report" traces the various stages of the journey. Its linearity is undercut, however, by constant oscillation between present and past, knowledge and imagination. The narrator highlights the constructed nature of chronological history and its problematic relation to the nonlinear character of myth. Following the "Travel Report" is a "Work Diary." This, too, takes a linear form, with dated entries arranged in chronological sequence. Yet the diary is also undercut, not only by complex movements among different time planes but also by a movement between personal memory and texts read.

In its penultimate part, immediately preceding the fictional narrative, the text again takes a personal form. Couched as a letter to a woman friend, it is essentially a piece of literary criticism. It frames a discussion of Goethe's Faust with a close reading of a poem by Ingeborg Bachmann and a study of Bachmann's unfinished story *The Franza Case* (published posthumously in 1979). It is significant that two works by a modern female author frame a canonical work by a male author. The letter-writer perceives close links between Helen, in Goethe's *Faust*, and Franza, in Bachmann's story, both of them, in her view, "colonized" by males for whom they act as embodiments of imagined womanhood. The letter refuses to accept the male paradigm that women must either "adapt" or "disappear" (*Cassandra*, 279–300). Instead, it argues that literature should present woman in her own right rather than as an ideal constructed by a patriarchal system.

Thus, before even reaching the *Cassandra* fiction proper, the reader has already worked through a complicated series of texts. The meandering route toward the *Cassandra* story is figured in terms of two different motifs from classical myth: Penelope's web and Daedalus's labyrinth. The tapestry Penelope weaves by day and unravels by night is an apposite image for this unusual text (the word "text" derives from the Greek word "to weave") that "unravels" traditional myths about Cassandra. Far from being the maligned women seer of classical tradition, Cassandra appears as a genuine visionary, the first in a long lineage of far-sighted, creative women. Wolf unravels familiar texts about Cassandra just as Penelope undid her daily weaving. The labyrinth metaphor suggests that it is precisely the nonlinear or labyrinthine course of her thinking and writing that allows her to reconstruct the original Cassandra of the Minoan period. Like Theseus feeling his way out of the labyrinth by following Ariadne's thread, Cassandra tells her story by groping backward "along the thread of [her] life" (*Cassandra*, 21). The story Cassandra tells will be a correction of the familiar myth.

Wolf's *Cassandra* (1983) shares several concerns with Julia Kristeva's "Women's Time" (1973). Kristeva's concerns about violence, motivated by the terrorist groups of the 1970s, are echoed by Wolf's fear of a possible nuclear war in Central Europe that might occur if the tenuous equilibrium between America and the Soviet Union were to be disturbed.[15] In the fictional narrative *Cassandra*, the Trojan War functions as a temporal displacement of this concern. Within the narrative, Cassandra passes through two phases similar to those outlined in Kristeva's: a desire to insert herself into male history, and an attempt to diverge from male conceptions of history by developing fundamentally different ideals. Initially, Cassandra wishes to be a seer: she is envious of her brother Helenus, actually a rather mediocre prophet, and even more so of the male visionary, Laocoon. Once she herself receives the "gift of prophecy," she becomes involved with a group of women who meet outside the caves on the slopes of Mount Ida. This is the "counterworld" of the narrative (*Cassandra*, 48).

As Cassandra exercises her visionary gift, she begins to develop something akin to what Kristeva terms "aesthetic practices" that will themselves constitute an intervention in political realities. Cassandra insists repeatedly on her marginal position in which she is not only "outside this final gate" (*Cassandra*, 8) but also "out of her mind" (*Cassandra*, 43). Yet her marginality is precisely what grants her access to modes of thought beyond the pale of ordinary logic. The fictional text forces the reader to enter into these new modalities through the complicated games it plays with temporality. The opening paragraph takes us rapidly from the present to the past, shifting almost imperceptibly from the pronoun "she" to the pronoun "I." At first, we seem to be standing with Christa Wolf in front of a ruined stone fortress whose gate is guarded by two stone lions that have lost their heads. Yet we are also there with Cassandra, back in the time when these monuments had not yet been reduced to rubble. Chronological time has elapsed, yet "the sky is still the same." The kinship with Kristeva's concepts of linear and monumental time is striking.

Expanding on ideas Wolf had already developed in an earlier novel,[16] Cassandra tries to develop an expressive medium more flexible than conventional language. Her prophecies appear in the form of images; and she believes, accordingly, that "the last thing in my life will be a picture, not a

word. Words die before pictures" (*Cassandra*, 21). Words, which demand
sequential arrangement, are associated here with the male sphere, whereas
images, which are not linear, are linked with the female sphere. The increasing emphasis on the visual rather than the verbal as the narrative nears its end
suggests the emergence of a new, female aesthetic. In this sense, we could say
that *Cassandra* takes up a question Luce Irigaray had raised in her *Speculum
of the Other Woman*: "But what if the 'object' [i.e., woman, subordinated in
patriarchal societies] started to speak?"[17]

Still, the story's attempt to leave linear time behind poses difficult narrative challenges. We are asked to imagine that told in over a hundred pages of
written text before Cassandra's imagination in a single flash. This works only
to the extent that we call to mind the traditional story of the Trojan War, yet
the fragmentary and shifting form of Cassandra's interior monologue continually frustrates our attempts to do so.

Conscious of the difficulties of presenting "women's time" in language at
all, Wolf draws on Ernst Bloch's *The Spirit of Utopia* (1918):

> I am by myself.
>   That I move, that I speak: is not there. Only immediately afterwards
> can I hold it up in front of me. Ourselves within: while we live, we do
> not see it; we trickle away. What really happened there, then, what we
> really were then, refuses to coincide with what we can really experi-
> ence. It is not what one is, and certainly not what one means.[18]

The opening passage of the *Cassandra* narrative signals this connection by
its clipped sentences and its movement between past and present: "It was
here. This was where she stood. These stone lions looked at her; now they no
longer have heads. This fortress—once impregnable, now a pile of stones—
was the last thing she saw. A long-forgotten enemy demolished it, so did the
centuries, sun, rain, wind. The sky is still the same, a deep, blue block, high,
vast" (*Cassandra*, 3).

For Bloch, memory was not merely backward-looking, but also an "antici-
patory consciousness" that allows us to imagine the future. He argues that
history should always be understood as if from its end, an end conceived also
as a future that opens onto an unlimited field of possibilities. Although Wolf's
Cassandra looks backward from the moment of her imminent death, her train
of thought permits us to imagine a new form of social organization in which
figures like Cassandra will not be put to death. Reflecting on the past while

envisaging a differently structured future, this Cassandra assumes her full powers as a woman visionary. As Kristeva had written in "Women's Time," "women are writing, and the air is heavy with expectation: What will they write that is new?" (32). Perhaps, Wolf suggests, it is something like *Cassandra*.

Museum Time: Maron's *Animal Triste*

In *Animal Triste* (1996),[19] Monika Maron took issue with precisely the kind of mythic vision that Christa Wolf had inscribed in *Cassandra*. Written after German reunification by a writer who had herself left the GDR for the west in 1988, the novel explores what had come to be known as *Ostalgie*: homesickness for the East German state that has been swallowed up in the new German republic (*Ost* means "east" in German). Because the German communist regime had presented itself as an idyllic society, untouched by what it regarded as the mercenary and egotistical aspects of Western society, some of its former citizens had trouble adjusting to reunification. From their perspective, they had lost a kind of security and predictability (even though that had been purchased at the price of oppressive surveillance by the state). Taking the familiar trope of lovers divided by cultural differences, Maron dismantles the utopian associations of "women's time" and suggests that it may be unwise to ignore chronological and historical time.

The narrator of *Animal Triste* is an elderly woman who was formerly the curator of an East German museum of paleontology. The novel is set well into the future. Claiming to have forgotten her age—she thinks she may be ninety or perhaps even one hundred years old—the woman looks back at her relationship with a man whose name she has also forgotten but whom, for the sake of narrative convenience, she decides to call Franz. Her affair with this man had begun just after the reunification of Germany. A common German term for reunification is *die Wende* (the turning point). Suddenly a man from the western part of Germany appears in her museum and the two begin a love affair that flourishes in the first instance because there is no state boundary, no political difference to separate them. After a period of ecstatic happiness, however, the relationship begins to fail, in part because of mundane cultural differences. One of the greatest problems for the lovers turns out to be their divergent relationships to time.

While she was still working in the museum, the narrator had a clear sense of the relation between present and past, encapsulated in a brachiosaurus skeleton housed beneath a glass roof. Although she enjoyed watching over the enormous skeleton, she had longed to be able to travel to the West. Her dearest wish had been to see the dinosaur tracks in South Hadley, Massachusetts, and walk on ground that the creatures had trodden in prehistoric times. Now, instead of spending her days in a glass-roofed museum space, she inhabits a kind of mental bubble in which time exists only in the vaguest of approximations. Thus, she remembers little of her life before Franz and before reunification. Scraps of memory concerning her parents do not form any kind of continuous story. Animals make isolated appearances: she recalls riding on the back of a large Saint Bernard; she once gave her daughter a pet tortoise; and another time she helped a friend to recover a stolen dog. But again, these images fail to make coherent meaning.

She calls the German Democratic Republic *die seltsame Zeit* (the strange time; *Animal*, 45). Like the glass room in the museum that houses the brachiosaurus bones, the communist state is an enclosed space, cut off from the rest of the world. Yet her love affair also appears to be sealed off from the flow of events. From her present perspective, it seems like "a timeless time not ordered by any cogwheels, a time in which I have been ever since as if in the airy interior of a sphere" (*Animal*, 126). Even long afterward, she remains in the bubble, suspended in a kind of fetal position.

The fall of the Berlin Wall means that the narrator can fulfill her lifelong ambition to travel to America to see the dinosaur tracks, but although she does get as far as New York, she turns back before setting out for Massachusetts. Pliny Moody's garden, the site of the prehistoric footprints, no longer holds the same fascination for her. In her mind, the dinosaur park has become an idyllic spot not unlike the traditional lovers' meeting-place or *locus amoenus*: "Pliny Moody's garden was a wild, paradise-like piece of land where a gentle wind tamed the heat" (*Animal*, 86). In actual fact, Pliny Moody was a young farm boy who found the dinosaur tracks while plowing a field in 1802.[20] The alteration to the historical story behind the strange markings Moody had found on a stone slab is characteristic of the narrator. She prefers to imagine a place untouched by time, the mythic home of the "ancient, atavistic power" she so often experienced in the museum's dinosaur room.

By contrast, Franz and his wife go on a trip to Britain because of their interest in recorded history. A highlight of the journey for Franz is Hadrian's Wall, the ancient dividing line between Roman and barbarian Britain. When the narrator reaches Franz by phone at his hotel, she refuses to listen to what he has to say about the wall. Angry that he has visited the site with his wife rather than with her, she believes that he sees her as a barbarian. The cultural divide between East and West Germany persists between them, a phenomenon popularly known as "the Wall in the head."

Underlying this novel is a seemingly simplistic opposition: while the man is firmly anchored in (chronological) time, the woman drifts in a timeless and undifferentiated realm. Since the end of their affair, the curator has been telling herself a story that turns out not to be true: that Franz just went away and never came back. At the end of the novel, however, we discover that she has been trying "not to know" what really happened. This is a fascinating variation of more familiar versions of unreliable narration. In a stunning last move, the narrator finally recalls what happened when she realized that Franz could never leave his wife for her. As so often, the lovers have spent the night together and are saying good-bye at the bus stop:

> The bus is almost here, I clutch Franz's sleeve between my fists. Stay here. Franz tries to get away. I fling myself around him with my own arms and with his. I'm coming back tomorrow. I know he's lying. Then go, go. A noise never heard before, as if wet cardboard were slapping against iron. Howling like the howling of a pack of dogs. Who's crying out like that. Someone is bleeding under the bus. A pool of blood appears in the gutter. The crushed arm of a man under the front wheel. (*Animal*, 238)

In her mind's eye, she herself seems to turn into an animal, a brown ape clutching herself with long furry arms.

This final image is profoundly troubling. The woman who has forbidden her daughter any pet other than a tortoise is now herself reduced to an animal-like existence. A question arises: can animals have feelings of guilt? Surely human consciousness divides us from animals in this regard. Becoming like an animal is nothing other than an escape into atavism, not unlike her earlier identification with the brachiosaurus. But her refusal of guilt in Franz's death under the bus is also similar to the refusal of communist Germany to admit its role in the Nazi past. Declaring itself the heir of the communist resistance to Hitler, the GDR had willfully obscured the fact that many of its citizens had in fact been complicit with Nazism. By the same token, former East Germans who claim that they were oppressed by a communist dictatorship may not be fully acknowledging their own passivity in refusing to protest against that government. The curator's narrative meditation—the entire monologue that comprises this novel—opens her mind briefly to the possibility of personal guilt. But in the end, she decides to close her eyes again and drift back into the protective, timeless bubble where she began her narrative. This may seem like an unduly harsh indictment of the GDR and its former citizens.

We need to remember, however, that Franz is also not free from guilt. After all, he has refused to leave his wife and move in with the narrator. It is not as if Maron has simply returned to an older tradition that values historical time over all else. The narrator's predicament at the end is quite moving. Read as a response to Christa Wolf's implicit proposal in *Cassandra* that "women's time" might serve as a remedy for the warrior societies constructed by men, Maron's *Animal Triste* suggests that there is in fact no simple solution. Neither the creation of a prototypically "women's" conception of time and language nor a return to "male" linear time and logic provides a satisfactory resolution to the most fundamental dilemmas of human existence. Maron's title indicates as much. It alludes, after all, to the Latin proverb attributed to Galen: *post coitum omne animal triste est sive gallus, qui cantat* (after coitus all animals are sad, except the rooster, who crows). Some versions of the saying include two exceptions, the rooster and the woman (*sive gallus et mulier*), which would introduce even greater irony to Maron's use of the truncated phrase in the novel's title.

In the final analysis, however, it would be misleading to privilege the personal over the political and historical strand of *Animal Triste*: the novel focuses equally on differences between the sexes and between the two state systems. The complex interweaving of the two themes is a significant part of the novel.[21] Insofar as *Animal Triste* engages with Christa Wolf's *Cassandra*, Maron's novel would seem to suggest that the women's utopia Wolf envisages in *Cassandra* is ultimately unworkable. Maron's *Animal Triste* seems to argue that utopian ideals come at the expense of historical consciousness.

Male and Female Historians: Kristeva's *Murder in Byzantium*

In her third detective novel, *Meurtre à Byzance* (2004; *Murder in Byzantium*), Julia Kristeva revisits "Women's Time" from a complex and sophisticated perspective that permits her to explore more closely the relation of sexual difference to the aesthetic. Once again, the journalist Stephanie Delacour and detective superintendent Northrop Rilsky stage the distinction between the male and the female psyche, a distinction now complicated by the fact that they have embarked on a love relationship. In this novel, as in Kristeva's previous detective fictions, love motivates various kinds of identification that enable the plot to move forward. In two intertwined subplots, two other male-female pairs add depth and detail to the novel's study of this problem: first, the twins Fa and Xiao Chang, and second, the historian Sebastian Chrest-Jones and his predecessor from the twelfth century, Anna Comnena. Emotional identification with a person of the opposite sex is involved in each of these pairings. The bond of affection between the twins is colored by fierce jealousy on the part of Xiao for his sister and intense anxiety coupled with a kind of rejection on the part of Fa for her intellectually handicapped and violent brother. In the other couple, the bond is purely imaginary and held together by written texts. Sebastian Chrest-Jones, a historian of migration patterns and racial intermarriage, has "fallen in love" with Anna Comnena (1083–1153) through her epic *The Alexiad*, a history begun but not completed by her husband. The epic recounts the events of her father's reign and his military campaigns against the West; it is the main source of Byzantine history and culture from the period. Sebastian's obsession with Anna Comnena offers a different way of understanding sexual identity while also situating this issue within a complex conflation of time and space. The form of identification between the two historians Sebastian Chrest-Jones and Anna Comnena is not unlike the one that Kristeva attributes to the pregnant woman in "Woman's Time": a "redoubling up [sic] of the body, separation and coexistence of the self and another, of physiology and speech." ("Women's Time," 31). A similar relationship exists between the twins Fa and Xiao Chang. In each case, the imagined relationships "are accompanied by a fantasy of totality—narcissistic completeness" ("Women's Time," 31).

While detective superintendent Rilsky attempts to discover the perpetrator of serial murders "signed" by the mark for infinity incised upon the victims' bodies, the journalist Stephanie Delacour tries to find out why Sebastian Chrest-Jones has suddenly disappeared. As in *Possessions*, the male detective employs reason to search for the serial murderer, whereas the female journalist uses psychological identification to discover the motivation of the missing historian. Significantly, her work proceeds by means of a text: Sebastian Chrest-Jones's computer files on Anna Comnena. From the tone of his writing, Stephanie discerns that he has fallen in love with his Byzantine precursor. This leads her to guess that he has decided to follow the trajectory of the First Crusade in reverse and to predict where his next stop will be. The narrative's crisis occurs in a dramatic moment that brings together Stephanie Delacour, Northrop Rilsky, Sebastian Chrest-Jones, and Xiao Chang.

A detective story naturally unfolds in time: a death has occurred or a person is missing, and the detective tries to explain what has led up to this situation by working backward from clues. As the detective reconstructs the prior story, his or her mental processes take place during time that is moving forward and in which other events can also take place. Linear time is at the base of the detective plot, but it is never approached in linear fashion. In *Murder in Byzantium*, these attributes of the detective novel are supplemented by Sebastian's research on Anna Comnena. Like most traditional epics, her *Alexiad* narrates the events of the First Crusade in historical order, in other words, in accord with linear temporality. Historical research such as that undertaken by Sebastian is not unlike detection in that it deals with its material in a nonlinear way, circling back to look again at puzzling events. In the case of Sebastian's obsession with Anna Comnena, he fills what he sees as a gap in the story with a love affair with Ebrard de Pagan (prior to her marriage at the age of fourteen to Nikephoros Bryennios). The passages in *Murder in Byzantium* where Sebastian's suppositions are spelled out are not likely to appeal to the conventional reader of murder mysteries, because even though they do tell a story, they make their way slowly and ponderously through it. The narrative becomes laborious because Sebastian is trapped in what Kristeva refers to as "obsessional time" ("Women's Time," 17). Projecting herself into Sebastian's psyche, Stephanie enters his experience of time, where the present folds itself back on the past and cannot be fully disentangled from it.

Linked with this peculiar temporality is the treatment of space. Kristeva's two earlier detective novels were set in a "corrupt seaside resort of a mythical town, where the boundaries between East and West, civilization and barbarian, and good and evil are erased."[22] This no-man's-land effect is intensified in the third novel, where the ambiguity of "Santa Barbara / Santa Varvara" is doubled by the presence of a nearby town called "Santa Cruz" and made even more mystifying by the existence of a place called "Stony Brook," where a university bestows an honorary degree on Sebastian Chrest-Jones. Given that Sebastian takes the plane to Stony Brook, the reader can be forgiven for thinking that it may be situated in North America, a confusion reinforced by the remark that the hood he receives belongs to the fraternity of "imaginary monks from time immemorial, a link that every university in the United States, Canada, and elsewhere wanted to cultivate so as to extend the honor of its vocation."[23] Having killed his pregnant lover, Fa Chang, and rid himself of her body by driving it into a lake inside her Fiat Panda, Sebastian flies back to Santa Varvara and takes the next plane to Milan. Renting another Fiat Panda, he traces the route of the First Crusade in reverse, starting at Philippopolis and heading for Puy-en-Velay. If this part of the novel is confusing, it is because Sebastian is beginning to lose his bearings. During the plane trip from Santa Varvara to Milan, "time seemed contracted—Sebastian had no idea how long a flight it was. A second, an hour, or eight hours—what did it matter, he held himself erect, perpendicular, for an instant" (*Murder in Byzantium*, 89–90). Similarly, he drives from Milan to Philippopolis "like a zombie without stopping" (*Murder*, 94). Because he doesn't use his email account, his ex-wife believes he must be dead, and metaphorically, he is. No longer simply a historian, Sebastian is now living his "Byzantine love story" (*Murder*, 101),[24] a story that, like any fiction, is located outside of time. By the same token, Anna Comnena's *Alexiad* has become, in Sebastian's mind as well as in his computer, *The Romance of Anne* (*Murder*, 40), the title it continues to bear in Stephanie's sympathetic retelling to the indifferent Rilsky (*Murder*, 183). As if to emphasize the difference between the fictive or imaginative space of Sebastian's obsession and the space of documented history, *Murder in Byzantium* also includes several maps of the Crusades and a photograph of a seal attributed to Anna Comnena.

In addition to the "transit zone" created by Sebastian's imagination and Stephanie's narrative recreation of it, there is also the virtual space of the computer, a medium that, like literature, allows one to leave real space and travel in a place "outside" the real. Stephanie has access to Sebastian's computer text because her adoptive son has enabled her to access it; but at the same time, the mathematician Xiao Chang has also hacked into Sebastian's computer. Both realize independently that Sebastian driving to Puy-en-Velay. In a wild imitation of a stereotypical crime plot, four people are now making their way to the same place: Stephanie, Rilsky, Xiao Chang, and of course Sebastian. Time continues to stand still as the reader waits for the anticipated showdown.

The opening of the novel has already allowed us a glimpse into the serial killer's mind; at that point, however, we know him only as the mysterious "Number Eight." The novel employs free indirect discourse to create the virtual space in which we gain access to the killer's thoughts: "Shouldn't he use those wonderfully medieval-looking gloves knit with stainless steel fibers that autopsy specialists used?" (*Murder*, vii). By amplifying computer space with both imaginative and narrative space, Kristeva enacts her principle of "aesthetic practices" and their importance as "the modern reply to the eternal question of morality" ("Women's Time," 35).

Two murderers are among the figures making their way to Puy-en-Velay: Sebastian, who has killed Fa Chang, and Xiao Chang, who has killed a whole series of victims. Both murderers are killed in the shoot-out at Puy-en-Velay. The famous cathedral, with its dark stones and bizarre "agglomeration of styles, stories, and passageways," strikes one of the tourists visiting the monument as "an ideal place for miracles. Or crimes" (*Murder*, 197). The deaths of the two killers in the shoot-out imitate a stock ending for a novel or film. As Kristeva observes about literature in general, it "redoubles the social contract by exposing the unsaid, the uncanny" ("Women's Time," 31).

The dénouement at Puy-en-Velay reveals the extent to which violence lies at the heart of social reality. "Anthropology has shown that the social order is sacrificial, but sacrifice orders violence, binds it, tames it," writes Kristeva in "Women's Time"; "refusal of the social order exposes one to the risk that the so-called good substance, once it is unchained, will explode, without curbs, without law or right, to become an absolute arbitrariness" ("Women's Time," 29). Significantly, Stephanie is the one who fires the first shot, impulsively forgetting Rilsky's command to use the weapon only for self-defense.

Murder in Byzantium goes beyond its predecessor novels in Kristeva's Santa Varvara series not only in its darker view of global interconnectedness but also in its exploration of the role of religion in an increasingly secular world. Sebastian's pilgrimage to Puy-en-Velay, reversing the direction of the First Crusade, is an objective correlative of the modern shift from religion to a more literary kind of affect. At the same time, remainders of archaic belief are embodied in the "New Pantheon" sect and its fanatical follower Xiao Chang, who sees himself as a designated "purifier" (*Murder*, viii). What the Kristeva of "Women's Time" had understood as an atavistic "sacrificial contract" that women in particular are called on to experience against their will ("Women's Time," 200), now emerges as a global phenomenon led by extremists. Her portrait of international criminality and psychological imbalance constitutes a powerful updating of her earlier theoretical essay.

III *Theories of Society*

5 *Systems of Constraint*

At the end of his book *Discipline and Punish* (*Surveiller et punir*, 1975),[1] Foucault declares that it should "serve as a historical background to various studies of the power of normalization and the formation of knowledge in modern society."[2] This description could equally well apply to Foucault's earlier books, which examine, through the lens of major social institutions and their history, the ways in which society organizes and polices itself. Focusing on the forms taken and the powers exercised in modern institutions, Foucault looks back over several centuries to establish when a new system emerged to replace an older form of organization. *Madness and Civilization* (*Folie et déraison*, 1961), *The Birth of the Clinic* (*La Naissance de la clinique*, 1963), and *Discipline and Punish* all follow this line of exploration, focusing in turn on the mental asylum, the hospital, and the prison. The penal system, to take the example most relevant to this chapter, underwent a radical change between the mid-eighteenth and the mid-nineteenth centuries: public displays of punishment such as torture and execution yielded to an apparently kinder form of control exercised within the prison itself. Jeremy Bentham's unrealized idea for what he called the Panopticon (1843), a prison building constructed with a central surveillance tower, was emblematic of the new system. Although the guard could not possibly observe all prisoners all of the time, no individual prisoner would know when he might be monitored; this architectural arrangement, Bentham argued, would establish order without physical violence or public castigation. Constraint would be shifted into the consciousness of the individual prisoner rather than manifested in external systems of punishment. In its opening chapter, *Discipline and Punish* dramatizes the contrast between the old and the new penal styles by contrasting a grisly public execution with the daily schedule of a house of correction. Punishment had shifted from the body to the mind. In the parlance of a mid-nineteenth-century prison reformer: "Punishment, if I may so put it, should strike the soul rather than the body" (*Discipline*, 16). Yet the apparently gentler approach to punishment still bore what Foucault saw as a lingering whiff of torture: "a trace that has not been entirely overcome, but which is enveloped, increasingly, by the non-corporal nature of the penal system" (*Discipline*, 16). The system has not so much become more lenient as displaced the locus to which punishment is applied (*Discipline*, 22).

Foucault's frequently anthologized essay "What Is an Author?" (1969) is best regarded as another part of his larger project on institutional change. The institution in this case is the system of legal protections that was developed once authors came to be seen as "owners" of their texts in the late eighteenth and early nineteenth centuries. In Foucault's view, copyright law did more than simply protect those who wrote and published: it also made it possible to recognize "initiators of discursive practices."[3] Only certain types of texts, Foucault observed, can be understood as having an author (the parties to a contract have standing, not its writer, for example; but for the present chapter, perhaps the most interesting example Foucault gave of an authorless text was "an anonymous text posted on a wall"[4]). When texts do have authors, the relationship between the two is historically determined, taking different forms at different times and in different cultures. Without explicitly mentioning Barthes's "The Death of the Author," Foucault's essay was in fact a response to it. One of the distinguishing features of Foucault's answer was its greater emphasis on historicity and on the social and institutional structures in which the author is situated. As Andrew Bennett puts it, "Barthes is both present as an antagonist in Foucault's essay and at the same time unacknowledged."[5] Whereas Barthes positions the "death of the author" within debates about the New Novel, Foucault attends less to the literary-historical and more to the socio-historical construction of the author. Despite some over-lap with his precursor, Foucault shifts his argument into a different intellec-tual sphere: the two essays take forking paths.[6] And although Foucault never expanded his essay into a book, it clearly springs from an impulse similar to those that underlie his other projects: the desire to understand the power formations that characterize modern society.

The essay emerged at much the same time as Foucault's book *The Archae-ology of Knowledge* (1969), and was followed by his essay, "The Discourse on Language" (1971).[7] These two texts spell out the central concept that runs through all of Foucault's work, the notion of "discursive formations." Under-lying the major institutions he studied was the language through which they were conceived and understood. In *The Archaeology of Knowledge*, he points out several advantages of the term "archaeology," one of which is its ability to reveal "relations between discursive formations and non-discursive domains (institutions, political events, economic practices and processes)" (*Archaeol-ogy*, 162). The concept of "archaeology" allows him to embed discourses in history without proceeding according to the discipline of history narrowly conceived. Similarly, his use of the term "archaeology" is much closer to "genealogy" as Nietzsche uses it than it is to archaeology as an academic dis-cipline. In "The Discourse on Language," Foucault declares that "the genea-logical aspect concerns the effective formation of discourse, whether within the limits of control, or outside of them, or as is most frequent, on both sides of the delimitation."[8] His unfinished later project, *The History of Sexuality*, of which three volumes were published before his death in 1984, shares some of the intellectual scaffolding of his other works: its interest in sexuality as a dis-cursive formation, its "genealogical" approach to the periods, cultures, and institutions where these discourses were formed, and its focus on the relation of discourses about sexuality to questions of power and control.

The compelling character of Foucault's work has much to do with its identification of modern social structures and institutions with a single prin-ciple: that of the "carceral network."[9] Characterized by "systems of inser-tion, distribution, surveillance, observation," it may be found in what he terms "compact" forms, such as prisons or mental hospitals, or in more "dis-seminated forms" that infiltrate society as a whole.[10] It subtends disciplinary mechanisms of all kinds,[11] and thus constitutes "one of the armatures of this power-knowledge that has made the human sciences historically pos-sible."[12] It is striking, then, that one of the institutions to which Foucault did not devote a separate book is the university. Novelists associated with the academic world seem to have noticed this lack. Let us begin by looking at a novel that imaginatively brings together almost the entire range of Foucault's intellectual interests.

The Carceral Network: Duncker's *Hallucinating Foucault*

Patricia Duncker's first novel, *Hallucinating Foucault* (1996), is narrated in the first person by a doctoral student at a British university: "Writing a thesis is a lonely, obsessive activity. You live inside your head, nowhere else. Universities are like madhouses, full of people pursuing wraiths, hunches, obsessions. The person with whom you spend most of your time is the person you're writing about."[13]

Topping off this description of the university, the narrator refers to a "sort of prison yard next to the tea room" to which graduate students who wish to smoke are relegated while they pursue their habit. The outdoor smoking area as prison yard and the university itself as a madhouse are of course clichés — until one discovers the topic of the narrator's dissertation, a project to which he feels metaphorically captive. The dissertation focuses on a fictive French novelist named Paul Michel. Through this device, a crucial link is established with Michel Foucault, whose given name was Paul-Michel. Among other texts by Foucault, *Madness and Civilization* is a significant intertext of Duncker's novel. On the microlevel, one might connect the play with the names Paul Michel and Michel Foucault with the discussion of the "paradoxical singularity of the author's name" in "What is an Author?" (178).[14] Where Duncker's novel engages more significantly with Foucault, however, is in its extension of issues raised in his *History of Sexuality* to accord with more recent understandings of sex and gender.

Duncker's most alluring achievement in *Hallucinating Foucault* is her creation of the fictive novelist's life and oeuvre: she evokes his individual works through luminous descriptions that convey the narrator's obsessive fascination for Paul Michel and his writing. The writer's kinship with Foucault emerge from the publication list the narrator supplies: between 1968 and 1983, the fictive Michel produced five novels and a collection of short stories: "His first novel, *La Fuite*, translated into English under the title *Escape* in 1970, was a set text on the modern French novel course when I was an undergraduate. He won the Prix Goncourt in 1976 with *La Maison d'Eté*, which all the critics say is his most perfect book. I wouldn't disagree" (*Hallucinating*, 5).

So compelling is the evocation of Paul Michel's life and works in *Hallu-cinating Foucault* that some readers have actually tried to locate his writings in bookstores and libraries. In fact, Duncker's construction of Paul Michel depends on her ingenious choice of titles for his works, which seem some-how familiar, and the close similarities in the dates of his literary career and the life of Michael Foucault, who began publishing in 1966 and died in 1984. Even the slight shift in the starting date of Paul Michel's fictive achievement is significant: 1968, the year of the student revolution in Paris. Unlike many other writers of his generation, for whom this moment was an important turning-point, Michel Foucault had been away from Paris that summer. Two years earlier, he had taken up a teaching position at the University of Tunis because his lover Daniel Defert had been sent there to do his military service (the two would remain together for twenty years). Profoundly moved by the news of the student revolution, Foucault returned to Paris in Autumn 1968. Not only does the dating of Paul Michel's works evoke Michael Foucault, but the real-life philosopher becomes in Duncker's text the secret addressee of the fictive novelist and short-story writer. The real and the fictive inter-twine in curious ways. Learning that the novelist has been consigned to a mental hospital following a breakdown after Foucault's death in 1984 (the novel uses the real date), the narrator of *Hallucinating Foucault* decides to locate Paul Michel and get him released from his psychiatric "prison" (*Hallu-cinating*, 106). Playing with Barthes's idea that it is the reader who constructs the writer, the narrator's owl-eyed girlfriend explains the trigger for Paul Michel's madness in terms of a bizarre relation between writer and reader: "For Paul Michel it was the end of writing. His reader [Foucault] was dead. That's why he attacked the gravestones. To dig his writing back up, out of the grave. Why bother to exist if your reader is dead?" (*Hallucinating*, 37).

The motif of the death of Paul-Michel's most important reader is of course a reversal of Barthes's conclusion to his famous essay: "The birth of the read-er must be at the cost of the death of the Author."[15] Here, the novel brings together the author-theories of Barthes and Foucault. Although this con-junction is not without basis, Barthes and Foucault give different emphases to their accounts of the "writer." For Barthes, the author was irrelevant to the reader's interpretive construction of a text. His argument took issue with a convention in contemporary French literary studies by which texts were viewed primarily as extensions of their authors. He wished to focus on texts as language, not as aspects of individual psychologies. In Barthes's view, a text does not fully become a literary work until it is read and interpreted. In contrast, Foucault's author is not "dead," nor does he need to be. Rather, the term "author" is enmeshed in social and legal formations and the ideologies that subtend them.[16] Duncker's novel freely modulates the theories of both Barthes and Foucault. The fictive Paul Michel cannot conceive of himself as an author unless his one most important reader is still alive to validate his authorship. The image of the crazed Paul Michel trying to dig his own writing (rather than his dead reader's corpse) "out of the grave" takes this notion *ad absurdum*. This extravagant portrayal of the author-reader relationship goes beyond identification as it is usually understood.

A series of long manuscript letters from Michel to Foucault seem to confirm the "constructed" relationship between author and reader. In one of these letters, the fictive Paul Michel explains that whenever he sits down at his desk, "I clear a space to write, for you, to you, against you"; his greatest fear all along has been that he will lose "the reader for whom I write" (*Hallucinating*, 73). The letters, however, appear never to have been sent to their addressee. If that is so, then it is even stranger that they seem to respond to answers from Michel Foucault. The dissertation-writer, who has found the manuscripts in a London archive, has no way to decide the status of the letters.[17] If the letters have not been sent, as he surmises, the references they contain to replies from Foucault can only be invented. Here the novel challenges Foucault's distinction between "authored" and "unauthored" texts. In Foucault's essay, a private letter has a signer, not an author: "A private letter may well have a signer—it does not have an author; a contract may well have a guarantor—it does not have an author. An anonymous text posted on a wall probably has a writer—but not an author" ("Author," 108).

This distinction is questioned again during the account of the narrator's visit to Paul Michel in the mental hospital. Several slogans and even a complete poem written on the hospital walls recall Foucault's concept of the "unauthored" text. Not incidentally, they also resonate with Foucault's exploration of language in *Madness and Civilization:* "*Language is the first and last structure of madness* . . . ; on language are based all the cycles in which madness articulates its nature" (*Madness*, 100). As a student of Paul Michel's fiction, the narrator immediately recognizes the graffiti on the hospital walls as the work of the novelist. One slogan, cleverly located above the receptionist's desk, reads: "Je t'aime à la folie" ("I'm madly in love with you"). No doubt it is to be read ironically, with "madly" understood in both its metaphorical and literal meaning. Another slogan contains a critical barb directed at the institution, whose arched doorway it decorates: "J'ai levé la tête et j'ai vu personne" ("I raised my head and saw no one"). Is this slogan a reproach to the indifferent care that the patients are receiving? Or does it testify to the writer's inability to perceive reality? The poem on the wall, finally, is a witty little piece that questions the right of the juridical system to incarcerate the mentally ill and the failure of society to answer questions posed by those it regards as outsiders:

> Who are you, question mark?
> I often ask myself questions.
> In your festive garb
> You look like a judge.
> You are the happiest of punctuation marks
> At least you get answers. (*Hallucinating*, 88)[18]

In addition to these three bits of writing on the wall, we also hear that Michel has written other poems in the men's toilets. Whatever the nature of these additional poems may be, it is clear from their placement that for Michel they are an act of protest, messages of frustration over the inability of those in charge to "see things differently" (*Hallucinating*, 92).[19] From the receptionist's point of view, Paul Michel is simply a "vandal" (*Hallucinating*, 90). For his admirers in the world outside, however, Michel represents the "revolutionary art of thinking differently" (*Hallucinating*, 13). Foucault regards madness as not simply the opposite of reason, but as its hidden twin. Delirium and hallucinations are forms of "dazzlement" that, while seeing daylight, also see nothing (*Madness*, 108). Duncker's evocative prose in *Hallucinating Foucault* attempts to render this paradox.

Yet bedazzlement, as Foucault notes, is also a kind of benightedness and entrapment. The receptionist's disapproval of Paul Michel's inscriptions reminds us that the mental hospital is part of a larger social system of constraint. In an article drawing attention to Paul Michel's plight, one of his supporters compares the hospital with a prison: "We are in danger of losing one of our finest writers to the white prison walls of a psychiatric unit, to the very institutional forces that he and Foucault have put so radically in question" (*Hallucinating*, 32). At one point, a psychiatrist with twenty years of government service gives the narrator a brief history of how paranoid schizophrenics have been treated from the era of the madhouse, with its straitjackets and barred windows, to the present-day mental facility, with its use of modern psychopharmaceuticals. "The madhouse wasn't a pleasant place," he says. "It was oppressive to both the staff and the patients. And we had bars on all the windows. Now we use drugs. But it boils down to the same thing in the end" (*Hallucinating*, 44). Today's form of treatment, he implies, merely involves a different kind of confinement.

Michael Foucault and Paul Michel may be seen as reason and its opposite; at the same time, they are two sides of a single person. The novel is marked throughout by coexistent structures of reciprocity and imbalance. This point is hammered home in the two columns at the end of the book that set the philosopher's biographical dates against the fictive writer's chronology. Activism during the revolution of 1968 is part of the real and the fictive life, but the novel also shows that each man thinks and writes differently. Michel Foucault's writing is dense, baroque, and alive with detail; Paul Michel's writing is spare, classical, and remote (*Hallucinating*, 6–7). Yet as the almost chiastic nature of their names suggests, they are also mirror images of each other. By the same token, the narrator and his girlfriend are both fundamentally different and alike. Both have been erotically involved with Paul Michel. The flashbacks to these earlier experiences reveal a fundamental fluidity of sexual identities.

Toward the end of the novel, the status of the "private letter" is once again put to the test. After the death of Paul Michel in a car crash, the narrator's girlfriend writes a letter to the deceased author. Although the original of the letter is already sealed, she shows the narrator a copy, claiming that "it's from you." To his objection that he didn't write it, she responds, "Doesn't matter. Pretend that you did. It will say what you wanted to say to him" (*Hallucinating,* 170).[20] The wording of the letter allows the narrator and his girlfriend to fuse into a "reader" who is at once an actual person and a "reader function." Mirroring the author function in Foucault's essay, this reader function "does not refer simply to a real individual, since it can give rise simultaneously to several selves, to several subjects—positions that can be occupied by different classes of individuals" ("Author," 113). The letter speaks, in other words, for any reader who has become involved with the texts of a writer. At the same time, it points up an imbalance in the reader-writer relationship. While literary writing is a "hand stretched out in the dark, into an unknowing void" (*Hallucinating*, 170), it does usually reach a reader. If the author is dead, however, the reader cannot complete the other half of the communicative circle. Planning to tape the letter to Paul Michel's coffin beneath a bouquet of roses, the two young people act almost as if they believe in the possibility of communication beyond the grave. Addressing a dead author, the letter remains stranded and thus takes on a literary rather than a communicative function.

Through the final letter, the two young people—the narrator and his girlfriend—merge into a single being, a voice that speaks unmarked by any signs that would identify its gender or other aspects of personal identity. The delicate handling of the complexly enmeshed love relationships in *Hallucinating Foucault* questions what may at times appear to be a somewhat schematic way of thinking in Foucault. The novel's nuanced treatment of porous boundaries recovers the poststructuralist elements in a thinker who began as a structuralist. In so doing, it also updates them for our own time.

Controlling Knowledge: Umberto Eco

Not all texts that reflect on social control through institutions of incarceration necessarily mention Foucault by name. Nonetheless, sometimes the best place to hide something is in plain view, as Poe's tale *The Purloined Letter* so deftly demonstrates. Such is the case with Umberto Eco's novel *Foucault's Pendulum* (1988), whose title refers to Léon Foucault (1819–68), scientist and inventor. Nonetheless, the later Foucault—Michel—is not far to seek.

Eco, a specialist in semiotics, had already alluded to the theories of Barthes and Foucault in his best-selling novel *The Name of the Rose* (1980).[21] Not for nothing does a medieval scriptorium—the workplace of scriptors in the medieval sense of the word—constitute the location where texts circulate in that novel. *The Name of the Rose* takes place in a fourteenth-century abbey, partly in its scriptorium and partly in its library. Supposedly to help the reader understand the mysterious happenings in the library, the novel includes a diagram illustrating a cross-section of the tower library with its central staircase and its separate rooms and multiple niches. The diagram bears a strong resemblance to the illustration of Jeremy Bentham's Panopticon in Foucault's *Discipline and Punish: The Birth of the Prison* (1975).[22] To be sure, the library in *The Name of the Rose* does not have a central system of optical surveillance; still, it is subject to the abbot's tight control. In *Discipline and Punish*, Foucault notes similarities between methods of control originally developed in the medieval monastery and those used in the prisons, hospitals, workhouses, and schools that came into being in the nineteenth century. One of these was the rigid daily schedule, adopted in workhouses and hospitals from the monastic communities to which they were originally attached (*Discipline*,

149). Eco includes a timetable in the opening sections of *The Name of the Rose* (xx–xxi) and then goes on to organize the narrative according to the set times for prayer. The fictional library is organized in an unusual way, however: not by author, but by the geographical places in which individual books originated. While this method of classification allows for anonymous texts and works collated from several different sources to be housed in meaningful groups, it gives more power to the librarian than is the case in a library where books are catalogued alphabetically by author. The librarian's control over the books—which ones may be read or copied and by whom—mirrors the abbot's control over the abbey to which the library is attached. Disguised as a detective story, *The Name of the Rose* explores problems of hermeneutics and literary history in the context of the larger social connections between knowledge and power.

Foucault's Pendulum (1988) extends this reflection on control. Displacing the scriptorium and library in *The Name of the Rose*, the conservatory of the Paris Musée des Arts et Métiers—housed in a former priory—is the backdrop for the action in *Foucault's Pendulum*. The large, glass-enclosed hall is full of strange machines, including, of course, the pendulum of the novel's title. Madness and reason combine in this place that is at once "a revolutionary museum and compendium of arcane knowledge" (*Pendulum*, 8).[23] It embodies in an extravagant way the deeper antinomies of the Enlightenment. Entering the display room, the narrator senses that he has penetrated "to the heart of a secret message in the form of a rationalist theatrum" (*Pendulum*, 15). His discovery of this duality leaves him at once impressed and appalled.

The novel itself is an assemblage of obscure knowledge, mobilized by three fictive book publishers and a young scholar, Casaubon, who is writing his dissertation on the history of the Knights Templar.[24] Driving the plot is Casaubon's attempt to discover whether the Knights Templar are still in existence today and if so, whether they are engaged in an obscure cabal designed to reach its culmination at the millennium.[25] The group of editors, Garamond, Belbo, and Diotallevi, concoct a publishing scheme to take advantage of the widespread interest among readers for books on the occult sciences. Their plan, "Project Hermes," is to be divided into two distinct series of books, one for a popular audience, the second for more scholarly readers. The division suggests that the occult sciences are what Foucault calls "orders of discourse." Egyptian hieroglyphs, astrological schemes for reading the stars, and symbols shared by quite different esoteric communities (such as the serpent and the swastika) are among the many sign systems the editors discuss. As Casaubon notes, even modern computer systems exert a powerful attraction on the nonrational as well as the rational mind. Diotallevi rather fancifully imagines that "the world of machines [is] seeking to rediscover the secret of creation: letters and numbers" (*Pendulum*, 248). Computer language becomes a point of contention among the editors because it does not conform to familiar expectations of language: one cannot read it, they contend, as one would a book manuscript or a set of printer's proofs.

Barthes's concept of the "birth of the reader" receives a thorough workout in *Foucault's Pendulum*. Illicitly accessed computer files that mimic the "found manuscript" motif of the traditional novel, a list-like text in medieval French replete with lacunae and illegible words, a map that is thought to show the location of the "Umbilicus Telluris" or navel of the world when placed beneath the pendulum on a certain date, hanging gardens constructed by the Rosicrucians and reputed to contain a hermetic message, the pendulum itself—all these seem part of a vast network of texts available for interpretation. The difference of opinion between the quack archaeologist Colonel Ardenti and Casaubon's wife Lia about whether the medieval list is linked to the Templars or merely a list of purchases for a wedding points up the question whether any and all interpretations are equally valid. Everything seems somehow readable, as if the entire world were composed of a secret code. "Let's not go overboard," one of the friends comments pertinently (*Pendulum*, 83).[26]

But of course the novel is not solely about acts of reading. It also explores issues of violence and control. Many of the machines in the Musée des Arts et Métiers suggest torture and the rack, and Casaubon also knows that some of their makers were put to death for their inventions, presumably because they had dared to venture beyond the bounds of the natural. In contrast to Michel Foucault, whose historical studies tend to locate the crucial point of rupture between older and newer institutions in the seventeenth or eighteenth century, Umberto Eco leads us into a more distant past. Although the opening chapters focus on the birth of the modern era, represented by the machines on display at the Musée des Arts et Métiers, the broader sweep of the narrative traces the genesis of power networks back into earlier and "darker" periods. By exploring ways in which secret societies like the Templars, the Freemasons, the Rosicrucians, the Druids, the Invisibles, and the Jesuits competed for domination, Casaubon presents a hidden continuity in the struggle for world power that links the Middle Ages with the present. If the Templars' secret plan were about to be realized in the present-day time layer of the novel, as Casaubon believes, that would only confirm this trans-historical continuum.

History, in this novel, is represented almost exclusively as a set of inter-twined semiotic systems. Each secret society has its own forms of expres-sion, its own special signs, its own hermetic rituals. Together, they form a dense tissue of relations linked by their common origins in esoteric knowl-edge. In this way, the novel corresponds with Michel Foucault's archaeol-ogy of knowledge, described as a process whereby discourse is not treated "as groups of signs . . . but as practices that systematically form the objects of which they speak."[27] At the same time, *Foucault's Pendulum* never remains entirely serious about its intricate mesh of discourses. The Sloane Bookshop, for example, complete with piles of dusty volumes, sticks of incense, and tarot cards in the display window, is a business designed to serve a gullible clientele. Its customers clearly do not all distinguish between historical fact and sensationalist trumpery.

In his essay "The Discourse on Language,"[28] Foucault introduces the concept of "genealogical" discourses, which he contrasts with what he calls critical discourses.[29] "Criticism," he states, "analyses the processes of rarefac-tion, consolidation and unification in discourse; genealogy studies their formation, at once scattered, discontinuous, and regular."[30] The two types of discourse, while not simple opposites, "alternate, support, and complete each other."[31] In *Foucault's Pendulum*, the word "oscillation" substitutes, as it were, for Michel Foucault's notion of alternation between two principal modes of investigation. In this way, the pendulum becomes more than a machine in a museum, but a thematic and structural principle of the novel. Belbo's "sacrifice" in the midnight ceremony that ends with his hanging from the pendulum exemplifies the principle of oscillation in a thoroughly grue-some way. Still, it is not entirely clear whether we should understand this scene as a real happening within the fiction of the novel or as something more metaphorical.

Indeed, the reader of *Foucault's Pendulum* comes to see that signification is not fixed, but rather constantly shifting. After Casaubon's terrible night that began in the viewing box of the ancient Periscope, he leaves Paris with a new understanding of perspective that does not depend on fixed points like the periscope and the pendulum. Although he still claims to think of himself as pursued by a diabolic society that has brought Belbo to his death, Casaubon also knows that the members of the sinister group (if indeed it exists) would attempt to give his account of his experiences a different meaning than he gives it himself: "They would only derive another dark theory and spend another eternity trying to decipher the secret message hidden behind my words" (*Pendulum*, 623). The novel ends in insoluble ambiguity. Rather than continuing with the impossible search for meaning, Casaubon concludes by admiring the landscape, an aesthetic rather than an interpretive act.

Policing Authorship: Hilbig

Like Duncker's *Hallucinating Foucault* and Eco's *Foucault's Pendulum*, Wolfgang Hilbig's novel *»Ich«* (1993; "I") explores the relationship between Foucault's ideas about authorship and his studies of power and control. Yet Hilbig's book can hardly be read by anyone not steeped in poststructuralist theory: the novel fairly bristles with it. Perseverance and not a little knowledge are required to make headway in *»Ich«*, but the reward is some very funny scenes and episodes.[32] Written after the unification of East and West Germany, the novel focuses on the period shortly before the fall of the Berlin Wall. Its action is set against the backdrop of the "alternative" cultural milieu of Prenzlauer Berg area in Berlin, to which Hilbig himself belonged. During the German Democratic Republic regime, the Prenzlauer Berg was home to writers whose work was situated on the fringe of what was officially permitted: in some instances, their literary experiments owed more to the West than to the GDR. Poststructuralist theory was part of the mystique in these enclaves. Drawing on the real history of the "scene," in which members of the East German secret police (Stasi) infiltrated avant-garde literary groups,[33] Hilbig creates a narrative that folds intricately back on itself, becoming a reflection on the nature of literary writing in circumstances of surveillance and control. Echoing Foucault, the historical setting is one of imminent change: a moment when a particular system of constraint has reached an extreme point and its innermost problems are revealed in the form of insoluble ruptures. Pressing upon the reader with the full weight of obsessive and often tedious sentences that continually loop through repetitive and obscure reflections, the narrative style of *»Ich«* imitates the oppressive verbosity of East German official jargon and the repressive structures of its ideological system. At the same time, this style also parodies the system: humorous formulations punctuate the narrative even as the reader feels suffocated by the text's dense and abstract manner. In one of these moments, the narrator (identified variously by the initials M. W., W., C., or the name

Cambert) describes a conversation with his Stasi handler, who likes to speak of Foucault as if his name were Le Fou, in the mistaken assumption that the French word *fou* means "fire" (he is confusing it with *feu*). His misapprehension derives from the fact that Foucault's ideas have suddenly come into fashion and are making the rounds like wildfire (*»Ich«*, 21). Of course, *le fou* really means "the madman"—again, not an inappropriate association with the author of *Madness and Civilization*. The narrator distances himself from the newfangled mania for Foucault, claiming to have read only the titles and a few opening sentences of his books:

> I didn't like the way some enclaves that belonged to the so-called "scene" justified a person's existence by the fact that he was an enthusiastic reader of Foucault, which consequently gave rise to the obligation of reading Derrida or Paul de Man as well—I didn't like books that were printed in Gothic script. It would have come to the point where I would have had to read Heidegger, too . . . and finally *Mein Kampf* as well. (*»Ich«*, 22)

Apart from this one reference to Foucault, the French thinker's name is not mentioned in the novel. The text does refer to other theorists, however, notably Barthes, Baudrillard, and Deleuze (*»Ich«*, 236, 335–342, 354–355). On one occasion the narrator refers to the "neostructuralists" (another term for the poststructuralists[34]) whom he suspects of feeling envious of the "totalitarian author personalities" they see in writers from the communist German state (*»Ich«*, 309); yet at another point he is convinced that he cannot make an impression on a certain young West German woman (he mistakenly thinks she is a student) unless he bones up on neostructuralist thought: "I might reject them [the neostructuralists], but I had to know something about them!" (*»Ich«*, 316). Such discrepancies contribute to the ironic effects created by the narrator's odd combination of constant philosophical reflection and sketchy scholarly knowledge. Compounding this effect is his bored recollection of his earlier exposure to Marxist ideology. His Stasi handler is named Feuerbach, an allusion to Marx's "Theses about Feuerbach" in *The German Ideology* (written 1846). Fearing that he might accidentally have mentioned the name Feuerbach in his sleep—at this point he is having an affair with his landlady—he consoles himself by reflecting that "if need be, one could say that the name *Feuerbach* was the onset of a snore" (*»Ich«*, 253).

It is unnecessary to discuss at length the depiction of political and social oppression in Hilbig's novel. What concerns me here is the way in which these systems of constraint inform the literary scene, in particular concepts of authorship and the authorial practices of both East and West Germany. Inducted into the Stasi as an "informeller Mitarbeiter" (unofficial informant), the narrator of *»Ich«* is assigned the task of observing a writer whose code name in the Stasi files is Reader (the name is in English in the German text, presumably to suggest the sheer absurdity of some Stasi cover names). This writer gives sporadic readings of his work in different parts of the city, always unannounced except by an underground grapevine. On the literal level, then, this writer is also a reader: one who gives readings. But the code name also alludes to the debate between Barthes and Foucault over the ways in which an author is constituted by his or her readers.

In *»Ich«*, the narrator does not actually read Reader's texts: he hears them. To be sure, he does understand that Reader is a creature of the Stasi, planted to entice people into attending officially forbidden events, where they can be observed by undercover officers. Despite clear signs that Reader has no genuine connection with the West—his "collarless black shirt of Russian cut, slightly shiny," for example—the narrator comes to envy and emulate Reader. In his attempt to capture the attention of the young woman he calls the student, the narrator begins to copy Reader's manner: "I adopted almost every one of Reader's attributes" (*»Ich«*, 310). Yet in distinction to Foucault's claim that an author is constituted by the system of copyright, Reader has never actually published anything in print form. In contrast, the narrator does manage to get his own texts published, though not without difficulty. Advised by his Stasi handler to write avant-garde pieces that can be published in the West to consolidate his cover as a dissident poet, the narrator struggles repeatedly to create suitable texts. Finally, he takes one of his rejected poems, cuts it down the center and reassembles each line in reverse order. When this and similar texts appear in oppositional journals, the narrator scarcely recognizes them as his own: "Were the texts really by him? If it was the case that his hand had committed them to paper, they had been authorized, by contrast, by someone other than himself. And then it occurred to him that all the reviews that he had seen were virtually identical: here the concept was even more apposite: they had been authorized!" (*»Ich«*, 202).

The shift from "author" to "authorized" in this clever passage gives an extra dimension to the debate about authorship conducted by Barthes and Foucault. In tightly controlled societies like that of the GDR, only what is authorized is permitted to appear. But what the Stasi authorizes is not always authentic, as the narrator discovers when he learns of letters that have been written in his name to his mother and when he is forced to sign paternity papers for a child he has not fathered. Both the letters and the paternity declaration are fabrications by the Stasi. The letters have provided cover for his whereabouts, and the paternity document provides material for future blackmail if the narrator tries to escape his handling by the Stasi. Even as they force him to sign the document, the Stasi representatives ask him to remain silent about the child and "really act as if he didn't have a child." After an elaborate and unintentionally hilarious exchange with them, the narrator declares the matter concluded and proposes that they should now "talk about literature" (»*Ich*«, 101).

The obscene drawing of a phallus, mysteriously signed with his own initials, that the narrator discovers on a wall in the basement of his building is another link in this chain of falsified writings. Settled in a womb-like red plush chair, the narrator spends long periods observing the sketch, reflecting that the wall on which it is placed is one that extends upward for several floors before becoming the dividing partition between Reader's apartment and those of his neighbors. Anyone else, seeing his initials next to a vulgar graffito, would be annoyed by this mocking gesture from an unknown intruder. But in an absurd epiphany, the narrator immediately thinks, "empty signifier." He has learned the lessons of poststructuralism all too well.

Toward the end of the novel, the narrator listens to a text Reader calls *Brief Movements of the Lower Part of the Face*. The title is actually taken from Beckett's New Novel *Comment c'est* (1961; *How It Is*), in which an unnamed narrator crawls slowly through the mud while engaging in a repetitive monologue. One kind of brief movement of the lower part of the face occurs when we chew or speak, as Beckett well knew when he coined this oddly behaviorist periphrasis. In this sense, the title of Reader's text alludes to the oral aspect of his literary readings. But it also suggests their mechanical nature, as if his readings were merely the actions of a marionette. We know, of course, that he is a puppet of the Stasi.

Early in the novel, Feuerbach gives voice to the official East German disgust at modernist writing like that of Beckett: "And Beckett, you said . . . his texts are like Beckett's? I continue to believe that that Irishman spoiled the literature of his island. And probably French literature as well. And exactly the same thing will happen here. That wasn't a good idea with these texts in the manner of Beckett! But what can we do? I for my part don't like that stuff of Beckett's at all . . ." (»*Ich*«, 39). If Reader has a reason for appropriating not only a phrase but also a style from a Western writer, the narrator cannot decipher it. Certainly, one question might be whether Reader is adopting or mocking experimental literature from the West. The narrator of Hilbig's novel never poses this more complex question about Reader's literary posture. The narrator can only come up with an allegorical reading in which the "brief movements" represent the fitful actions of the secret police organization in its final death throes. Yet perhaps this is precisely the reason why the narrator has been fascinated by Beckett for so long.

Toward the end of the novel, the narrator is suddenly arrested and inexplicably thrown into prison. After a few weeks in isolation, he again signs a document without having really read it closely: all he knows is that he has pledged to remain silent about anything he may have witnessed while in prison. But of course he has not seen or heard anything in the isolation cell. The absurdity of the document is indeed comparable to the absurdity of the situation in Beckett's *How It Is*. After a terrifying night in which he hears the sounds of menacing footsteps in the corridors, he flees to his mother's house in a town designated by the initial A. As Peter Cooke writes, "ultimately Beckett fails him. Neither the Stasi, nor Reader nor the world of literature can overcome the narrator's sense of crisis. Beckett's work too becomes a constraining structure, which prevents the narrator from finding an autonomous voice."[35] But could the narrator have found such an autonomous voice within the constraints of the GDR system? Profound contradictions between what GDR ideology called the "postfascist subject" and what Western poststructuralism regards as the postmodern subject are the cause of the narrator's confusion.

»*Ich*« ends on a deeply ironic note. The novel's empirical author and reader know, of course, that the Berlin Wall has fallen and that the two German states have been united; but the narrative itself does not proceed this far. Instead, it stops just short of the fall of the Wall. The narrator's new Stasi handler still employs Marxist ideas about the dialectical workings of history even though he senses that political reality is about to change. "Always remember," he advises the narrator, "that history is on our side, we have time . . ." Stepping to a broad window that looks out onto the street below he contrasts the city of A. with the big cities further north: "Berlin, Leipzig, Rostock, it's starting to boil and bubble there, you don't really want to look too closely. Bear in mind that down here we have lots of time, we'll come up with something . . ." (»*Ich*«, 377). The contradiction between the notion that history proceeds inexorably according to its own rules and the opposing idea that individuals are capable of changing history is part of the irony of the novel's last pages. By concluding the novel with this scene, Hilbig returns us to the real world and to an awareness of our paradoxical behavior within existing systems of constraint.

Complicating Foucault: Coetzee's *Waiting for the Barbarians*

Coetzee's remarkable *Waiting for the Barbarians* (1980) is one of the most deeply probing novels written in the wake of Foucault. *Waiting for the Barbarians* confirms postcolonial theories developed by Homi Bhabha and Gayatri Spivak, while also reaching down to their conceptual underpinnings in Foucault. Coetzee's novel engages Foucault's entire corpus. Ideas from his books *Madness and Civilization, The Archaeology of Knowledge, Discipline and Punish,* and *The History of Sexuality* come together in a fictional narrative that tests them by transposing them to a rather different context. Unlike much of Coetzee's other fiction, *Waiting for the Barbarians* is not set in a clearly locatable time and place. On the face of it, that seems at odds with Foucault's emphasis on the historical nature of institutions and the moments when distinct ruptures can be observed in their development. Instead, Coetzee shifts our attention to less easily definable transitions in both time and space. As war looms between the inhabitants of a garrison at the border of Empire and the barbarians whose arrival they fear, skirmishes take place with a mixture of weapons ranging from spears to muskets, with men on horseback wearing shining helmets and armor, sounding trumpets and carrying banners. Descriptions of the troops consist of an odd medley of medieval and nineteenth- or early twentieth-century elements. When the magistrate crosses into enemy territory to bring the barbarian girl back to her people, one of the barbarians points at him "an ancient musket nearly as long as a man, with a dipod rest bolted near the muzzle."[36] Looking up the slope, he sees the barbarians silhouetted against the sky in a formation that seems to belie their sheepskin coats and caps and the shaggy ponies on which they are mounted. "I count three of the long-barrelled muskets; otherwise they bear the short bows I am familiar with" (*Barbarians*, 77). Power relations reveal themselves as shifting and paradoxical. Upon the magistrate's return to the garrison, he expects that he and his men will be warmly greeted, although this does not happen because their meeting with the barbarians in the desert places them under suspicion at home:

> The thin tones of a trumpet reach our ears; the horsemen of the wel-
> coming party issue from the gates, the sun flashing on their helmets.
> We look like scarecrows: it would have been better if I had told the
> men to put on their armor for these last few miles. I watch the horse-
> men trot towards us, expecting them at any moment to break into a
> gallop, to fire off their guns in the air and shout. (*Barbarians*, 82)

What the text does here and in similar descriptions is transpose familiar images of colonial wars onto an underlying military ethos loosely derived from the medieval period.[37] Similarly, Colonel Joll's dark glasses are both a modern invention—the magistrate has never seen such glasses before—and an avatar of dark glass that were worn by judges in ancient China. Whereas Chinese judges used dark eyepieces to obscure their facial expressions, the present-day apparatus is intended to protect the eyes from glare. Yet even indoors, Joll does not remove his glasses, giving rise to the impression that he, too, wishes to shield his expression from others. When Joll calls upon the magistrate to interpret the strange script on some pieces of poplar wood, Joll speaks from behind his dark glasses and the magistrate "stare[s] into the black lenses" (*Barbarians*, 120). At the same time, Joll's dark glasses form part of another network that involves the partial blindness of the tortured native girl and the metaphorical blindness of the magistrate himself. Such details allude only obliquely to historical realities; their more significant function is to hold open a more capacious space within which the relation of impe-rial territory to bordering territories can be imagined less reductively. These descriptions contain within them archaeological layers that only gradually come into sight.

The fact that the entire novel is narrated by the unnamed magistrate of the imperial outpost—and narrated, strangely enough, in the present tense—is one primary reason for the slow uncovering of these layers. Present-tense narration that is supposed to occur simultaneously with the narrated events blocks retrospection. To deprive a first-person narrator of genuine retrospec-tion is to curtail the tradition hope for narrative: that it can somehow find out the truth or show the way to redemption. That is true, for example, of novels like Beckett's *How It Is*. As Matt DelConte comments, simultaneous present-tense narration "tends to restrict its narrator's function to that of reporting, inviting the reader to supplement the other two functions, inter-preting and evaluating."[38] Although it is true that narrator and reader subsist on two different ontological planes, the onus falls more heavily on the reader because the narrator is unable—or only partially able—to reflect on what is happening while it happens. In a sense, this makes us complicit in the events narrated.[39] Certainly this is part of the force of *Waiting for the Barbarians*: that we are drawn much further into the power structures it depicts than might have been the case had the story been told retrospectively. Of course, any work of fiction will call on our faculties of empathy and judgment in a way quite distinct from, say, Foucault's studies of punishment systems; but Coetzee has chosen here one of the most compelling techniques for doing so.

Discussing Foucault in his book of essays *Giving Offense*, Coetzee elabo-rates on his "elevation of paranoia into the animating principle of historical awareness." He goes on to show how such paranoia is linked in Catherine MacKinnon's work on pornography with the way in which "male power, as a kind of first principle, creates and uses desire for its own ends."[40] The way in which the magistrate treats the tortured girl in *Waiting for the Barbarians* can profitably be seen in this context. Also pertinent to the novel is Coetzee's discussion of Erasmus, whose *Praise of Folly* he sees as consonant with Fou-cault's project, which, in Coetzee's formulation, aims "to return authority to madness as a voice counter to the voice of reason" (*Offense*, 84). We can see this in the magistrate's protest against Colonel Joll's torture of the barbar-ians. Although the colonel later accuses him of wishing to be "the One Just Man" (*Barbarians*, 124), the magistrate voices his protest less from a position of reason that out of an almost insane rage that makes him he feel that "God-like strength is mine" (*Barbarians*, 117). The ambiguities of *Waiting for the Barbarians* mirror Coetzee's recognition that "Foucault was not unaware of the paradoxical nature of his project" (*Offense*, 86), and he points out that in his response to Derrida's critique of *Madness and Civilization* "Foucault con-cedes that the philosopher trying to enter madness *inside* of thought can do so only as a fictional project."[41] Further, Coetzee argues, Foucault's *Madness and Civilization* helps us see "why it is that the actions of reason come to look more and more like madness, just as madness, and particularly the madness of paranoia, looks like an excess of reason: because each is imitating the other" (*Offense*, 91). These remarks about Foucault, written over a decade later than *Waiting for the Barbarians*, illuminate some of its most striking paradoxes.

In the novel itself, Coetzee heightens his appeal to the reader's judgment by having the magistrate reveal some of his shortcomings. The magistrate fails to understand the hand gesture with which the tortured girl tells him that she is a prostitute and thus may not be welcome in his house (*Barbarians*, 29). We see the magistrate puzzling over his own motivations in his relationship to her, as well as to the prostitute whom he still visits from time to time during the barbarian girl's stay in his house. We read signs that he cannot: for instance, his constant washing of her feet. These ablutions allude to Christ's washing of Mary Magdalen's feet; yet the magistrate is no Christ-figure. The foot-washing seems to be a displacement of sexual desire; yet he also feels that he wishes to "obliterate" the girl (*Barbarians*, 50). Her tortured body with its broken feet and burn-mark near the eye are not just a permanent record of the torture she bore, but also become for him a kind of writing that he cannot decipher. Finally, when Joll asks him to interpret the script on the poplar slips, he is painfully aware that he has not cracked the code.

Intimately linked with the problem of reading the girl's body is his interest in archaeology. Ruins in the sand dunes south of the garrison prove that the imperial outpost is not the first settlement in these territories. One large structure that he has managed to excavate "stands out like a shipwreck in the desert, visible even from the town walls" (*Barbarians*, 15). And while he does imagine layer after layer of former magistrates beneath him in the ruins, he does not seem to come to the obvious conclusion suggested by the architectural structure that stands out like a shipwreck. Moreover, he is unable to decipher the inscriptions on the poplar slips he has found in the ruins, despite his almost scientific attempt to collect as many slips as possible. His enthusiasm for the archaeological project leads him to an ingenious plan by which he sentences petty criminals to digging there and even sends soldiers "on punishment details" to work on the excavations (*Barbarians,* 15). Caught up in the penal system himself, he imagines that the previous settlers may have built not only houses but a fort not unlike the garrison of his own time, "so that their masters, their prefects and magistrates and captains, could climb the roofs and towers morning and evening to scan the world from horizon to horizon for signs of the barbarians" (*Barbarians*, 16). Simultaneous present-tense narration does not allow him time to do much more than pose questions and make suppositions: like the sand in the dunes, events keep shifting before he can fully evaluate them. Even when he writes a letter of protest, he tears it up almost immediately. And during the entire time that the girl spends with him, he never thinks once of asking her to teach him her language (as he realizes when he is about to turn her over to the barbarians).

In "The Discourse on Language," Foucault asks a series of rhetorical questions: "What civilization, in appearance, has shown more respect towards discourse than our own? Where has it been more and better honoured? Where have men depended more radically, apparently, upon its constraints and its universal character? But, it seems to me, a certain fear hides behind this supremacy accorded, this apparent logophilia" (*Archaeology*, 228). This paradox is elaborated in the novel's final sequences involving Colonel Joll and the magistrate. The crucial scenes play out against Joll's inhumane treatment of a group of prisoners. The violence is stopped neither by the magistrate's instinctive protest "No!" nor his attempt to force Joll to recognize those he has tortured as "men." In a subsequent scene, Joll forces the magistrate to confess that his collection of poplar slips from the dunes is actually a set of messages passed between him and the barbarians. In a brilliant gesture of defiance that is also a parody of scholarly interpretation,[42] the magistrate mocks Joll by providing fake translations of the inscriptions, claiming for them a high degree of semantic ambiguity: "Now let us see what the next one says. See, there is only a single character. It is the barbarian character *war*, but it has other senses too. It can stand for *vengeance*, and, if you turn it upside down like this, it can be made to read *justice*. There is no knowing which sense is intended. That is part of barbarian cunning" (*Barbarians*, 122).

The punishment that Joll metes out to the magistrate (who has already been severely beaten by a hammer) involves what the colonel describes as two different forms of "flying" (*Barbarians*, 132). One is a near-lynching, in which the magistrate is forced to balance on a ladder with a noose around his neck and a hood over his face; from time to time, his torturers tighten the knot. The second act of torture involves tying his wrists together behind his back and making him hang by the arms, thus dislocating his shoulders. The onlookers greet the sound that comes out of his throat with jeers and laughter: "That is barbarian language you hear" (*Barbarians*, 133). In this scene, the novel extends its probing of colonial torture by reading it through later scenes of torture.[43] In particular, we may think of Jean Améry, whom the Nazis tortured in precisely this way during his detention in Fort Breendonk, Belgium, in 1943. Coetzee, however, is also familiar with more recent torture and brutality in South Africa: Derek Attridge refers to Steve Biko's murder by South African security police while he was being held in detention.[44]

Complicating the novel's exploration of punishment and torture are the difficult relation between sadism and desire. Sexuality is at the center of the magistrate's peculiar relationship with the barbarian girl, with whom he makes love for the first time just before he gives her back to her people. In his first approach to her, he claims that "this is not what you think it is" (*Barbarians*, 29). Yet it is undeniably sexual, all the same. To his mind, the barbarian girl is the opposite of the prostitute he occasionally visits, who charms him with her tiny, bird-like body and fluttering movements. He knows that the prostitute is merely simulating sexual desire and satisfaction, but for him her performance is more attractive than the stolid body of the barbarian girl. "With this woman," he says of the barbarian, "it is as if there is no interior, only a surface across which I hunt back and forth seeking entry. Is this how her torturers felt hunting their secret, whatever they thought it was?" (*Barbarians*, 46). Frustrated in his attempt to move the barbarian girl, he sees "a face masked by two glassy insect eyes from which there comes no reciprocal gaze but only my doubled image cast back at me." The horrifying mirror image leads him to a crucial question: "What depravity is it that is creeping upon me?" (*Barbarians*, 47). One symptom of his depravity is his inability to recall the face of the girl as it appeared before she was tortured. All he can remember is the face of her father next to her. In one of his repeated dreams, however, he sees the image of a hooded child that may be a trace of his irretrievable memory: "The face I see is blank, featureless; it is the face of an embryo or a tiny whale; it is not a face at all but another part of the human body, that bulges under the skin" (*Barbarians*, 40). It is a face, in other words, that resembles the female genitals. In other dreams, the girl "changes shape, sex, size" (*Barbarians*, 95), finally swelling to fill his throat and choke him. In the last scene of the novel, he sees children building a snowman in the town square. They fetch objects to represent the snowman's facial features, but neglect to give him arms. The scene reminds him of his dreams in which children were playing in the snow; yet "it is not the scene I dreamed of" (*Barbarians*, 170), and he is unable to make any sense of its relation to his previous dreams. As Derek Attridge notes, in this series of scenes the magistrate "finds interpretation simultaneously invited and baffled."[45] The novel itself remains open ended, inviting further thoughts on the part of its readers.

As Foucault formulates it, "the disciplinary gaze did . . . need relays" (*Discipline and Punish*, 174). *Waiting for the Barbarians* is structured by various types of relays: the magistrate's series of puzzling dreams is only one of several such mechanisms. The Panopticon, represented in *Waiting for the Barbarians* by the garrison's watchtowers, is designed to induce in the inmate a state of conscious and permanent visibility that assures the automatic functioning of

power" (*Discipline*, 201). The relay of power is replicated structurally in Coetzee's novel by the transfer of the magistrate's story to the reader. The magistrate's dreams and their troubling overflow at the end into a strangely unreal
reality remain resistant to interpretation, not only for him. Certainly, they
cannot be reduced to unambiguous meaning. While the novel clearly engages with Foucault's ideas, it also refuses to boil them down to some simplistic
schema. At the same time, *Waiting for the Barbarians* is an attempt to think
the implications of institutionalized violence beyond the end of Foucault's
own writing by delineating its position in colonialism and postcolonialism.

Disciplinary Architecture: Sebald

Two remarkable narratives that engage with Foucault's ideas on "the carceral network" are W. G. Sebald's *The Rings of Saturn* (1995) and *Austerlitz*
(2001).[46] Both texts explore the workings of power and its common structures over several centuries. *The Rings of Saturn* focuses primarily on colonial
power networks and their continued presence in today's world; *Austerlitz*
explores the history of fortifications, dungeons, and prisons from Casano-
va's incarceration in Venice in 1755 to the Nazi concentration camps in the
twentieth century. The theoretical foundation for both books is provided in
part by Foucault's *Discipline and Punish*, in particular the discussion of Jeremy Bentham's plan for the panopticon.[47] Among the illustrations to *Discipline and Punish*, Foucault reproduces a cross section and a floor plan of the
Panopticon, an 1840 sketch of a prisoner praying before a central inspection
tower, and a photograph of the interior of the Stateville Correctional Center
in Illinois, showing the glass cupola above its panoptical observation post.
In Sebald's *Austerlitz*, related illustrations include diagrams of fortresses, the
floor plan of Theresienstadt, and the inner courtyard of the Prague Karmelitska with its glass cupola. These illustrations clearly allude to those in *Discipline and Punish*, though they are drawn from other sources (the diagram
of Theresienstadt, for example, is taken from H. G. Adler.)[48] When Sebald's
eponymous protagonist consults the Prague archives at the Karmelitska in
order to find out his mother's address before she was deported to Theresienstadt, he describes the building's inner courtyard as reminiscent not
only of a prison, "but also of a monastery, a riding school, an opera theater,
and a madhouse" (*Austerlitz*, 213). Austerlitz's observation recalls Foucault's
claim that the panoptical system is "polyvalent in its applications: it serves to

reform prisoners, to instruct schoolchildren, to confine the insane, to supervise workers, to put beggars and idlers to work."[49] The seemingly irrelevant mention of a "riding school" is an allusion to a scene in Kafka's *The Missing Person (Amerika)*, where the young immigrant to America is virtually held hostage by his purported uncle and forced to learn English while taking riding lessons. Kafka's fascination with penal systems forms an undercurrent throughout Sebald's *Austerlitz*.[50] The eponymous Austerlitz is a historian of architecture engaged in research for a book on what he calls the "family resemblances" between different types of nineteenth-century structures: "law courts and penitentiaries, railway stations and stock exchange buildings, opera houses and insane asylums, and the rectangular grids of housing settlements for workers" (*Austerlitz*, 52). Foucault regards the common architecture of such buildings as "the diagram of a mechanism of power reduced to its ideal form,"[51] a "network of mechanisms that would be everywhere and always alert, running through society without interruption in space or time."[52] The idea of a network is a central image in Sebald's works, appearing in *Austerlitz* in the form of railway lines crossing the country or the pneumatic message tubes connecting the reading room with the stacks in the old Bibliothèque Nationale. Networks of control demonstrate the imbrication of power and knowledge from the eighteenth century to the present day. In this respect, Sebald accomplishes what Foucault's study of the carceral system explicitly refrains from doing: examining the carceral system as it emerged in the twentieth century. The final sentence of *Discipline and Punish* declares only that the book "must serve as a historical background to various studies of the power of normalization and the formation of knowledge in modern society."[53] *Austerlitz* traces the lines forward from where Foucault leaves off to the Nazi period and beyond. Following Kafka's example in such texts as "In the Penal Colony," Sebald also augments Foucault's theories by examining in some detail the forms of imperialism that flourished in the late nineteenth century. The description of Antwerp's central railway station is a key moment in Sebald's development of this theme. How much still remains of the controlling networks that helped imperialism to flourish? To what extent did imperialist power structures pave the way for the Nazis' crimes against humanity? Was it a factor in racial "cleansing" in Bosnia? In posing these questions, Sebald points up the continuing relevance of Foucault's theories of surveillance and control.

Exploring these questions leads Sebald's narrators into controversial territory. The lengthy treatment of Roger Casement in *The Rings of Saturn* is a case in point. Casement, on whom George V had bestowed a knighthood for his work in uncovering abuses of the Puntamayo Indians in the Amazon at the hands of a cruel rubber baron, was later hanged for high treason as a result of his collusion with Irish Revolutionaries and his attempt to supply them with German guns. In the course of his trial, Casement's "black diaries," a record of his homosexual encounters in the Congo, surfaced and were used as an additional reason for condemning him. The authenticity of the diaries was much debated at the time as well as later: were the diaries a forgery that had been planted in order to discredit Casement, or had they been written in his own hand? Sebald's narrator comes to the latter opinion. Regardless of which side one agrees with, Casement's fate is a clear indication of one of Foucault's key points: that sexuality is also a nodal point for the exercise and often the abuse of power. What appears to be a lengthy digression in *The Rings of Saturn* is in fact an important link in the network the book sets up.

The nonlinear method by which *The Rings of Saturn* is structured leads to effects that are not only provocative, but that also offend against strongly held beliefs. When the narrator of *The Rings of Saturn* writes about the dangers of overfishing in the Atlantic, he reproduces a postcard showing a fisherman standing proudly with his herring catch.[54] He then writes in the accompanying text about documentary films from the Nazi period designed to make schoolchildren proud of their country's industries (*Rings of Saturn*, 54); only a few pages later, he includes as a double-paged spread a photograph of dead bodies lying on the ground among trees at the concentration camp Bergen-Belsen (*Rings of Saturn*, 60–61). No explicit identification of the Bergen-Belsen photograph is given, but it is included at the point where the narrator introduces Major George Wyndham LeStrange, who had served in the British antitank regiment that liberated Bergen-Belsen in April 1945 (*Rings of Saturn*, 62). The narrator includes a peculiar item here: a photocopy of a newspaper article that tells how LeStrange had rewarded his housekeeper in his will for having remained silent at dinners with him since 1955. A cluster of questions arise from this bizarre juxtaposition. Is there a connection between the massed herrings in the photo of the fishing catch and the massed bodies at Bergen-Belsen? Who could have the temerity to compare the overfishing of the ocean with the Nazis' genocide of human victims? Is Major LeStrange's fifty-year dinnertime silence the result of trauma from the sight of the dead at the concentration camp? Does he wish to exclude himself from ordinary human converse? The burden this cluster of pages places on the reader is almost unbearable. We are called to pass judgment on incommensurable situations. Are we expected to arrive at a particular solution? The problem is virtually intractable.

The narrators in both *The Rings of Saturn* and *Austerlitz* draw connections between the abuses of power during the colonial period and those inflicted by the Nazis. The narrators do not propose causal connections, but they do seem to regard the violence of the two periods as part of the larger network that informs their respective narratives. Where do these narrators stand with respect to the debates about the singularity or historicity of the Holocaust? *Austerlitz* in particular is fraught with ambiguities. At the end of the book, the narrator believes that he has no other choice than to continue searching for traces of his father and his friend Marie de Verneuil. The book's open ending suggests that it still subscribes to a belief in the power of narrative to bring hidden things to light, while at the same time putting this very capacity seriously into question.

Sebald's Austerlitz experiences throughout his life a variant of what Foucault terms the "carceral continuum." As Foucault formulates this idea, "prison continues, on those who are entrusted to it, a work begun elsewhere, which the whole of society pursues on each individual through innumerable mechanisms of discipline" (*Discipline*, 303). Austerlitz's carceral continuum takes the form of psychological rather than physical imprisonment. Believing that he had escaped death in a concentration camp by means of the *Kindertransport*, he still resents the dour household of his adoptive parents in Wales. In many respects he never escapes from psychological imprisonment except for rare moments. At various points, he is immobilized by depressions that prevent him from conducting his life in a normal fashion.

As we have seen, Foucault's *Discipline and Punish* stops short of considering the twentieth century. The last dates he gives in the book are from the mid-nineteenth century, and the last actual quotation he adduces is an anonymous text of 1836 that speaks ironically about the failure of reforms in Paris and the death of the ideals that motivated the reformers. Ending with this text, Foucault comments:

We are now far away from the country of tortures, dotted with wheels, gibbets, gallows, pillories; we are far, too, from that dream of the reformers, less than fifty years before: the city of punishments in which a thousand small theatres would have provided an endless multicoloured representation of justice in which the punishments, meticulously produced on decorative scaffolds, would have constituted the permanent festival of the penal code. The carceral city, with its imaginary "geo-politics," is governed by quite different principles. (*Discipline and Punish*, 307)

Indeed, if Foucault had extended his study to the twentieth century, he would have had to deal with issues, such as the Vichy government, that are still not easy to speak about in France today. He would also have had to address the larger history of National Socialism and its abuses. Instead, he concludes with an indirect reference to the Nazi *Gleichschaltung* (literally "synchronizing" all German citizens to the same ideology) by stating that his book "must serve as a historical background to various studies of the power of normalization and the formation of knowledge in modern society" (*Discipline and Punish*, 308). Sebald's *Austerlitz* confronts precisely the later developments of the power structures Foucault had studied and that he had refrained from pursuing in *Discipline and Punish*.

As Ann Laura Stoler comments, "there are several ways to think about a colonial reading of Foucault."[55] This task is precisely what Coetzee and Sebald take on. Kafka's earlier investigations of power, violence, and sexuality in his novels and stories are one of the stepping-stones that both Coetzee and Sebald use to bring Foucault's theories into conjunction with the history of colonialism and postcolonialism. This is not to say, however, that Foucault had no thoughts about these connections. On the contrary: toward the end of *Discipline and Punish*, Foucault writes that "the penalty of detention seems to fabricate . . . an enclosed, separated and useful illegality." He goes on to say that "the establishment of a delinquency that constitutes something like an enclosed illegality has in fact a number of advantages" (*Discipline*, 278). This kind of illegality has the effect of keeping delinquent behavior in check in other parts of society. He is thinking here of penal colonies and overseas colonies in general: "The example of colonization comes to mind," he writes (*Discipline*, 279). Yet he quickly moves away from colonialism as such. Instead, he talks about the regulation of prostitution in the late nineteenth century, as well as arms and drugs trafficking in more recent times. His allusion to the "power of normalization" in the final sentence of *Discipline and Punish* shows he is thinking of such formations as Nazism. But he leaves to his readers the task of thinking through the implications of this allusion.

Hilbig, Coetzee, and Sebald engage with Foucault precisely by extending this line of thought and questioning its validity in contexts different from those Foucault directly studied. Hilbig's juxtaposition of Western poststructuralist theory (with a substantial focus on Foucault) with what was called the "actually existing socialism" of the German Democratic Republic focuses primarily on the fault lines created in individuals by the proximity of two ideologically opposite states and the complex nature of the political and ideological borders between them. Coetzee's novel, set in no identifiable time or place, is strongly suggestive both of the nineteenth-century colonization of Africa and the political situation of South Africa during apartheid. Sebald's narratives look backward from the present day to British and Belgian colonialism, the "semicolonial" situation of Ireland, and the period of German territorial expansion from the late nineteenth century to the Holocaust. To my mind, Coetzee's *Waiting for the Barbarians* is the most remarkable of this set of novels for its ability to engage theory in its particulars and in its broader sweep and to blend its narrative into a compelling unity that continues to resonate long after the reader has laid down the book.

6 Simulacra and Simulation

In contrast to Foucault, Jean Baudrillard maintained as early as his 1981 book of essays, *Simulacra and Simulations,* that contemporary society had arrived at "the end of the panoptic system."[1] Representation in the common sense of the term, he argued, has been supplanted by a system of "simulation" that radically negates the conventional idea that signs refer to something outside the sign system itself. "The transition from signs that dissimulate something to signs that dissimulate that there is nothing marks a decisive turning point," he writes. "The first reflects a theology of truth and secrecy. . . . The second inaugurates the era of simulacra and simulation . . ." (*Simulacra,* 6). In this new system, he claims, reality is replaced by nostalgia, a mode of recalling the past that nullifies traditional distinctions between the original and its replica, making both appear equally artificial. We have come to think of simulations as somehow more "real" than the things they simulate. The replica of the Lascaux caves, situated alongside the original underground formations, not only serves to protect the ancient rock drawings from damage, but also to resituate the monument within present-day culture. Whereas we must observe the original through a peephole, we are allowed to enter the simulated caves and experience them from close at hand. Formulating this phenomenon a little differently and using another example, Baudrillard argues: "Everywhere we live in a universe strangely similar to the original—things are doubled by their own scenario. But this doubling does not signify, as it did traditionally, the imminence of their death—they are already purged of their death, and better than when they were alive; more cheerful, more authentic, in the light of their model, lie the faces in funeral homes" (*Simulacra*, 11).

Indeed, we may conclude that embalmed faces in funeral homes are more "cheerful" and "authentic" not because they accord more closely with the former real appearance of the deceased, but because these reconstituted, unchanging faces remain within our visual and emotional control. Simulacra conform to already formed expectations, and thus they cannot ever really surprise. Yet Baudrillard also argues that simulacra exert influence over the shape reality takes for us. The metaphor he uses is that of a map that determines the territory to be surveyed. This is what Baudrillard means when he writes of the "precession of simulacra": that the map precedes the area it is understood to be mapping.

Julian Barnes's *England, England* (1998) presents an ironic version of the "precession of simulacra" by introducing us to its protagonist, Martha, as a child trying to assemble an educational puzzle in the form of a map of England.[2] Later, she works as a consultant to an entrepreneur developing a theme park on the Isle of Wight that is to be more like England than England itself. The two different kinds of simulacra represented by the map and the tourist replica are arranged in the novel as if Martha's jigsaw puzzle were somehow a precursor of the tourist attraction. In case the reader doesn't recognize the allusion to Baudrillard's theory of simulacra, Barnes introduces an unnamed French intellectual who explains that people these days prefer replicas to the original. Even as the replica of England establishes its appeal with jolly pubs and faux beefeaters, the mainland countryside comes to seem like a travesty of an English rural haven: the formerly "real" England now functions as a nostalgic utopia. Baudrillard's theory of the movement from original to simulacrum and back again is consummately rendered in Barnes's novel.

We do not have to wait until the late 1990s, however, to find novels that rework Baudrillard's ideas. Baudrillard's writing was quick to appear in English translation: *The Mirror of Production* was published in the United States only two years after the original French edition (1973).[3] Two of the essays in *Simulacra and Simulation* made their way into English translation via the "Foreign Agents" series, published in 1983 under the aegis of the magazine *Semiotext(e)*,[4] and another set of essays appeared in the same series in 1988.[5] These were rapidly picked up by science fiction writers like Samuel R. Delany and William Gibson. As Sylvère Lotringer notes, "part of the response to *Simulations* had to do with the quasi-fictional or science-fictional character of the book."[6] Delany's *Stars in My Pocket Like Grains of Sand* (1984) is one of the most interesting and ambitious of the science fiction novels that engage with Baudrillard's ideas about simulation. The simulation system of *Stars in My Pocket* fulfills the role that reading has traditionally done in our own culture, a notion that allows Delany to develop an intriguing connection between simulation and intertextuality.

The years around 1984 were a high period in Anglo-American literary reflections on Baudrillard. This may have something to do with the arrival in reality of the date in which the George Orwell's *1984* had been set. Early glimpses of his ideas on death could already be found in *Simulations and Simulacra*.[7] In the German-speaking domain, major works by Baudrillard appeared in translation between 1978 and 1987.[8] We will begin this chapter by looking at two examples of Baudrillardian novels from the German-language sphere.

Simulation and Identity: Two Berlin Novels

Bodo Morshäuser's *Die Berliner Simulation* (1983; *The Berlin Simulation*) is set in 1981, the year when Baudrillard's *Simulacra and Simulation* was originally published in France.[9] The novel is a relatively early engagement with the concept of simulation. Morshäuser's narrative[10] pivots on a central tenet of Baudrillardian theory: the idea that nostalgia has come to supplant what used to be understood as reality. A conventional description of the novel might present it as taking place on two time planes, that of 1981 and that of 1966/67. But in fact, these two temporal moments cannot be fully disentangled. Not only does the narrator continually map events of the second time plane onto those of the first, he sees the later experiences as ghostly reenactments of the earlier ones. The effect resembles what Baudrillard means when he writes of a new kind of fiction as a "desperate rehallucination of the past."[11] This occurs, Baudrillard explains, because reality has become a "lost object" for us, a utopia that can only be dreamed of, never directly experienced (*Simulacra*,

123). In Morshäuser's novel, the "lost object" takes the form of a young Englishwoman named Sally who is the subject of a (simulated) public announcement that opens the narrative: "Seeking Sarah, who calls herself Sally; last seen at subway station Wittenbergplatz getting into a train in the direction of Ruhleben. Born and raised in London, she is twenty years old, about 165 centimeters tall, and slender. She speaks hardly any German and is presumably not armed" (*Berlin*, 9).[12]

We are later told that Sally had come to Berlin from "swinging London" (*Berlin*, 99), a reference that places the opening announcement in the 1960s. Yet the narrator's search for Sally after her disappearance from Berlin continues into the time of narration, 1981. His frequent conflation of the sixties and the eighties, motivated by the idea that "remembering is making things present" (*Berlin*, 10), results from a failure on his part to distinguish between the present of actuality and the present of memory. Although he often speaks as if Sally were literally present in 1981 Berlin, his friends of that period call her "the phantom" (*Berlin*, 35–36). In occasional, more lucid moments, the narrator speaks of time he spends with the remembered Sally "in the form of her absence" (*Berlin*, 36). At such times, he seems to understand that his attempts to recapture recollections of Sally are no more than desperate hallucinations. His discussions with friends about Sally are recounted in a chapter titled "Talking Heads," as if conversations among individuals were merely a television show. In addition to television, a key source of simulations in Baudrillard's analysis of modern society, the novel also alludes to computers, then quite new as a medium available to individuals. The division of the book into two parts titled "Input" and "Output" enables memory and imagination to be configured as computer-like processes.

In flashbacks to 1966/67, we see Sally and the narrator pantomiming the scene from the musical *Sweet Charity* (1966) in which the protagonist sings the Cy Coleman song, "Big Spender." Imitating Charity, Sally pretends to pull a beret down over her forehead and to prance seductively in high heels; the narrator struts with an imaginary walking stick, whirling it from time to time in the air. Performing this act in a variety of public places like bus stops and subway stations, the two create surprise and amuse people around them. "Simulations make you feel good right away," notes the narrator (*Berlin*, 73). In Baudrillard's theory, this effect of simulations is due to their apparent "weightlessness" (*Simulacra*, 34) or lack of firm moorings in reality.

Increasingly, the narrator reduces everything to simulations, refusing to believe that there is any kind of concrete reality behind the mediated images of modern technology. He begins to think of television news not as a representation of real events, but as one simulation in an endless sequence of simulations:

> I see the model of a television program about the model of a demonstration. What is real slips, as usual, back behind the screen, and in the main what is said is what has already been said in some other context. That's how it goes, day after day. Not events, but models are repeated. For a long time now they have dominated what happens. Emotions are restricted, in any given instance, to two possibilities. We are obliged to keep to these models as if in a hamster's wheel, for nothing real remains in them; only simulation. (*Berlin*, 97)

These dizzying effects are akin to those Baudrillard describes in *Simulacra and Simulation*. Knowing that the simulation mimics reality while also seeming to *be* reality, Baudrillard explains, can cause the viewer to enter a state of "vertigo" (*Simulacra*, 34). In certain instances, real events, such as sending a man into space and having him walk on the moon, seem to take place not so much for their own sake as for their recreation on television. "Their truth," Baudrillard writes, "is to be the models of simulation" (*Simulacra*, 35). The "phantom" existence of Sally during the narrated time of *Berlin Simulation*, August and September 1981, simulates the narrator's friendship with her some fifteen years earlier.

Yet even the events from the 1960s are a repetition of previous models, as in the case of the reenactment of the scene from *Sweet Charity* (1966).[13] Christopher Isherwood's "Sally Bowles" (1937)[14] is another model for *The Berlin Simulation*. Just as Sally and the narrator reenact the "Big Spender" scene from *Sweet Charity*, they also relive the story of Sally Bowles and Isherwood's narrator, Chris. Behind Isherwood's light-hearted plot lurks the more sinister reality of Germany before the Nazi takeover, marked by sudden bank crashes, constant financial struggles, and the mysterious disappearance of friends who owe Sally money.

Isherwood's story and Coleman's musical determine the way Morshäuser's characters understand their lives and shape their relationships to the urban world around them. The receding sequence that passes from the phantom Sally of 1981 to the experienced Sally of 1967, from her to Charity in the 1966 musical and then to the Sally of Isherwood's 1937 story is a good example of what Baudrillard calls the "precession of simulacra." Hints at even earlier models are given by allusions to Gérard de Nerval and André Breton. The story's epigraph is a quotation from Nerval's *Aurélia* in which he claims to have adapted an ordinary person from his own time to make a modern version of such idealized loved objects as Laura and Beatrice. Similarly, a reference to Breton's *Nadja* (1928) also evokes the theme of a lost love. Describing Breton as a "projector" who fills his screen maniacally with other people, the narrator declares: "Seldom has anyone spoken so honestly of the process of projection, as deadly as it is productive" (*Berlin*, 42). This comment helps us understand what might perhaps be dangerous about the "unarmed" Sally in *Berlin Simulation*: it is her existence as a projection.

Morshäuser's narrative ends with an episode in which Sally, the narrator, and their American friend Terry attend an anti-Vietnam demonstration in 1966. When the police use tear gas to disperse the participants, the three friends take refuge in a department store, a central emblem of Baudrillard's consumer society. Terry has with him a makeshift bomb—some explosive material in a bottle—which he activates in a fitting room while pretending to try on a pair of trousers. The heat of the explosion sets off the fire sprinklers, but for Terry, Sally, and the narrator, the water coming from the ceiling just sets the stage for another one of their high-spirited theatricals. As if the sprinklers were nothing more than convenient shower heads, Terry announces that he needs to buy shampoo. Sally protects herself from the water with her newly purchased "Sally Bowles" hat. As the three of them step off the escalator, they break into improvised song and dance. "We aren't outraged any more," says the narrator, in the final sentence of the book. Indignation over the Vietnam war gives way to a frivolous subversion of consumer society. And the menacing function of shower heads under Nazism is not even mentioned. The ludicrous reversal from a serious political protest to an ineffectual travesty of the world of consumption is thoroughly in tune with Baudrillard's theory about how easily simulacra take over from reality.

The strange way in which simulation and identity are intertwined is also the subject of a later book about Berlin: Georg Klein's *Barbar Rosa: A Detective Story* (2001).[15] The publication date of this novel is somewhat misleading, since it was actually written in 1991. Only after Georg Klein's brilliant novel about German multiculturalism, *Libidissi* (1998), received several major literary awards[16] did publishers evince an interest in the manuscript of *Barbar Rosa*. Just as Morshäuser's *Berlin Simulation* works backward from the 1980s via the 1960s to the late 1920s, so Klein's *Barbar Rosa* hinges on a conception of history as a kind of temporal archaeology.

In this respect, the novel builds on Reinhart Koselleck's important study of historiography, *Zeitschichten* (layers of time).[17] The cityscape of what is referred to only as "the capital" (the name Berlin is never used) consists in a conflation of two temporal levels. A former men's public convenience now houses a video rental business that specializes in films for certain kinds of sexual fetishists; a former nightclub called "Bettina's Bar" has become a hangout for people addicted to an "alcohol intensifier" called "sucko" that is made on the premises; an abandoned parking garage is now owned by two brothers who sell used comics and printed materials. Corresponding to these temporal layers are spatial layers. Only some of these are functional, even if no longer used for their original purpose. The converted two-story men's toilet is one of the few such two-story buildings still in existence. Other layers of the cityscape have been abandoned: the unused elevated railroad track, for example, and the water-damaged lower levels of the parking garage. An important scene takes place in an enclosed public swimming pool that has fallen out of use.

The city is deftly sketched with sparse details suggesting the decline of a formerly vibrant metropolis. The narrator-protagonist, Mühler, moves through a shadowy and often sinister underworld populated by sucko addicts and violent youth gangs made up of disaffected immigrants from other countries. Technology ranges from dysfunctional public telephones and ancient television sets to fax machines and computers with the latest graphic software. Yet despite the threadbare present through which fragments of the past continually emerge, the inhabitants of the city appear to have little historical awareness. The narrator's peregrinations are in large measure a search for his personal, as well as a larger national, past. Numerous aspects of the novel identify the larger context as that of "Vergangenheitsbewältigung" or coming to terms with the guilt of the Nazi period. In this respect, the novel positions itself in a dominant mode of German literature since 1945. But rarely has the confrontation with the Nazi past taken such a zany form.

The novel consists in a parody of psychotherapy that uses simulations and other modern media instead of the Freudian "talking cure." Mühler's efforts to find out what has happened to a missing money transport vehicle, along with two drivers and an enormous amount of cash, turns out to be a flashback into his childhood. Using first computer graphics that create a visual image of the vehicle, turning it on its axis in all directions as in a television car advertisement, Mühler goes back in time to print media. To locate appropriate images, he visits a "used text" shop. "I only come here," he says in an echo of the postmodern penchant for textual borrowings, "when I need material for my work."[18] Soon he has several strong paper bags full of relevant "material," much of it in the form of old comic books. Only gradually does this bizarre sequence begin to make sense.[19]

The novel is a farcical transposition of Baudrillard's theory that modern simulations have radically changed our understanding of the relation between reality and appearance. The familiar detective story represents an earlier phase in which a search for the truth is conducted using evidence from reality. The shift to the age of simulation reverses the coordinates. In *Barbar Rosa*, the underground tunnels and covered swimming pools where much of the action takes place suggest a reality hidden from the clear light of day. Yet when that reality is revealed, the money transporter turns out to be nothing other than a toy vehicle, just like the ones Mühler collected as a child. The therapeutic process has successfully excavated Mühler's repressed memories. The search for the money transporter is merely a stage in Mühler's rehabilitation from addiction to sucko and a traumatic car accident. The reminders of childhood are an updated version of psychotherapy in which "video simulators" are employed as stimuli to memory (*Barbar Rosa*, 108). Mühler's adventures underground suggest that the attempt to locate the missing vehicle is also a journey through his own unconscious.

Art and literature enable his journey to recombine past and present. Paradoxically (or so one might think), the comic books are a key to this development. A Polish woman who reads one of the comic books along with Mühler notes that its text employs turns of phrase reminiscent of fine literature. "She suspected, rightly, that this comic-book author had plundered dialogues from famous novels. And laughing, baring her large teeth, she added that it was as if the speech bubbles had stolen gold in their mouths" (*Barbar Rosa*, 50). The motif of the gold fillings recalls the Nazis' plundering of the Jews who had been deported to concentration camps. But the language in the speech bubbles alludes to Erika Fuchs's renowned German translations of Walt Disney's Mickey Mouse and Donald Duck comics.[20] Fuchs, known for introducing into German grammar such exclamations as *seufz* for the English "sigh,"[21] had elevated the level of the comic books by inserting quotations and allusions to classical German literature. Donald Duck, in particular, adapts quotations from Schiller and Goethe in speech that Fuchs "translated" for him from the English. Her texts for the Disney comics kept German cultural tradition alive by transmitting it to an entire generation of young readers. Indeed, Fuchs's versions rapidly became a cult that was cited even in the distinguished German newspaper, the *Frankfurter Allgemeine Zeitung*.[22] The "used material" in the form of comic books is part of Mühler's psychotherapeutic journey, which takes him back, not to the German classics, but to popular echoes of them.

To translate this somewhat clumsy allegory, we can say that the novel asks whether art is in fact a good medium for coming to terms with the past. Although Mühler is now restored to full health, the owners of the used paper store have disappeared from the city. Rumor has it that they "have gone back to the east for good" and are enjoying "lengthy cures in that famous open-air spa" (*Barbar Rosa*, 203). The language here echoes that of the Nazi period, in which unwanted people were deported to places like Theresienstadt, the city Hitler claimed to have built as a "gift" to the nation's Jews. The novel implies that healing Germany from the trauma of its past may be possible only at serious cost.

The title of Klein's novel evokes the legend of Barbarossa. According to folk belief, Frederick I (known as Frederick Barbarossa) did not really die; rather, he fell under a spell that left him asleep, sitting at a massive stone table through which his red beard kept growing over the years. One day, as legend has it, he will awaken and restore the Holy Roman Empire just as it was during his reign in the twelfth century. In an allusion to this legend, "Operation Barbarossa" was the name the Nazis gave to their invasion of Soviet Russia in 1941. To evoke the legend of Barbarossa just after the unification of the Federal Republic of Germany and the German Democratic Republic, as Klein's book does, was to evoke the notion that reunification might reconsolidate German power in the center of Europe. Indeed, many East Germans regarded unification as a sort of imperialism in which the more prosperous West took over the powerless and rather decrepit East. In one of the last chapters of *Barbar Rosa*, Mühler sees a tiny desk, made of some older kind of plastic (Klein uses the East German *Plaste* instead of the West German *Plastik*), at which sits a transparent child, probably a boy. Could it be a replica of his childhood self? From the child's chin, a flesh-colored growth penetrates downward through the table and lies in circles on the floor. "It seemed to me," writes Mühler, "that a thousand years of disgust, an empire of aversion and repugnance, hung upon this growth" (*Barbar Rosa*, 188).

This scene is the penultimate stage in Mühler's journey toward recovery. Yet in the end, the return to normal life is disappointing. Although Mühler is free from the trauma that had prevented him from performing his job as a truck driver, some things are missing. The Ilbich brothers, owners of the "used text" store, have disappeared from the city, and they are rumored to have gone to a renowned spa in the east (Theresienstadt casts a sinister shadow over this change). Furthermore, Mühler is troubled by a stubborn spot of dried paint that cannot be removed from the back of his suit jacket. Can the new simulation therapy really effect a complete cure? The ending of the novel is decidedly troubling.

Simulacra of Death: Don DeLillo's *White Noise*

When *Simulacra and Simulation* first appeared in America in 1983, it tended to be understood as a critique of consumer society rather than as a more widely reaching analysis of the problem of authenticity in contemporary life. Familiarity with *The Mirror of Production* (first published in America in 1973) set the terms for many readers of *Simulacra and Simulation*, which was read as a continuation of the earlier discussion of consumer society. The American writer who seems most akin to Baudrillard is Don DeLillo in his novel *White Noise* (1984). Many scholars who write about *White Noise* note its affinities to Baudrillard.[23] One reason for these affinities may be a common interest in the ideas of Marshall McLuhan, whose book *Understanding Media: The Extensions of Man* (1964) rapidly became a foundational work in communication and media studies. In 1967, Baudrillard had written a critical review of the book, but he eventually came to adopt some of its ideas.[24] As Andreas Huyssen observes, "Baudrillard's texts are full of references to McLuhan's work."[25] In America, McLuhan was a point of reference throughout the 1960s and 1970s for anyone interested in media: indeed, he was a "popular phenomenon, beloved by Hollywood, the popular press, and the talk-show circuit."[26] Huyssen says that "it would be too easy to speak of a return of McLuhan in the guise of French theory,"[27] yet this is not entirely wrong, either. Peter White remarks that the publication of *White Noise* "coincided with great academic interest in the ideas of Baudrillard and other theorists of postmodernism."[28] Simulation and its effects in contemporary consumer society are clearly a central issue for DeLillo, who, like Baudrillard, connects them with an ill-defined fear of death. At the time when *White Noise* appeared, Baudrillard's *L'Echange symbolique et la mort* (1976; *Symbolic Exchange and Death*) was known in English only in the form of excerpts.[29] DeLillo identifies a book on a related topic, Ernest Becker's *The Denial of Death* (1973), as an influence on his writing, but even this admission is highly unusual for him.[30] Whether or not he read Baudrillard, DeLillo's talent lies in his perceptive understanding of the effects of pervasive consumerism on individual human psychology. More originally, he also captures the elusive glimmerings of meaning that seem to flash forth from the most humdrum moments in everyday life.[31]

In "The Precession of Simulacra," Baudrillard devotes a subsection to the problem of simulated illness, a topic also addressed in *White Noise*. "Simulation" in this sense was doubtless the first usage of the word, before it came to be used in connection with mechanical simulators such as air pilot training programs, and then employed in social theory in a broader sense. Baudrillard argues that if a person who intends merely to feign illness actually produces physical symptoms characteristic of the disease, the simulation puts into question the accepted relation between true and false:

> Psychology and medicine stop at this point, forestalled by the illness's henceforth undiscoverable truth. For if any symptom can be "produced," and can no longer be taken as a fact of nature, then every illness can be considered as simulatable and simulated, and medicine loses its meaning, since it only knows how to treat "real" illnesses according to their objective causes. (*Simulacra*, 3)

White Noise addresses this problem in two ways: first, in the way the narrator's daughters respond to the "airborne toxic event" by manifesting the latest symptom of exposure to the poisonous cloud that is being described on the radio; and second, in the plot strand involving the narrator's wife and her treatment for fear of death by a quack doctor who supplies her with a supposedly experimental medication, ironically named Dylar.

White Noise opens with a depiction of students arriving at the College-on-the-Hill at the beginning of the academic year. The lineup of shiny cars and its replication of college arrivals from fall semesters past can be seen as a version of the phenomenon Baudrillard describes in his essay "The Precession of Simulacra." As Jack Gladney watches parents and students greeting one another, he notices the way the vehicles reflect images of people and things, refracting them in multiple variants: "The parents stand sun-dazed near their automobiles, seeing images of themselves in every direction."[32] The Gladneys' own life takes place mainly at home, with the television set constantly on, or in the supermarket, surrounded by showcased produce and intermittent loudspeaker announcements. The effect resonates with Baudrillard's comments in *Simulacra and Simulation*: "Inside, a whole panoply of gadgets magnetizes the crowd in directed flows—outside, solitude is directed at a single gadget: the automobile" (*Simulacra*, 12).

In the Gladneys' chaotic household, snatches of speech from the TV set mingle with conversation as if the device were another member of the family. These scenes recall the television filming of the Loud family, a much-discussed event in the early 1970s, and one on which Baudrillard also comments. Bill and Pat Loud of Santa Barbara, California, along with their seven children, were filmed in 1971 during a critical time in their family life, and although the show was actually reduced from hundreds of hours of raw footage, it was disseminated on television in 1973 as if it were an unedited cultural document. The show, "American Family," proved immensely controversial, largely because of Pat's request for a divorce, which became a focus of debate among viewers and in the news media. As Baudrillard notes in his discussion of the show, television abolishes traditional distinctions between passive and active, obliterating all possibility of locating a clear center of power. Television leaves behind "only 'information,' secret virulence, chain reaction, slow implosion, and simulacra of spaces in which the effect of the real again comes into play" (*Simulacra*, 29, 30).

In *White Noise*, Babette subscribes to a then popular belief that watching television together as a family once a week will "de-glamorize the medium" in the children's eyes (*Noise*, 16). Jack Gladney, chair of the "Hitler Studies Department" at the College-on-the-Hill, likes to follow the regular television-viewing by reading "deeply in Hitler well into the night" (*Noise*, 16). Yet despite their attempt to reduce the aura associated with television, the medium still permeates their understanding of the world around them and the way they conduct themselves in public and private. Television is both a model to be imitated and a lens through which events are viewed and evaluated: one of Jack's daughters, Steffie, likes to move her lips in synchrony with television announcers (*Noise*, 84) and another daughter, Bee, is disgusted when a group of airplane passengers who had just endured a near crash is not met by the media: "They went through all that for nothing?" she comments (*Noise*, 92). In one amusing vignette, the family watches a televised session of Babette's posture class for the elderly. Taken aback by this program, for which Babette has not prepared them, they spend some time following her movements with the sound turned off, trying to understand what is happening. Jack finds it impossible to believe in the material reality of his wife: "I'd seen her just an hour ago, eating eggs, but her appearance on the screen made me think of her as some distant figure from the past, some ex-wife and absentee mother, a walker in the midst of the dead. If she was not dead, was I?" (*Noise*, 104).

Jack feels that what he is seeing is "her spirit, her secret self . . . , set free to glide through the wavebands, through energy levels, pausing to say goodbye to us from the fluorescent screen." He believes that she is not only disembodied, but actually dying, if not already dead. The youngest child, Wilder, takes the opposite position, trying to speak to the televised image of his mother, uttering fragments of language that are "sensible-sounding" but "mainly fabricated"; when the program comes to an end, he begins to cry. Jack's and Wilder's responses to the appearance of a familiar person on the screen suggest two possible ways of understanding the relation between the real and the simulation; but a more accurate understanding is given by Jack when he notes that his wife's image "was projected on our bodies, swam in us and through us" (*Noise*, 104).

Baudrillard's observation that we live "in a universe strangely similar to the original—things are doubled by their own scenario" (*Simulacra*, 11) is, in essence, the basic supposition on which DeLillo's *White Noise* is constructed. Public announcements invariably involve repetition, whether they are supermarket requests for a van to stop obstructing a delivery entrance or bullhorn calls for people to evacuate their homes in the trail of a catastrophe. The toxic event at the center of the novel bears a bizarre relationship to simulated disasters. Officials attending to those who have been evacuated wear armbands with the initials SIMUVAC and explain that the experience they are gaining in this real event can serve as a model for subsequent simulations. "Are you saying," Jack asks them, "you saw a chance to use the real event in order to rehearse the simulation?" Resorting to bureaucratic phrasing, a frustrated official answers that there is, unfortunately, a "probability excess," compounded by the fact that "we don't have our victims laid out where we'd want them if this was an actual simulation" (*Noise*, 139). Later, when the SIMUVAC team stages a simulated emergency in which Jack's son and stepdaughter participate, Jack asks the officials scornfully, "Are you people sure you're ready for a simulation? You may want to wait for one more massive spill. Get your timing down" (*Noise*, 204). As it turns out, some first responders never do arrive at the scene of the simulated disaster. In these episodes, reality and simulation appear in the relationship of "operational negativity" that Baudrillard describes in "The Precession of Simulacra": "Who will unravel this imbroglio? The Gordian knot can at least be cut. The Möbius strip, if one divides it, results in a supplementary spiral without the reversibility of surfaces being resolved" (*Simulacra*, 17–18). He goes on to illustrate this intertwining by showing how terms that used to be regarded as opposite now relate to each other as if situated on a Möbius strip: sex and work, history and nature, desire and power are some of the traditional oppositions that Baudrillard sees as engaged in an "exchange of signifiers and . . . scenarios" (*Simulacra*, 18). Part of the poignancy of *White Noise* is the discovery Jack and Babette make about these eerie interconnections.

Jack's colleague Murray Jay Siskind, replaying a discussion with his students, takes a less complicated view of simulation and reality that still depends on conventional oppositions. His example is that of simulated car crash scenes in movies, which his students regard as a sign of "civilization in decay" (*Noise*, 218).[33] Murray, in contrast, sees them as part of a grandiose dream of technological perfection, as moments of optimism rather than as signs of an unhealthy interest in violence:

> I tell them they can't think of a car crash in a movie as a violent act. It's a celebration. A reaffirmation of traditional values and beliefs. . . . We will improve, prosper, perfect ourselves. Watch any car crash in any American movie. It is a high-spirited moment like old-fashioned stunt flying, walking on wings. The people who stage these crashes are able to capture a lightheartedness, a carefree enjoyment that car crashes in foreign movies can never approach. (*Noise*, 218–219)

Murray is caught up in what Baudrillard calls "the perfection of the programming and the technological manipulation, . . . the immanent wonder of the programmed unfolding of events" (*Simulacra*, 34). Murray's position on technology may be optimistic, but it is not unintelligent. He understands that "it's what we invented to conceal the terrible secret of our decaying bodies," while still arguing that "it's also life, isn't it?" (*Noise*, 285). He sees technology as a kind of prosthetic that enables us to circumvent in some sense our gradual physical decline, another manifestation of "God's own goodness" in the form of "light, energy, dreams" (*Noise*, 285). Similarly, Baudrillard analyzes the simulated reality of America as a way of eradicating consciousness of death. When things are doubled by technological means, this "does not signify, as it did traditionally, the imminence of their death—they are already purged of their death, and better than when they were alive; more cheerful, more authentic, in the light of their model, like the faces in funeral homes" (*Simulacra*, 11).

In one of several important conversations between Jack and Murray, the two colleagues discuss the phenomenon of nostalgia (*Noise*, 257–258). The Hitler specialist Jack recalls Albert Speer's architecture, with its ambition to create structures that would eventually become imposing ruins. Arguing from this example, he claims that "a certain nostalgia" lies behind the "power principle" (*Noise*, 258). Murray presents a more sophisticated position, in which he understands nostalgia as a "settling of grievances between the past and the present" (*Noise*, 258). He sees it as the first step on a scale that ultimately leads to violence, a physical equivalent of the irritation caused by a feeling that the past was superior to the present. This is a fascinating diagnosis. But ultimately, it is augmented by Jack's discovery, in the course of his long struggle with the fear of death, that simulation can also be consoling. Visiting a hospital in the old German quarter of town, he asks a nun whether devils, angels, and heaven actually exist and is shocked to receive her reply that she does not believe in these things. Pretending to believe, she explains, is the way in which she expresses her dedication to a social role whose meaning lies in its ability to reassure those who find their own failure to believe unsettling. The nuns' profession of faith is a simulation through which they "surrender [their] lives to make your nonbelief possible" (*Noise*, 319). DeLillo's presentation of simulated belief in this episode stands in distinct contrast to Baudrillard's contention that a "visible myth of origin" substitutes in modern consumer society for lack of belief (*Simulation*, 10).

DeLillo's Jack Gladney understands life as a narrative we tell ourselves, a linear sequence that moves from a beginning to an ending. Lecturing to the students in his course on "Advanced Nazism," he finds himself uttering, to his own surprise and bewilderment, ideas he had not prepared to say: "All plots tend to move deathward. That is the nature of plots. Political plots, terrorists' plots, lovers' plots, narrative plots, plots that are part of children's games. We edge nearer death every time we plot. It is like a contract all must sign, the plotters as well as those who are the targets of the plot" (*Noise*, 26). These words that seem to come from somewhere else play on the double meaning of "plot," shifting along a spectrum that extends from "political plots" to "narrative plots." The idea of the "contract" invokes the idea of contract killing while also recalling Lejeune's concept of the "autobiographical pact" between author and reader. The idea that all plots move deathward recalls Kermode's *The Sense of an Ending*, a study of apocalypse in fiction. The "airborne toxic event" in the middle section of *White Noise* conjures up just such an apocalypse. But although Jack Gladney discovers that he suffered a brief exposure to the poisonous chemical while he was filling his car's gas tank and thus may have impaired his health, no one actually dies—at least in the short run—from the noxious spill. Unable to bear the thought that his exposure may have shortened his life expectancy at some distant future date, Jack becomes easy prey for Murray's theory that "there are two kinds of people in the world. Killers and diers" (*Noise*, 290).[34] Murray explains that the act of killing is a way of controlling one's fear of death by letting one's victim stand in, as it were, for oneself. Killing thus becomes, paradoxically, a life-affirming act. Amusingly characterizing himself as just a theorist, Murray nonetheless plants the seed in Jack's thinking that leads to his killing of the mysterious man who provided Babette with the experimental Dylar pills. Jack performs this killing deliberately, as part of a carefully conceived "plan" (*Noise*, 304) that is the equivalent of the plots he had spoken of in his lecture. Equipped with his father-in-law's ancient automatic pistol, he confronts the phony doctor in his motel room and contrives to shoot him in a way that will disguise murder as suicide. The scene, a parody of familiar episodes from popular novels and films, is itself a kind of simulation based on preceding models. Yet Jack's attempt to create an ending to the plot in which he is living fails to succeed. Willie Mink, the purveyor of Dylar pills, is badly hurt and will need to spend time in hospital; but he will not die of his wounds. Neither a killer nor a dier, Jack himself is left to the "ambient roar" of the supermarket, with its computerized scanners and tabloid newspapers, encoding the "cults of the famous and the dead" (*Noise*, 326).

Baudrillard sketches the darker side of his simulation theory in his essay "Holocaust" (*Simulacra*, 49–51), a response to the American television series of that title, broadcast in Europe in 1979. Talking about our tendency to forget—or desire to forget—about the exterminations carried out by the Nazis, Baudrillard comments that "this forgetting is still too dangerous, it must be effaced by an artificial memory" located in what he terms the "cold" medium of television (*Simulacra*, 49). He goes on to say: "one would like to have us believe that TV will lift the weight of Auschwitz by making a collective awareness radiate" (*Simulacra*, 49–50). Yet, as he also points out, the responses evoked by television in its representation of the Nazi period are fleeting: they make us pay merely the "price of a few tears" (*Simulacra*, 49) for "a tactile thrill and a posthumous emotion" (*Simulacra*, 50), leaving us with a spurious sense of having developed a good conscience. In *White Noise*, the link between the "toxic airborne event" and the Holocaust is made through Jack Gladney's invention of "Hitler Studies," his inability to learn German, and his laughable attempt to be taken seriously in that field by developing a false persona. Sinister intimations emerge in his discussions with Murray Jay Siskind and throughout the entire Dylar sequence. In the final chapter of the novel, Jack avoids seeing his doctor who, he feels, "is eager to see how my death is progressing" (*Noise, 325*). Paradoxically, DeLillo is able to turn his narrative meditation on the problem of simulation into a probing and ultimately touching psychological novel. The wit and humor of *White Noise* act as a foil for its deeper understanding of human motivation. Starting out as caricatures, Jack and Babette ultimately become figures with whom we can (almost) identify. The wry pathos of the novel has a staying power that goes beyond its time-bound setting in the early 1980s. This remarkable achievement allows the reader to see the culture DeLillo presents on two levels at once: as a parodic scenario that enacts the shallowness of contemporary life and as an affecting study of deeper and more threatening fears.

Dystopian Simulations: Christoph Ransmayr

Perhaps the most densely textured fictional engagement with the concept of simulation is *Morbus Kitahara* (1995; *The Dog King*), by the prize-winning Austrian novelist Christoph Ransmayr. The German title is the name of an eye disease otherwise known as chorioretinitus centralis serosa, a disorder whose pathogenesis is still not fully understood. The name "Kitahara" recognizes a Japanese doctor who worked on the disease. With some reluctance, I will refer to the novel henceforth by its English title. *The Dog King* is an alternative history that imagines what might have happened if the Morgenthau plan had been imposed on Germany after its defeat in World War II. In September 1944, Henry Morgenthau Jr. elaborated a plan for turning Germany "into a country primarily agricultural and pastoral," without any "warmaking industries."[35] Although this plan was abandoned in reality, Ransmayr uses it as the basis for his dystopian vision of a postwar world in which American occupation of Germany and Austria continues for well over two decades after the end of the war. Ransmayr introduces several other changes to recorded history: in particular, the war between America and Japan continues without resolution for the same period of time. Eventually, the Americans succeed in forcing the Japanese to surrender by dropping an atomic bomb on Nagoya. The desolation of a nonindustrial Germany/Austria, the catastrophic bombing of Japan, and the protagonist's terrifying experience of the retinitis named after a Japanese doctor all come together in a complicated network of disasters.

The fictive place where most of the action occurs is a lakeside city called Moor, formerly an elegant spa, but also the site of a granite quarry in which the Nazis used forced labor from a concentration camp nearby. The quarry is modeled to some extent on the real camp Ebensee, a satellite of the concentration camp Mauthausen, in upper Austria. The excessively steep stone stairs up which the prisoners had to struggle bearing huge block of stone recalls the steps at the concentration camp Treblinka, but the stone memorial, except for its height, differs in crucial respects from the monument at Treblinka. The name of the fictional town, Moor, evokes a song that was sung in numerous Nazi concentration camps and continued to be sung by young people in a gesture of empathy with the victims of the Holocaust after the end of the war: "We are the moor soldiers . . ."

Early chapters in *The Dog King* describe the erection of a granite memorial on unused terraces of the Moor quarry in accord with the wishes of the (fictional) American commandant, Major Elliot. In huge stone letters each the size of a man, the monument spells out the number of prisoners killed while performing forced labor: "Here/eleven thousand nine hundred seventy-three/people lie dead/slain by the inhabitants of this land/welcome to Moor."[36] Four times a year, Elliot requires the people of Moor to stand in the quarry for a roll call that imitates those of the former concentration camp. Once he discovers old photographs of camp life, he introduces another memorial ceremony in which the residents of Moor are required to dress as concentration camp inmates and adopt the poses of the men in the pictures. One of these images, called "The Stairway," shows prisoners hauling loads of stone in barrows on their backs up the seemingly interminable steps. The forced labor of the simulation is in no way equivalent, however, to the labor of the original victims: "Elliot demanded only an external illusion this time as well, and forced none of his supernumeraries to heave onto his barrow one of the genuine ponderous hewn stones still lying scattered at the foot of the stairs like monuments to the agonies of death endured there. Elliot simply wanted the pictures to look alike and did not insist on the unbearable weight of reality" (*Dog King*, 36).

The memorial events, called "Stellamour parties" in recognition of the (fictional) American high court justice Lyndon Porter Stellamour, are in fact only partial simulations. While waiting for the roll call to begin, women and children are permitted to wait in tents and to huddle under blankets if the weather is cold; the participants in the stairway climb are allowed to carry stones made of papier-mâché, and those who stumble on the steep and irregular steps are not beaten, kicked, or shot as were the concentration camp laborers. These adjustments are not merely a reflection of Major Elliot's humaneness, but also an indicator of the problematic nature of simulations under conditions that have fundamentally changed.

Later in the novel, television images take up the theme of simulation. When Bering, the novel's the protagonist, finally visits the city of Brand, in the lowlands, he finds a world much less primitive than that of Moor. There, in a department store window, he sees row upon row of television screens, each displaying the bombing of Nagoya. Even these images, however, are replays of an event that had occurred two days earlier. Each time the screens show the blinding flash of the bomb, the mushroom cloud that rises up, and the flaming coastline that results, the crowd rejoices as if it were happening for the first time.

When Bering consults a doctor about his vision problems, the specialist compares the shape of the lesions on his retina to "the mushroom over Nagoya" (*Dog King*, 280). He claims that the disease is most frequently seen in people like trench soldiers or sharpshooters who have "stared a hole in their own eyes" (*Dog King*, 280). Although the doctor reassures Bering that his eyes will ultimately heal themselves spontaneously, he also suggests that the problem is more than merely physical. "What is it you can't get out of your head?" he asks (*Dog King*, 280), hinting that Bering has been damaged by some obsession or trauma.

The concentration camp reenactments in Moor and the television replays in Brand are versions of what Baudrillard describes as a tendency for real events to appear like mere models for their subsequent simulations, as in the case of the moon landing "made for television." The novel's opening bears affinities with Baudrillard's explanation of his concept of the "precession of simulacra" as the "map that precedes the territory" (*Simulacra*, 1). This map, Baudrillard writes, is almost more real than reality itself, which he calls "*The desert of the real*" (*Simulacra, 1*). In *The Dog King*, the first chapter presents a brief vignette that seems, on first reading, cryptic and disconnected from what follows. In a bird's eye perspective that is not quite identical to that of a plane pilot surveying an island off the coast of Brazil, we see the bodies of three dead people, two men and a woman. The pilot, who cannot see these bodies from the height at which he is flying, records in a radio message the same word he sees written below the name of the island on his map: "*Deserto*.

Uninhabited" (*Dog King*, 4). We do not find out until we have reached the end of the novel that this episode postdates the other events narrated in the book, which culminate in the deaths of three characters on this island. By placing this episode first, Ransmayr creates a "map that precedes the territory" but that gives us parameters we only understand at the end. We need to double back in order to make meaning out of this opening passage.

The entire novel is structured around a complex set of correspondences and doublings. One example is the train that brings Bering's father back from the war in North Africa at the beginning of the novel and the train that takes Bering away from Moor at the end. Bering's infancy, spent hanging in a basket above the chicken coop, gives him the skill to imitate the sounds of birds, a "natural" ability that is repeated in the mechanical facility with which he turns an old automobile into a bird-like machine. The green granite that is Moor's principal product is found only in one other place in the world: a small town in Brazil that bears the name Pantano, meaning the same thing as the German word "Moor," in other words a marsh or swamp.[37] Bering's friend Lily is known as "The Brazilian" because of her belief, when she arrived in Moor as a child with a group of families fleeing from Nazi Germany, that they had already reached their ultimate destination, Brazil. At the end of the novel, which actually takes place in Brazil, she is doubled by the native woman Muyra. In a terrible reversal, Bering, unaware that Lily has given her raincoat to Muyra, shoots the native woman thinking that she is Lily. These and other doublings give a sinister aspect to the concept of simulations, removing them from an association solely with modern media like television and linking them with consciousness, memory, and murder.

In the novel, there are two ships called *The Sleeping Greek Maid*, one covered with algae and sunk beneath the surface of the lake in Moor, the other a recent gift from a Greek town in payment for a shipment of granite. The ships' name is that of a geographical feature of the Traunsee, the real place on which the fictional lake of *The Dog King* is based. A mountain configured like a woman's profile turned toward the sky is popularly known in the region as the *schlafende Griechin* (sleeping Greek woman): it is one of a number of tourist sites in the mountainous Gmunden region surrounding the Traunsee.[38] By invoking this natural landscape formation, Ransmayr implies a hidden connection between technology (the two steam boats) and nature. He also suggests a mythic heritage that slumbers beneath the surface of the natural environment. This mythic substratum is reinforced by allusions to such mythic figures as Orpheus (in the figure of the singer Patton[39]), and

Hephaestus (in the figure of Bering himself). By locating myth at the deepest level in the "precession of simulacra," Ransmayr alludes to Baudrillard's contention that "history is a strong myth, perhaps, along with the unconscious, the last great myth" (*Simulacra*, 47).

Ransmayr has a long-standing interest in classical myth and the literature of classical antiquity. His previous novel, *Die letzte Welt* (1991; *The Last World*), was based on a fantastic penetration of the ancient and the postmodern worlds. There, the underlying model was the life of Ovid, including his exile from Rome, and the stories told in his *Metamorphoses*. In *The Dog King*, Virgil's *Georgics* have become the underlying literary model in the "precession." Inspired by Octavian's victory over Antony, the *Georgics* relate a return to ancient agricultural ideals that had been set aside during the many wars fought by the Romans. Like the *Georgics*, *The Dog King* begins with a much-desired peace treaty. But what follows from this treaty is not told from the perspective of the victors. Furthermore, its transposition into the modern world turns agricultural life into a punishment instead of a reward for hard-fought battles. In other respects as well Ransmayr turns the model of the Georgics inside out. The industrious colonies of worker bees that Virgil admired for their defiance of mortality take on a sinister connotation when we think of Nazi prisoners forced into hard labor. What the *Georgics* presents as the bees' miraculous survival of individual death by repopulating their hives appears in *The Dog King* as the bestial secret of the concentration camps that lies beneath the surface of present-day Austria.

Both Moor and Brand stand for aspects of Austrian culture today. Brand, whose name means "fire," is the opposite of Moor, meaning "swamp." The two locations are separated by almost impassable mountain tracks. The Americanized city of Brand bears an obvious connection to the world of supermarkets and consumer goods that Baudrillard describes in *Simulacra and Simulations*. Bering's reconstructed automobile, "The Crow," is another version of this phenomenon. After the Americans have left Moor, Bering creates the vehicle using scrap metal. It is a virtual parody of a 1950s American car. He creates tail fins so extended that they "look like tail feathers"; he builds doors that resemble "a bird's wings tucked tight to dive," and shapes a tapering hood that looks like a crow's beak (*Dog King*, 75). We might recall a passage from Baudrillard's *The System of Objects* (1968) that describes American cars with tail fins as a "compensatory mode of being in a world deprived of symbolic dimension."[40] Baudrillard writes: "Tail fins were a sign not of *real* speed, but of a sublime, measureless speed. They suggested a miraculous automatism, a sort of grace. It was the presence of these fins that in our imagination propelled the car, which, thanks to them, seemed to fly along of its own accord" (*Objects*, 63).

In *The Dog King*, Bering's refashioned car is an emblem of his rejection of the decree that Moor should "go back to the Stone Age." A crucial component of his transformation of Major Elliot's legacy, it testifies to ingenious coupling of technology with creative imagination. It is also, however, an embodiment of history as it is often understood today: as a "retro scenario" (*Simulacra*, 43). Imbued with mythic significance—the text alludes to the phoenix but also to Icarus—the car avoids what Baudrillard calls "cool" simulation because of the strong emotive associations it bears for Bering. Driving the car is for him a kind of flying. When he takes his first flight in a helicopter, he experiences only disappointment: this has "nothing to do with real flying, nothing to do with the magic of a bird in flight" (*Dog King*, 286). Looking down from the helicopter, he sees his precious car in flames, maliciously set alight by quarry workers: "Bedded in a nest of fumes lay the Crow, lay the hallmark of the Dog King, lay Bering's most ingenious work, rolled over, its open hood a gaping beak" (*Dog King*, 289). Back on the ground, Bering roams among the stone nymphs, weathered fauns, and classical columns of the Villa Flora mourning his destroyed automobile as if it were the lost Eurydice (her name is not mentioned, but the scene is explicit enough; *Dog King*, 297). The plume of smoke that rises from the burnt-out vehicle recalls the mushroom smoke sent up by the bomb in Nagoya; and later, it will be doubled again by the plume of smoke from the brushfire on Dog Island, halfway round the world from Moor. By means of these correspondences, *The Dog King* keeps looks repeatedly back to the myths that precede them.

History, in *The Dog King*, is a backward gaze to a point where time seems to reverse itself. After his discovery of an old record player left behind in Villa Flora, Bering gains access to the music of a former age. Similarly, during performances of Patton's Orchestra, he "sometimes slid back deep into years past, back to the darkness of the forge, and was floating and rocking again in his cradle suspended above cages of chickens" (*Dog King*, 118). The songs of the American army bands that perform in Moor tell of an undefined place "where everything was not only better but always *in motion*, too, and where time did not stand still and run backwards as it did in Moor" (*Dog King*, 118). The burden of these songs is "Keep movin'" and "Movin' along!" (*Dog King*, 119). Yet it is on the road, driving his precious Crow, that Bering first discovers the dark spots before his eyes that are the symptom of morbus Kitahara. When he and Ambras (along with their friend Lily) actually move from Moor to Brazil, they do not have time to embark upon a new life: instead, they find their deaths during the ramble on Dog Island. In his book *The Illusion of the End* (1992), Baudrillard elaborates a theory according to which time reverses itself ("The reversal of history," 10–13).[41] Ransmayr's novel replicates this idea by folding the last pages over onto the first, in which the Dog Island incident of the book's apparent ending is continued.

History runs backward in another way as well. Obsessed by the machines that have been banned under American occupation, Bering begins to commit acts of violence. First he kills an intruder using his father's old army pistol; later he fires the same weapon at an itinerant chicken thief. His association with Lily brings him into even closer contact with violence. Lily has discovered a cache of old guns, grenades, and ammunition in one of the deserted underground bunkers, and she finally exchanges some of this material in the lowlands for a modern sharpshooter's rifle. On her intermittent "hunting" expeditions, she uses this weapon to gun down members of wild gangs, looters, and hooligans who stray into the mountains. Oddly, it is not Lily the sharpshooter but Bering himself who contracts the eye disease normally caused by staring for too long at a single focus. During the period when Bering is most hampered by his retinitis, his father, the former blacksmith, gradually becomes senile. When Bering and Lily are forced to make an arduous trip across the mountains to place him in a veterans' hospital in the city of Brand, the old man believes that he is still fighting in North Africa. For him, too, time runs backward, and it is as if the Peace of Oranienburg (the fictive treaty that ends the war in this novel) had never existed. Finally, once the Americans have brought Japan to its knees in unconditional surrender, the army command decides to convert the whole of Moor, including the now exhausted granite quarry, into an exercise terrain. A decades-long war has yielded to world peace, but the conquerors believe that they must start once again to prepare for an unknown military threat. The area that was the site of a concentration camp during the Nazi regime and the quarry that was the location of Ambras's torture in the device called "The Swing" (which cracks the joints of its victim's shoulders) will become a place where simulated violence—military exercises—is enacted.

Like many of the novels we have looked at, *The Dog King* understands its underlying theory of simulation through the filter of other discourses. There are two major filters at work in *The Dog King*: first, Walter Benjamin's concept of the "memory-landscape" and second, the memorialization debates of postwar Germany and Austria. Benjamin developed his idea of "memory-landscape" in response to World War I, with its trail of ravaged terrain inaccessible to traditional ways of perceiving and understanding nature. Whereas in the nineteenth century, landscape was seen as a symbolic setting for an individual's passage through time, the wastelands left by World War I seemed to have become depersonalized. They appeared like correlatives of what was widely felt as a diminishing of experience. T. S. Eliot's *The Wasteland* expresses similar dismay at the way in which the landscapes of modern life seemed to have been emptied of meaning, and it is surely not wrong to take the figure of Major Elliot in *The Dog King* for an allusion to the poet. World War II left behind ruined cities as well as ravaged countryside. Rebuilding tended to take precedence over the erection of memorials to the dead, but once the question was raised of what kinds of monuments were best suited to express the German situation, debates were intense.[42] In comparison with Germany, Austria broached this question belatedly: it had, after all, been treated as a victim by the Allies in 1945. Ransmayr's fictional occupation of Austria by the Americans thus forces his countrymen to experience imaginatively a period of forced domination by a conquering power. Since Austrian guilt during the Nazi period had been officially played down, it was not until around 1983 that discussion about appropriate memorials and monuments entered the Austrian public arena.[43] The question of words versus images—inscriptions versus sculptural forms—was central to discussion in both Germany and Austria. In *The Dog King*, the two forms of memorial are fused together: granite sculptures become letters in a text inserted into the landscape itself. Furthermore, the quarry is neither countryside nor cityscape: in essence, it is a hollowed-out landscape, ravaged not by war but by the forced labor of concentration camp inmates. In this sense, the novel itself becomes yet another answer to the debate on memorialization, a textual monument to the guilt that Ransmayr's native land has only belatedly begun to acknowledge.

Thinking backward through the "memory culture" of today, Ransmayr transforms Baudrillard's theory of simulation into a vehicle that has relevance beyond the world of modern media it was first developed to explain. In Ransmayr's fictional world, objects do not "shine in a sort of hyperresemblance" (*Simulacra*, 45); instead, the violence that is aestheticized by mediated simulations is brought to the fore in all its traumatic force. By placing a restaged version of concentration camp reality at the very opening of his novel, he makes it possible for his readers to look behind the screen of what Baudrillard terms "artificial memory" (*Simulacra*, 49). The lack of referentiality that

Baudrillard sees as the root problem of contemporary fascination with the fascist period is dismantled, as it were, by Ransmayr's elaborately referential narration. When Bering falls from a cliff in the final chapter of *The Dog King*, he feels as if he is flying; Ambras's fall, coterminous with the ending of the novel, is a step "into emptiness," in which "everything that burdened and tormented him loses weight" (*Dog King*, 355). For the reader, however, this conclusion only adds to the almost unbearable weight of the past that has been the principal obsession of *The Dog King*. Replacing traditional desires for narrative fidelity to the facts and details of history, Ransmayr uses an almost entirely fantasized reality to draw our attention away from conventional representations of the Third Reich. The dialectic he sets in place between familiar images of the ways in which that past infiltrates our present and his dystopian reimagining of that relationship causes the reader to ask complex questions about causality, continuity, and memory. Although his narrative is an alternative history that includes numerous fantastic elements, it is densely textured like the thick description of the realist novel, cross-hatched by multiple networks of association and layered with historical and mythic strata. Ransmayr has developed, in *The Dog King*, a way to reach behind the "cold media" of today's technology while also experimenting with new ways of conceiving our historical embeddedness.

The Search for Ecstasy

The search for meaning takes a different form in *The Dog King* than in *White Noise*. Both novels are concerned with the interplay between simulation, desire, and death. In both cases, the protagonist longs for some kind of transcendent experience, an epiphany that would lift him out of his everyday life. In both cases, however, this quest ultimately fails. With virtuoso lucidity, DeLillo weaves simulation theory into a narrative that keeps its finger on the pulse of life as many American families experience it. In contrast, Ransmayr's darkly imagined novel overlays simulation theory with a thick impasto of imagined history. On this level, the two novels seem diametrically opposed.

Toward the end of *White Noise*, Jack lets Murray convince him that he is gaining in charisma and even acquiring an aura: "You're creating a hazy light about your own body. I have to like it" (*Noise*, 284). As Jack gets ready to confront the fraudulent doctor Willie Mink, he feels that his consciousness is expanding and opening to new insights. "Things glowed, a secret life rising out of them" (*Noise*, 310). Approaching Mink with a borrowed gun, Jack's relationship to the world of things intensifies: "I knew who I was in the network of meanings. Water fell to earth in drops, causing surfaces to gleam. I saw things new." After he fires at Mink, "I saw beyond words. I knew what red was, saw it in terms of a dominant wavelength, luminance, purity" (Noise, 312). Soon afterward, "the extra dimensions, the super perceptions, were reduced to visual clutter, a whirling miscellany, meaningless" (*Noise*, 313). As Leonard Wilcox points out in a perceptive article, what Jack experiences here is the other face of the alienation he had felt before: now he is overwhelmed by an "undifferentiated flux of pure signifiers, an 'ecstasy of communication' in which conventional structures of meaning dissolve and the ability to imagine an alternative reality disappears."[44] The term "ecstasy of communication" is Baudrillard's, as is the description of the way in which ecstasy emerges as signifiers proliferate to a point where they finally become meaningless. As Wilcox observes, however, there is a crucial difference between the views expressed in *White Noise* and those of Baudrillard himself. Baudrillard's stance, Wilcox says, is ultimately one of "radical skepticism," whereas DeLillo's writing "reveals a belief that fictional narrative can provide critical distance from and a critical perspective on the processes it depicts."[45] In this regard, we need to look carefully at the ending of *White Noise*. The final chapter opens with an episode in which Jack and Babette's young son Wilder escapes what might have been a fatal accident while crossing a highway on his plastic tricycle. When Wilder is rescued by a motorist from his fall down the embankment, "the sky takes on content, feeling, an exalted narrative life" (*Noise*, 324). The ironic sentence suggests that the parents' heightened sense of relief is predetermined by narrative conventions. In the last lines of the novel, we see them standing in a supermarket line, gazing at the tabloid newspapers and their never-ending stories about celebrity cults and miracle cures. Jack's life has returned to its previous routine, but he is more aware than before of its mediated nature. The toddler Wilder has no awareness of his escape from possible death on the highway, but Jack knows that his own survival depends on an ironic awareness of the ways in which narrative shapes our lives. Baudrillard writes that "in survival, death is repressed; life itself, in accord with that well-known ebbing away, would be nothing more than a survival determined by death."[46] In *White Noise*, DeLillo answers such pessimism with an ironic espousal of the power of narrative.

In "The Ecstasy of Communication," Baudrillard comments on a shift away from traditional modes of ambitious struggle such as "the Faustian,

Promethean, (perhaps Oedipal)"[47] and toward a looser understanding of subjectivity as continually moving and changing interconnectivity. *The Dog King* explores a similar idea when it presents Bering's life in Moor as a mythic struggle between a single individual and his world. Although the novel itself, as we have seen, presents Bering's story in terms of classical mythology—himself as a kind of Daedalus and his car, Crow, as a version of Icarus[48]—it can also be seen in terms of a rebellious individual like Faust. In Goethe's version of the Faust myth, the wager between Faust and the devil has precisely to do with the desire for epiphany. Romantic poets called the epiphanic moment "the eternal moment," meaning not that it *is* eternal, but that it seems eternal to one who experiences it. Goethe's Faust agrees that the devil may have his soul if he ever wants the moment to linger. Bering's longing for experiences in which he feels as if he is "flying" can be understood as a desire for such an epiphanic moment. Yet each experience of this kind is connected with American culture: the charismatic singer of "Patton's orchestra," the reconstruction of the car in a virtual parody of American automobile styling, and the wall of brightly lit television screens that enraptures Bering when he first sees them in a department store window in Brand. The television episode, in particular, exemplifies an experience akin to Baudrillard's "ecstasy of communication," which occurs when an individual is confronted by an overwhelming proliferation of images and other forms of information. In this scene, ecstasy is not a positive phenomenon: in effect, it is a false sense of exaltation. By connecting these experiences with Americanization, Ransmayr puts into question their validity as ecstatic experience in the traditional sense of the word. It is also on the way to Brand that Bering first becomes a killer: equipped with Lily's rifle, he kills a group of skinheads who are stealing chickens. Looking through the lens of the rifle's scope, Bering believes that he sees the same images that she has seen. Becoming a sharpshooter, he acquires the eye disease that causes gaps in his field of vision. It is an allegory for his loss of moral sense.

Ransmayr's fundamental divergence from Baudrillardian theory is closely connected with morality. Bering's trip to Brazil with Lily is motivated by their search for the green granite that is running out at the quarry in Moor: the Brazilian town Pantano has the same kind of granite, with plenty still to be carved out of a huge natural stone monolith that rises from the ground. The hints of colonialism in these final scenes recall Faust's exploitation of land in Goethe's *Faust II*. When Bering mistakenly kills Lily, he commits the equivalent of Faust's crimes against an old couple on his newly acquired land. The last chapter of *Dog King* consists of a complex interweaving of reality and hallucination, but it is clearly designed to provoke the reader to deeper reflection on Bering's actions. The chapter not only presents obstacles to full understanding on first reading, it also sends us back to the novel's first section, which presents a view of the place where Bering met his end from the perspective of a surveyor in an airplane. It is not clear whether the dead bodies can be seen from the plane, but when the surveyor marks the territory as "uninhabited," he effectively leaves Bering's final moments unrecorded. The reader is impelled to ask how and why Bering could have taken the course that turned him into a sharpshooter and led him to incur guilt.

Like DeLillo, Ransmayr believes in the power of narrative to engage productively with important questions of our day. Where DeLillo's tool is irony, Ransmayr's tool is complexity. Both leave us with conclusions that make us "think beyond the ending."[49] Whereas Baudrillard ultimately found no better solution to the situation he had analyzed than to drive the culture of simulation to such an extreme that it would self-destruct, DeLillo and Ransmayr continue to work toward the moral education of their readers by posing problems in their novels that awaken our consciences and call for further thought.

7 *Lines of Flight*

A hilarious mafioso wedding scene in Pynchon's *Vineland* (1990) set on the fictitious Wayvone estate just south of San Francisco revolves around a band of popular musicians called Billy Barf and the Vomitones. Disguising themselves as an Italian group by means of ill-fitting wigs and costumes, the Vomitones are forced to play a set of Italian tunes they do not know in order to palliate the older generation at the reception. Luckily, the host owns a copy of "the indispensable *Italian Wedding Fake Book* by Deleuze & Guattari," which the bride brings out to the musicians in an attempt to save the day (*Vineland*, 97). A Web guide to the novel by John Diebold and Michael Goodwin comments on this passage by saying, "If this book isn't real, it oughtta be."[1]

Following in Pynchon's wake, David Foster Wallace nods to Deleuze in his novel *Infinite Jest* (1996) by means of a title mentioned seemingly in passing. In this case, a minor character named Molly Notkin is revealing to some secret service agents what she knows about the deceased filmmaker James Incandenza, versions of whose unreleased movie *Infinite Jest* are involved in political machinations they are investigating. According to Molly, a student in an MIT doctoral program who is thoroughly conversant with modern theoretical language, "the entire perfect-entertainment-as-*Liebestod* myth surrounding the purportedly lethal final cartridge was nothing more than a classic illustration of the antinomically schizoid function of the post-industrial capitalist mechanism, whose logic presented commodity as the escape-from-anxieties-of-mortality-which-escape-is-itself-psychologically-fatal, as detailed in perspicuous detail in M. Gilles Deleuze's posthumous *Incest and the Life of Death in Capitalist Entertainment*" (*Infinite Jest*, 792). Both references to Deleuze are couched in a familiar mode: that of academic parody. Yet in each case, what seems at first to be just a laugh is ultimately revealed as crucial to the novel's larger significance.

Vineland and *Infinite Jest* expose the pressures contemporary social structures place on the individual to conform to the "post-industrial capitalist mechanism." The logic of this system presents itself as a modern version of enlightenment reason, but instead of freeing people to act as they wish, it holds them firmly in its grasp. The result, as Deleuze and Guattari describe it, is a double-bind in which individuals are made to feel desires that they might not otherwise have had, while at the same time they attempt to escape the system in the hope of discovering what they imagine to be their more authentic selves. The feeling of being caught between these impossible alternatives is what Deleuze and Guattari, in a departure from the psychoanalytical use of the term, call "schizophrenia." This chapter will focus on the workings of schizophrenia, in this special sense, in several recent novels, including *Vineland* and *Infinite Jest*. It will also look at the ways in which novelists have dealt with other aspects of the two theorists' thought: first, their ideas about the relation between human beings and robots, and second, their concepts of the rhizome and the nomad.

The Man–Machine Interface

Among the first novelists to engage with Deleuze and Guattari were writers of science fiction, especially those interested in cybernetics.[2] For writers in this field, the principal text of reference was an essay that appeared for the first time in Félix Guattari's *Molecular Revolution* (1977).[3] It was titled "Concrete machines."[4] Here, key elements in Deleuze and Guattari's *Anti-Oedipus* (French, 1972; English 1977)[5] were formulated more accessibly. Distinguishing between "concrete" and "abstract" machines, Guattari laid the groundwork for his conception of the world as a network in which human bodies, the social fabric of human life, and modern machines were connected by what he called "flows." These were at once the psychological mechanisms of human desire and the electrical impulses that make computers function and connect them with other computers. The expanded concept of "machine" that underlies Guattari's discussion of "concrete" and "abstract" machines in this essay connected for many readers with ideas that had already been developed in science fiction about the nexus between human beings and machines.

From Asimov's short story "I, Robot" (1950) to Samuel R. Delany's novel *Nova* (1968), a distinctive narrative tradition had already been established on the question of human-machine relations. *Nova* is an early development of the idea that the world is a "great web that spreads across the galaxy."[6] Like a fishing net, it can be "spread out," made to "ripple," and be "torn." Ideas from computer technology prior to the development of the Internet help to visualize complex interrelations in which human beings and machines function as parts of a single system.

Delany's *Dhalgren* (1974), now something of a cult novel,[7] moves closer to French theory. Teaching comparative literature and English at several universities brought Delany into contact with French poststructuralism, which leaves clear traces in his fiction.[8] *Dhalgren* shows close affinities with Deleuzian thought. The novel depicts life in Bellona, a fictive American city that has been struck by some kind of disaster. Within this city, electric power has been all but completely shut down; linear temporality has dissolved, and space has become distorted so that the familiar rules of optics no longer hold. Visitors to Bellona must traverse rough terrain and pass smashed tollbooths.[9] The city's isolation suggests Deleuze and Guattari's concept of "deterritorialization." The novel begins with the protagonist crossing over the border into Bellona, and ends with his departure by the reverse route. This character acquires a strange weapon from a woman who is on her way out of the afflicted city. Called an "orchid," it is a metal implement that opens and shuts like a flower and is strapped onto its bearer's arm by means of a chain and leather harness. Although not actually a part of the wearer's body (the word "orchid" comes from the Greek for testicle), the weapon is not far removed from the prosthetic machines that had already become a staple of science fiction.

Cybernetics fans began to make explicit reference to Deleuze and Guattari as English translations of their work appeared.[10] In 1983, the essay "Rhizome" appeared in the Foreign Agents series published by *Semiotext(e)*. The metaphor of a rhizome, which Deleuze and Guattari opposed to that of a root, represented a mode of thinking that broke with hierarchical structures. What had previously been envisaged as a net is reconceived as a structure that spreads, like crabgrass, in irregular and jagged shapes. At the same time, energy is understood in terms of "flows" that produce dynamic, nonhierarchical forms of connection. In Bruce Sterling's *Islands in the Net* (1988), for example, a multinational cyber-communications corporation bears the name Rizome. Sensory transmission equipment permits the corporation to maintain a disseminated presence throughout the "Net." As long as they wear special videocamera sunglasses, the main characters function as prosthetic sensory organs for the company. In this way, the corporation becomes the equivalent of what Deleuze and Guattari call a "body without organs."[11]

William Gibson's *Neuromancer* (1984), one of the best-known novels involving cyberspace, is probably the most distinctive fictional transposition of the "body without organs."[12] This was the novel that first introduced the term "matrix" in the sense of a vast network sustained by computers. It is an important predecessor to the sequence of films that began with *The Matrix* (1999). In *Neuromancer*, a system called "simstim" (simulated stimulation) enables one person to experience the sensory field of another. But the difference between the material body and the virtual reality to which it is connected causes conflicts that put into question the apparent directness of the connection. By means of simstim, the novel's main character, Henry Dorsett Casc, becomes a kind of futuristic Tiresias, able to know the experiences of the opposite sex.[13] Drawing on Deleuze and Guattari's *Anti-Oedipus*, Gibson creates a world controlled by robotic constructs, in which Oedipal desire is a relic of a rapidly receding past. Human desires are replaced by desires implanted in Case by the vast conglomerate that rules the matrix.

Kathy Acker's *Empire of the Senseless* (1988) draws substantially on Gibson's *Neuromancer*, especially in its development of a technological interface between humans and robots.[14] *Empire of the Senseless* portrays social life as debased by violent incestual relationships that she regards as inherent in patriarchal traditions. Acker claims not to have read French theory until after she had published significant works of her own. In an interview with Sylvère Lotringer, Acker says that "French philosophies . . . gave me a way of verbalizing what I had been doing in language. . . . And then when I read *Anti-Oedipus* and Foucault's work, suddenly I had this new language at my disposal."[15] It is difficult to judge how genuine this claim may be.

Schizophrenic Cultures: Pynchon's *Vineland*

Deleuzian concepts by no means need to be housed in cybernetic fiction. In Pynchon's *Vineland* (1990), for example, the way in which desire in the nuclear family and desire in the larger social body are traced to mechanisms of consumer society is part of the very fabric of the narrative. The conflicting desires instilled in individuals by means of media advertising was a central concept in Deleuze and Guattari's *Anti-Oedipus*; it is gradually becoming a critical commonplace that "Pynchon knows their work well."[16] At the center of Pynchon's complicated plot is a threesome composed of Zoyd Wheeler, Frenesi Gates, and their daughter Prairie. The novel, set in 1984 but with lengthy flashbacks to the 1960s and shorter recollections of previous periods, depicts a fundamental tension between a continuing adherence to the nuclear family and a view in which it no longer remains intact. When Frenesi leaves Zoyd, crossing over from the revolutionary counterculture to the repressive culture of the FBI, she unwittingly reconfigures desire in her daughter, who now longs more than anything to meet and know her mother.

Vineland opens with an extravagant display of apparent insanity. In fact, Zoyd is just acting insane in order to ensure the regular arrival of his government disability checks. His shenanigans manifest an abandonment of fixed structures in order to participate in the unformed chaos of free-flowing desire, in other words, what Deleuze and Guattari term "schizophrenia." According to their theory, the proliferation of conflicting desires created by capitalism not only gives rise to "schizophrenia" and "paranoia," but can also cause "catatonia." This last occurs when individuals experience in acute form the double bind created by the system's simultaneous encouragement and repression of desire. The psychological result is complete withdrawal. In *Vineland*, the "Thanatoids," who spend most of their time mindlessly watching television, represent catatonia in this sense. The Thanatoids, defined as in a state "like death, only different" have all but cut off their connection with the capitalist world.[17] They have learned how to shut down most of their feelings: their main emotional responses are resentment and a desire to take revenge on the system that has precipitated their withdrawal.

In a series of important flashbacks, *Vineland* explores several historic moments marked by conflict between the forces of liberation and the forces of repression. These moments represent precisely the kind of situation that Deleuze and Guattari see as the cause of paranoia. The student unrest and anti-Vietnam protests of the late 1960s receive the most detailed presentation, but the narrative also reaches further back to the McCarthy era of the 1950s and the repression of the union movement in the 1930s. Frenesi Gates' family history provides a genealogy for American society over several generations: born to leftist parents active in the union struggle of the thirties, Frenesi begins her career by capturing the student movement of the sixties in a documentary film. When she turns informant and is placed in the federal witness protection program, both she and her former family (Zoyd and Prairie, who remain linked to the New Left) experience paranoid responses. Even when she seems secure in her reconstructed life, Frenesi is conscious of the "merciless spores of paranoia" that drift through every part of American society (*Vineland*, 239).

Repressive authority is embodied in Brock Vond, whose position of political power is linked with his dominating sexual personality.[18] Brock is more than the rebels' political enemy; he also understands the complex psychological workings of the revolutionary movement: "Brock Vond's genius was to have seen in the activities of the sixties left not threats to order but unacknowledged desires for it," we read, in a particularly Deleuzian passage. He regards the students' actions as the expression of a need to "stay children forever, safe inside some extended national Family" (*Vineland*, 269). This analysis is what makes it possible for him to bring Frenesi over to the government side. Initiated by Brock Vond's political manipulations, Frenesi's paranoia intensifies under the Witness Protection Program, which, though keeping her real identity invisible to her friends and neighbors in her new life, nonetheless subjects her to permanent observation by government authorities. Similarly, her former husband, Zoyd, also remains under observation while "protected" by the fraudulent mental disability scheme that permits him to continue a seemingly free-form life in the alternative culture of Vineland. Outwardly living what Deleuze and Guattari call "schizophrenia," Zoyd is haunted by paranoia as well. Pynchon's psychological portraits of Frenesi and Zoyd bring to life the inner dialectics of capitalist society as presented in *Anti-Oedipus*.

In the novel's elaboration of these issues, we can also detect elements of Horkheimer and Adorno's *Dialectic of Enlightenment*,[19] a theory that underlies Deleuze and Guattari's *Anti-Oedipus*. Not by accident is the younger, leftist Frenesi an experimental filmmaker. Light, the traditional emblem of enlightenment, is the instrument she uses to document the campus unrest of the late 1960s. During her revolutionary period, Frenesi and her crew argue over whether to work with "available light" or artificial illumination. Whereas her

assistant espouses the cheaper method, Frenesi opts for electric light, "drain-
ing off whenever possible the lifeblood of the fascist monster, Central Power
itself" (*Vineland*, 202). In her later life under witness protection, Frenesi mar-
ries Fletcher Desmond, familiarly known as Flash. The film camera, illuminat-
ing and revivifying reality, forms a counterpoint to the deadening television
sets that hold the Thanatoids in thrall. The two machines make energy flow in
different directions, creating intricate and at times contradictory connections
within the "plugged-in" society.[20]

Zoyd is also linked with a machine: the synthesizer he played in a band
during the early years of his marriage. No longer in good repair, the synthesizer seems to have acquired almost animate features: "The critter liked to
drift off pitch on him, or worse, into that shrillness that sours the stomach,
curtails seduction, poisons the careful ambience. Nothing he could find in
the dash-one under the seat ever corrected what he more and more took to
be conscious decisions by the machine" (*Vineland*, 62). Later on, his daughter
Prairie is herself associated with a band: the Vomitones of the Wayvone wedding episode. Music pervades the novel in the form of Pynchon's signature
song lyrics, performed by characters from various different social milieus.
Like other media, music sets up flows of energy through which desires are
created. It is another modality involved in the formation of what Deleuze
and Guattari call "desiring machines."

The interaction of machines with desire also gives shape to another strand
in the novel involving a woman named DL Chastain and her bizarre relationship with a Japanese man named Takeshi Fumimota. Commissioned to
assassinate Brock Vond, DL has disguised herself as Frenesi in order to attract
Brock sexually; but unbeknown to her, Takeshi has taken Brock's place. In a
grotesque parody of the sexual act,[21] a farcical machine called the Puncutron
sets up an electrical current that "recalibrates" Takeshi's brain waves after DL
has accidentally given him the "Ninja Death Touch" during intercourse. This
complicated plot strand is indebted to Deleuze and Guattari's notion of the
"body-without-organs" even as it also makes fun of it.

One of Deleuze and Guattari's most influential ideas, developed in *Anti-
Oedipus* but elaborated in their later writings, is that of "territorialization."[22]
In their usage, the term refers to the process of labor and production and
thus indirectly to the way in which conventional frameworks of thought are
established by the social order. We can think of the capitalist system as taking
over and occupying spaces both literal and metaphorical, turning them as it
were into "territories" over which it holds dominion. By dissolving conven-

tional associations, "territorialization" provokes its opposite, "deterritorialization." This in turn is met by a reaction that immediately tries to reestablish the old parameters, reshaping up identities, redrawing boundaries, and reassigning stable positions to individual elements within the social, economic, and political nexus. Deleuze and Guattari call this "reterritorialization." Even though these movements and countermovements may appear as successive historical phases, they are in fact constantly in tension with one another. Pynchon's novel gives vivid shape to this idea.

Territorialization becomes more clearly a spatial concept, reinforced by the imagery of plateaus, nomads, and rhizomes, in Deleuze and Guattari's volume, *A Thousand Plateaus* (French 1980; Eng. trans. 1987).[23] Here, geographical space becomes increasingly important. The title of *Vineland* alludes to the controversial Vinland map, thought by some to provide evidence of fifteenth-century Viking exploration on the East coast of North America.[24] In the late 1960s and early 1970s, a view of America as an "imperialist" nation was a central belief of those involved in the student revolution. In *Vineland*, Pynchon alludes to this view when he describes the "secession" of the fictional College of the Surf from California to form "a nation of their own, which following a tumultuous nightlong get-together on the subject they decided to name, after the one constant they knew they could count on never to die, The People's Republic of Rock and Roll" (*Vineland*, 209). When Frenesi disappears with Brock Vond to a "National Security Reservation" hidden in a secluded valley that does not appear on any map, her friends try to find her by entering the area in a four-wheel drive 1957 Chevy Nomad (*Vineland*, 250). The choice of vehicle is, of course, a nod to Deleuze and Guattari's concept of "nomadism."

When Zoyd needs to disappear with the infant Prairie, his mother-in-law tells him about Vineland, which she used to visit on summer vacations when Frenesi was a child. She describes it as a vast tract of land that has never been fully surveyed. Zoyd does not go there at first, however. Instead, he and Prairie stay in a commune in the Sacramento Delta that serves as a "sanctuary for folks on the run from court orders, process servers, and skip tracers, not to mention higher and more dangerous levels of enforcement" (*Vineland*, 306). But ironically, this commune is itself lodged in a military installation complex whose airplanes and helicopters cause noise that infiltrates the supposed sanctuary day and night. After some further traveling, Zoyd and Prairie end up settling in Vineland, situated on a bay designated in an 1851 survey map as a "Harbor of Refuge" for ships buffeted by headwinds along the coast. Yet capitalism, in the form of developers and real-estate speculators, soon begins its counter-offense. Long after Zoyd has abandoned his makeshift house, he sees it as something that needs to be "released from its captivity" (*Vineland*, 374). This sequence of events illustrates one of the central ideas in *Anti-Oedipus*: the fact that all movements away from capitalist structures transform themselves into other versions of the same structure; and these, in turn, call for yet another act of dismantling. The alternation between "deterritorialization" and "reterritorialization" finds its narrative equivalent in Zoyd's changing allegiance to alternative and more settled lifestyles.

Boundaries, in *Vineland*, are both literal and metaphorical, fixed and fluid. City limits, unincorporated country, state borders, and gated communities are interspersed with "other states of mind" (*Vineland*, 206), the "realm of the chemical" (158), the place "behind the Thorazine curtain" (260), the worlds of television and film, and various imagined alternative worlds or parallel universes. Pynchon clearly understands that "territories" can take both geographic and imaginary forms and that to occupy a territory means to invest it with specific social meanings.

The conflicting desires and contested territories of *Vineland* put flesh on theoretical bones. The novel enlivens the daunting ideas of Deleuze and Guattari by linking them with outrageous characters and preposterous scenarios. The sheer zest with which Pynchon creates the action of his novel gives the lie to the notion that theory must inevitably be turgid and arcane.

David Foster Wallace's *Infinite Jest*

David Foster Wallace's *Infinite Jest* (1996) also engages with ideas from both *Anti-Oedipus* and *A Thousand Plateaus*. Territoriality in the geographic sense is addressed in the novel's political thread. Set in the early twenty-first century (mainly 2002–2010), *Infinite Jest* constructs a "reconfiguration" of North America in which Canada and Mexico have joined with the United States to create the Organization of North American Nations (ONAN). Far from a simple confederation, however, the redrawing of national boundaries has led to a total secession of Maine to Canada and the placement of a good deal of the rest of New England, demarcated by a line from Syracuse, New York, through Ticonderoga, New York, and on to Salem, Massachusetts, into a kind of no man's land that officially belongs to Canada but is used by the United States as a dumping ground for toxic waste. For obvious reasons, this area is known in the United States as the "Concavity" and in Canada as the "Convexité." Inevitably, the reconfiguration of the North American map leads to complicated relations between the United States and Canada. A group of Quebec terrorists known as the wheelchair assassins (in the Québecois version of their name, "Les Assassins des Fauteuils Rollents" *[sic]* or the AFR—the initials recall the German terrorist group of the 1970s known as the RAF). These terrorists, who have lost their legs in terrifying initiation rites that involve throwing oneself in front of oncoming trains, are working hard to infiltrate the United States and to force its inhabitants into a state of mesmerized torpor. They aim to do this with the aid of a film called *Infinite Jest,* which reputedly has such seductive powers that its viewers watch it over and over again like addicted laboratory rats. By this means, Quebec hopes to gain the ascendency in the ONAN.

Territorialization also plays a role in a key episode of the novel where the students of a tennis academy cum prep school play a game they call Eschaton. This, as its name suggests, has to do with last things: it is a game about nuclear war, conducted on tennis courts temporarily converted into a replica of the *Rand McNally Map of the World*. Divided into teams representing different nations, the students use dead tennis balls as stand-ins for nuclear warheads. On one occasion, snow begins to fall while the children are still playing the game. A discussion breaks out about whether the snow is falling on "the map" or "the territory." Although this distinction derives from Borges's story "Of Exactitude in Science,"[25] the debate that ensues also bears a relation to the debacles that followed from Saussure's theories of referentiality in language. As Mark Currie puts it in his accounts of the linguistic debates, "Stupid arguments broke out in university bars. If you die of exposure in a snowstorm, is it exposure to language?"[26] As the snow comes down during the Eschaton game, the tennis students wrangle over problems of representation: "It's snowing on the goddam *map*, not the *territory*, you dick!" yells Pemulis; "Except is the territory the real world, quote unquote, though!" retorts Axford; "The real world's what the map here *stands* for!" argues Lord; "Real-world snow isn't a factor if it's falling on the fucking *map!* . . . It's only real-world snow if it's already in the *scenario!*" rages Pemulis.[27] The dispute degenerates into fisticuffs. Meanwhile, the narrative continues to confuse the imaginary world of the Eschaton map with the real world of the boarding-school tennis courts: one boy "is throwing up into the Indian Ocean" while another hurries off "across Indochina toward the southern gate" (*Infinite Jest*, 341, 342). When some of the youngsters end up hurt and bleeding, it becomes clear that they have taken too literally the "deterritorialization" involved in the game of Eschaton.[28]

An unnamed narrator tells us that a similar phenomenon occurs during states of anhedonia experienced by some psychiatric patients. Kate Gompert, a former junior tennis player who is living in a halfway house for alcoholics and drug addicts, regards anhedonia as "a hollowing out of stuff that used to have affective content." As a result, she explains, "Everything becomes an outline of the thing. Objects become schemata. The world becomes a map of the world. An anhedonic can navigate, but has no location" (*Infinite Jest*, 693). The younger tennis students attribute this kind of anhedonia to James Incandenza (maker of the film *Infinite Jest*), describing it as the reason for his suicide in, of all things, a microwave oven. His son Hal, the protagonist of the novel, ends up becoming anhedonic himself. Through the figure of Hal, Wallace builds on Deleuze and Guattari's view of catatonia as a direct result of capitalism's simultaneous creation and repression of desire. Hal's psychological withdrawal during his senior year at school expresses his sense of being in a double bind situation: his tennis career is a trap from which he cannot escape but to which he has also been encouraged to have affective connections.

In parallel with Deleuze and Guattari's description of the mutually destructive (but also mutually constitutive) interaction between capitalism and the nuclear family, damaged and damaging family relationships abound in *Infinite Jest*. Many of these have Oedipal aspects. There is the drunken Irishman who abuses his son sexually each night, the father who molests his paraplegic daughter, the radio personality whose face is destroyed by her mother. One angry father even gets his son to help him fix the squeaking parental bed.

Hal also needs to rethink family relationships. The psychological impact of his alcoholic, cinema-obsessed father, who seems not to hear Hal when he speaks, and his overly tolerant and noninterfering mother, who supplies her children with excessive amounts of food, combine with the academy's rigorous training to counteract Hal's belief that his early life was bathed in parental affection. At a therapy session Hal attends, the group's leader uses a teddy bear to encourage participants to return to childhood memories. Manipulating the stuffed animal as children do, "waggling the bear's arms back and forth and making his voice high and cartoon-characterish" (*Infinite* Jest, 805), the therapist tries to get the participants to admit their repressed desire for ʼntal love. Later, "waggling" is precisely the action Hal is accused of in the ʼ where he is interviewed by admissions officers at the University of Arizona. Hal would like to escape from this meeting, too, but he is afraid to do so. Sending his headmaster and tennis coach out of the room, the admissions officers perceive Hal as "flailing," and "waggling" while making unintelligible animal-like noises (*Infinite Jest*, 14).[29] At this point, Hal himself has regressed to an infantile status—indeed, to a preinfantile and not even totally human condition. This scene, the last in the chronology of the novel's plot, is placed at the beginning of the novel, but it only becomes intelligible when we have finished the book.

Hal's regression is in part the result of his possible ingestion of an "incredibly potent" drug called DMZ (*Infinite Jest*, 170).[30] Unlike the many other drugs mentioned in *Infinite Jest*, DMZ is never identified as the product of a specific pharmaceutical company. We know only that Hal's friend Michael Pemulis has acquired the drug from some Canadians, that it is synthesized from an obscure mold or fungus, and that it is "apparently classed as a paramethoxylated amphetamine" (*Infinite Jest*, 170). Pemulis has heard terrifying stories about the effect of the drug which, when administered experimentally to U.S. soldiers, may have caused some of them to lose their minds. The reader recognizes the abbreviation DMZ as an acronym for the demilitarized zone, where drug use was rampant in the Vietnam and Korean wars. But the term DMZ is also used to refer to a "place" on a computer server that lies outside a firewall and can be used as an indiscriminate dumping ground—just like the "Concavity" in the reconfigured America of this novel. The fictive drug is thus connected with places that are "off the map." People who take DMZ are reported, in one of the novel's many endnotes, as having altered temporal perception: one compares himself to a "Futurist sculpture, plowing at high knottage through time itself, kinetic even in stasis, plowing temporally ahead, with time coming off him like water in sprays and wakes" (*Infinite Jest*, 996n57). This may be one reason for the "missing year" between Hal's admission to an emergency room in November 2009 and his interview at the University of Arizona in November of 2010.[31] Further, if Hal's name is an allusion to the intelligent computer HAL in Stanley Kubrick's *2001: A Space Odyssey* (1968), Hal Incandenza's catatonic state would be a parallel to HAL's shutdown at the end of the film. Like Kubrick's HAL, Wallace's Hal suffers from a kind of emptying-out of the brain.[32]

The DMZ theme goes beyond these relatively obvious connections, however. The novel's voluminous endnotes draw explicit attention to the fact-fiction matrix; but they do not reveal everything we need to know. In this instance, there is in fact a drug known as DMZ: dimetrizadole. In the United

Kingdom, it is an antibiotic formerly used in chicken production; it has been suspected of being a carcinogen and a cause of birth defects.[33] In *Infinite Jest*, the "Concavity" is known for monstrous feral infants, severely deformed, who roam the toxic area (*Infinite Jest*, 1056). Hal's brother Mario is himself deformed, and the tennis academy is about to admit a blind player, born in the Concavity, who has a huge soft head without a skull and "several eyes in various stages of evolutionary development" (*Infinite Jest*, 518). The young tennis players themselves are described in a film made by Mario and narrated by Hal as "feral prodigies" (*Infinite Jest*, 172).

In addition to the theme of toxicity, a chicken motif also runs throughout the book and is evidently connected with the toxic antibiotic DMZ. One of the years of "subsidized time" is the Year of the Perdue Wonderchicken; in a chase scene, signs for "Fresh Chicken" and "Complete Destruction" flash by the runners (*Infinite Jest*, 720); and during Hal's panic attack, when he lies down in his room and is unable to get up, he imagines the total amount of "lightly breaded chicken fillets" he would eat in the course of a lifetime (*Infinite Jest*, 897). In fact, he begins to see himself as "the meat in the room's sandwich" (*Infinite Jest*, 902). This vision of himself as chicken meat[34] is only an extension of another aspect of the tennis academy, in which the young players are asked to give up their individuality "before the age when the questions *why* and *to what* grow real beaks and claws" (*Infinite Jest*, 900). The students' life at boarding school resembles in many ways the caged existence of factory-raised chickens, which are in fact debeaked and declawed. Among other things, this may be one reason why James Incandenza, the academy's first director, makes so many films called *Cage*. To use Deleuze and Guattari's terminology, the tennis academy itself is a place that deterritorializes its students and staff.

Infinite Jest not only engages with Deleuze and Guattari's concept of territoriality, it also takes up their ideas about the man-machine interface. Mario Incandenza, born prematurely, has withered arms and strangely square feet, and his spine is incapable of holding him upright. To support Mario, his father constructs a large metal pole attached at the top to a vest and at the bottom to a heavy lead block. Strapped in this apparatus, Mario helps his father with sets and lighting for his films. For his thirteenth birthday, he receives a large "Bolex" camera bolted to an old leather aviator's helmet. The camera is adapted so that Mario can operate it by an attached sewing-
hine treadle. In this outfit, Mario acquires considerable filmmaking abil-
id eventually makes documentaries for the academy. But in many ways,

he looks more like a machine than a human being. Similarly, the blind student, with his soft skull and deformed eyes, can only function by means of a rolling IV stand attached to a metal circle that supports his enormous head. When playing tennis—which he does with sonic balls—the boy has the use of only one hand because he has to roll the metal stand around with him at all times. The sinister Wheelchair Assassins from Quebec are virtually one with their machines. Even characters without physical disabilities have been turned into one or another kind of machine. Hal, for example, has been so thoroughly trained that the tennis racket is virtually an extension of his arm (*Infinite Jest*, 689). He sees himself as "robotic" and emotionally empty inside (694). Nonetheless, during the admissions interview in Arizona, he insists that he is "not a machine" (12). To formulate his predicament in Deleuzian terms, Hal has suffered a kind of psychological deterritorialization.

Infinite Jest not only embodies Deleuzian theories, it points up the sheer horror of the social distortions these theories analyze. In spite of its many comic moments and bizarre episodes, it does not share *Vineland's* zany exuberance. While *Vineland* give us repeated glimpses into the exhilaration that can accompany the free flow of desire, *Infinite Jest* leaves us with its darker side. Neither novel, however, presents a positive picture of society in the wake of *Anti-Oedipus*. Nor do they present a viable resolution of the tensions that beset this society.

Mapping the Territory: Pynchon's *Mason & Dixon*

In *Mason & Dixon* (1997), Pynchon extends these ideas about the relation between geographic space and cultural mindsets. The world of the novel, set in the period around 1750, is undergoing a mapping process that delineates space in new ways. In addition to the visible marks on the earth's surface— rivers, mountain ranges, and other geographic features—a network of invisible lines creates new understandings of territory. On Mason and Dixon's voyage to Africa in order to observe the transit of Venus, the crossing of the equator is celebrated on board ship by the usual sailors' pranks: the "Ritual of Crossing Over," complete with an appearance by King Neptune, gives definition to a boundary that is, in fact, a mere "Geometers' Abstraction."[35] Similarly, the line that Mason and Dixon are charged to draw between Pennsylvania and Maryland is an artificial demarcation unrelated to the geographic features of the terrain it traverses: it needs to be marked by cutting down trees along its entire extent. The Indian tribes, concerned about the possibility that this line will cross a traditional war path that is invisible to white surveyors, send a delegation to protect the sacred trail. Boundaries and crossings are not limited to space alone, however: they are also connected with time as it is conceived in this novel. A major focus of bewilderment is the year of the shift from the Julian to the Gregorian calendar, 1752, when eleven days appear to have disappeared without trace. Using terminology reminiscent of Deleuze and Guattari, the narrative describes the time of the calendar change as "that Schizochronic year of '52" (*Mason*, 192).

In America around 1750, the encounter of modern science with other kinds of knowledge questions conceptual boundaries that had previously been taken as fixed. Astronomical discoveries and the development of specialized machines are contrasted with superstition, magic, and fantasy among the white population and the non-Western belief systems of the American Indians. In addition to serious machines such as the equipment used for laying down the latitudinal line, the surveyors encounter numerous curiosities and automata typical of the period: Vaucanson's mechanical duck is one of these.[36] Distinctions between the human and the machine are put to the test by such robots, as well as by other fantastic phenomena such as the talking dog.

Toward the end of the novel, the two surveyors argue about whether the distinction between Pennsylvania and Maryland is naturally given or artificially imposed. When Mason claims that the two provinces "are as alike as Stacy and Tracy," Dixon retorts that slavery exists on one side of the line but not on the other (*Mason*, 615). Similarity and difference are thus part of the dialectic that underpins the concept of territorial division. A place called "the Delaware Triangle," known to surveyors as the "Wedge," complicates the understanding of space. As its name suggests, this territory shares the same properties as those said to obtain in the Bermuda Triangle: it is an area where people and things mysteriously disappear and where familiar categories of thought are strangely set aside. Like the "Concavity/ Convexité" in Wallace's *Infinite Jest*, the "Wedge" is a place whose boundary lines are in dispute, giving rise to proliferating lawsuits. A fraudulent local surveyor known as R.C. infuriates his colleagues by relying on guesswork rather than instrumental measurements: he claims that the Wedge is not accessible to scientific mapping.

A central metaphor in *Mason & Dixon* is that of movement across terrain. Broadly speaking, the narrative presents two different ways of traveling

across the land: those of the Indian tribes and those of the American settlers. We might also see this fundamental dichotomy as a conflict between
goal-oriented travel and what Deleuze and Guattari term "nomadology."
The slow and exacting process of defining the latitudinal line that will divide
Pennsylvania from Maryland finds its counterpoint in divagations of various
kinds: literal, imaginary, and narrative. Cherrycoke, the narrator, is described
as a "nomadic Parson" (*Mason*, 9). The surveyor Mason, whose name leads
some people to think he is a member of the freemasons, is greeted with the
Masonic password, "are you...*a traveling Man?*" (287). In a parody of the
eighteenth century's interest in "mobility," the mechanical duck takes to pursuing a French chef (449). The surveyors' work, while dependent on the
apparatus of science, also prevents science from becoming reified by keeping
open unlimited possibilities.

Deleuze and Guattari understand the self as ideally "nomadic" and constantly changing, rather than "sedimented," or bound by traditional modes
of classification. A "nomadic" vision of the world is one that is liberated from
conventional categories and in a constant state of change.[37] One historical
fact that contributes to the "nomadic" structure of *Mason & Dixon* is the shift
from the Julian to the Gregorian calendar that results in an apparent "loss"
of eleven days. The two ways of conceiving time are two different ways of
mapping the same temporal "territory," but paradoxically, the two maps cannot be superimposed on one another. The lost eleven days create a disjunc-
ture between the two that cannot be erased or even adequately explained. In
his dreams, Mason finds himself wandering aimlessly through the "Loop" of
lost days in the labyrinthine city of London (*Mason*, 556–561). Yet more than
ordinary people, Mason understands the reasons behind the calendar reform.
Astronomical observations and measurements have necessitated the new calendar, which will bring the religious, social, and economic year into harmony
with the actual duration of earth's rotation around the sun. Astronomy also
provides the points of reference with respect to which Mason and Dixon
establish the latitude they have been ordered to use as the boundary between
the two states. The "transit of Venus," which the two have observed on an
official trip to South Africa, is a trajectory that holds the key to solving an even
more difficult problem: that of mapping longitudes. Through this emphasis
on astronomical science, Pynchon expands the concept of territory beyond
the earth itself. Mason and Dixon perform a simultaneous mapping of earthly
and celestial territory. Unlike the rotation of the earth, of which we are only
intellectually aware, celestial space appears to be in constant motion: the plan-

ets themselves are like "nomadic" bodies wandering through the sky. Observing celestial space is not unlike observing the human imagination, always mobile and constantly making new connections. Structurally and conceptually, *Mason & Dixon* challenges the reader to retain this intellectual mobility.

Nomadic Narrative: W. G. Sebald's *The Rings of Saturn* and *Austerlitz*

Located in a literary filiation outside that of Pynchon or Wallace, W. G. Sebald also engages with Deleuze and Guattari's theories of "territorialization" and the "nomadic." He was familiar with the latter from their book *Kafka: Toward a Minor Literature* (French 1975, English 1986).[38] It is not clear to what extent Sebald knew other publications by the two theorists; the Kafka book is the only one of their works included among volumes from his private library currently housed at the German Literary Archive in Marbach.[39] He read and marked the Kafka book intensively. Careful study of his annotations reveals not only how closely he read the book, but also how many of Deleuze and Guattari's later concepts are already contained in *Kafka: Toward a Minor Literature*. The notion of the "nomadic," for example, subsequently developed at length in *A Thousand Plateaus*, is already present in the Kafka book. Sebald's book *Vertigo* (first published in 1990 under the German title *Schwindel. Gefühle.*) includes two texts that revolve around Kafka; it could well be described as a "nomadic" work.[40]

The Rings of Saturn (1995) is the best example of Sebald's engagement with Deleuze and Guattari. The book, with its German subtitle "eine englische Wallfahrt" (an English—or angelic—pilgrimage),[41] recounts a walking tour in Suffolk made by the narrator in an attempt to dispel a mental slump following completion of a substantial piece of work. It is not a novel, but a strange mixture of travel narrative, personal and historical reflections, and accounts of books, newspaper articles, and related items. Walking in Suffolk rather than in Norfolk, where Sebald himself lived, is one part of the "deterritorialization" the book enacts; the narrator's hospital stay one year after the walking tour is another deterritorialization that significantly inflects his mood as he writes up his travel notes. When the narrator enters the maze on the grand estate of Somerleyton, yet another form of "deterritorialization" comes into play. Similarly, his foray into the area from which British planes took off to engage in the carpet bombing of German cities during World War

II, a place only recently made accessible to the public, also involves a kind of deterritorialization. The book includes descriptions of numerous such locations that are profoundly disturbing—and dislocating—to the narrator. Territory in the larger sense is at issue in much of the information Sebald gathers, notably the accounts of the imperial and colonial endeavors exemplified by Joseph Conrad and Roger Casement, on both of whom *The Rings of Saturn* reflects at length. Kafka's presence is apparent at several junctures, notably when the narrator observes a small boat seemingly becalmed on the ocean like the ghostly bark in Kafka's "Hunter Gracchus."

With his introduction of the term "extraterritorial" in *The Rings of Saturn*, Sebald adds an additional dimension to Deleuze and Guattari's description of Kafka's geographic and cultural location in Prague, where German speakers were in the minority. "Extraterritorial" means "situated outside the limits of a jurisdiction."[42] Concentration camps, represented in *The Rings of Saturn* by the double-spread photograph of dead bodies at Bergen-Belsen, are places where those in charge disregard ordinary jurisdiction and those imprisoned cannot be reached through legal intervention. Theresienstadt, which plays an important role in Sebald's later book *Austerlitz*, exemplifies this problem in an especially vivid way through the film made about it by the Nazi authorities in preparation for the Red Cross inspection of the hastily cleaned and beautified "Jewish ghetto" in 1942.

The route the narrator takes on his walking tour through county Suffolk and the trajectory of his thoughts, readings, and investigations in the course of the journey might be said to be rhizomatic. The narrator comments, for example, on the erratic systems of footpaths in England, the complicated networks created by radar, and the way in which interwoven tree roots contributed to the spread of Dutch elm disease. The very structure of the book challenges familiar ways of ordering thought, and any attempt to trace it approximates the jagged lines of the foot journey that subtends the book's reflective content.[43] Like Deleuze and Guattari's concept of the rhizome, the irregular and seemingly wayward arrangement of ideas in *The Rings of Saturn* has the effect of undoing logical hierarchies. A scholarly monograph organized in this way would almost certainly meet with rejection. By enacting the rhizomatic movement of thought promulgated by Deleuze and Guattari, Sebald's narrator also forces us to question whether or not the crab-like creep of its mental trajectory succeeds in escaping the oppressive logic exerted by modern forms of power.

In a 1999 radio interview, Sebald used the word "nomadic" in a way that seems to echo Deleuze and Guattari.[44] Photographs, he claimed, lead a "nomadic existence" as they wander from personal collections to junk stores, often turning up unexpectedly between the pages of old books. He had already included numerous photographs in *Vertigo* and *The Rings of Saturn*, and unbeknown to his interviewer, he was engaged in a project that would deploy photographic material in an even more extravagant and provocative way. *Austerlitz* (2001) was to interrogate more intensively than his previous work the status of photography as documentation, evidence, and testimony. Sebald liked to prowl for old photographs in antiquarian shops and reuse them in his own writings. The origin of many of these images remains unknown, but they come to be imbued with new associations, suppositions, or fantasies as they are positioned into the complex networks of Sebald's own texts. In this way, the photos travel from one context to another, much like his nomadic protagonists and narrators. Anonymous images acquire the same status as identified or identifiable ones, forming part of multiple questions about personal identity, family and social relationships, and linguistic, cultural, and national affiliations. Any attempt to map, as it were, the arrangement of these different types of photographical material in the texts in which they are embedded would doubtless produce an irregular diagram akin to Deleuze and Guattari's rhizome.

In *Austerlitz*, Sebald continues his engagement with Deleuze and Guattari in other ways as well. Two locations depicted in that narrative illustrate complex histories of de- and reterritorialization. One of these is Fort Breendonk, in Belgium, constructed as a fortification, later used by the Nazis as a concentration camp, and more recently turned into a museum and memorial. The other is the terrain behind the Austerlitz railroad station in Paris, used during the Nazi occupation as a collection point for confiscated Jewish belongings destined to be sent to Germany. The protagonist reports that a librarian has told him that the new Mitterrand National Library stands on the same place where these items were collected. (In actual fact, the collection point was located not beneath the new library complex, but a few blocks to one side of it.[45]) In *Austerlitz*, these places used for different purposes at different times are brought into conjunction with journeys that traverse wider geographical spaces, such as Austerlitz's travels within Europe and between Europe and England. In addition to the networks created by these real and imagined connections, the unnamed narrator seems to think quite specifically of Kafka when he terms Fort Breendonk a "penal colony." A sense of marginality in his relation to the culture around him and with respect to the long history of Europe pervades much of Sebald's writing: in effect, his work is almost paradigmatic of what Deleuze and Guattari term "minor literature." In no way does the term involve a value judgment. Rather, "minor literature" is "impregnated with a profound sense of its marginalized position," by virtue of which it "forces individual experience to resonate with larger political concerns."[46] The protagonist of *Austerlitz* spends his adult life attempting to reconstruct his family history and consolidate his psychological identity. When he discovers his real name, Austerlitz, toward the end of his high school years, its first resonances for him are with the famous battle his history teacher has recounted so often in class. What does it mean when a personal name is also the designation of a historical event that occurred in a specific place? Later, he encounters the train station of that name in Paris, still a place of departure for many long-distance trains, but historically the station from which French Jews were deported to concentration camps in Eastern Europe. As he tries to find out about himself, Austerlitz travels restlessly in irregular patterns, passing through territories that are simultaneously parts of today's world and sites of crimes under the National Socialist regime. Much of what he finds out, or thinks he has found out, emerges through accident or contingency: his journey of discovery takes a rhizomatic shape.

By placing the ideas of Deleuze and Guattari into a post-Holocaust context, as Sebald does in *Austerlitz*, he brings out an important aspect of their thinking, namely their wish to understand what had happened during the Third Reich. Their choice of Kafka's narratives as exemplary texts is not random: as a lawyer, bureaucrat, and avid reader of colonial history, Kafka was well placed to diagnose social conditions that can be understood in hindsight as precursors of Hitler's Germany. Two aspects of Kafka's presentation of this precursor history were important to Deleuze and Guattari: first, how the manipulation of desire led to the extermination of entire ethnic groups, and second, the ways in which territory was configured within those manipulated desires.[47] The nomadic trajectories of Austerlitz and the unnamed narrator who mediates his story mirror their attempts to unravel the mystery at the heart of National Socialism by placing it into larger historical contexts of oppression. Locations and buildings in *Austerlitz* such as the many forts and fort-like structures that are described in words, rendered by diagrams, or represented through photographs, form self-contained spaces that in many instances have been sites of oppression. The narrators' irregular movements between territorialization and deterritorialization give the book its unsettling character.

In *Austerlitz* we find a photograph of a tree the protagonist notices on a walk through a park in Prague with the woman he believes is his former nanny. Or rather, the photograph is placed in the text in such a way as to suggest that it is a picture of the tree in Prague. The photograph focuses on the tree's tangled roots, rambling over the surface of the ground. Austerlitz associates these tree roots with the mosaic pattern in the tiled entry hall of his former house, and by extension with the complicated sets of networks that reflect both his personal travels and the interlocking power structures that he observes in the places he visits and reads about. The photographed tree roots, extending above ground far out from the trunk, look less like roots and more like Deleuze and Guattari's erratically spreading rhizome. In a world where it has become fashionable to seek one's roots, the rambling above-ground roots do not suggest the kind of firm anchoring that we normally attribute to the family tree. In *The Rings of Saturn*, another snapshot shows Sebald leaning against the enormous trunk of an ancient tree. The narrator tells us, however, that only a few years after the photograph was taken, the tree was completely uprooted in the terrible storm that blew through southeast England and on into France.

The more closely we read Sebald's work, the more we feel impelled to question the effectiveness of his narrators' rambling journeys. Does the narrator of *The Rings of Saturn* really discover the truth about Roger Casement? Does Austerlitz truly find his former home, or is he simply misled by an overwhelming desire to put to rest his uncertainty about his family origins? To what extent are the multiple journeys through real and imagined space in Sebald's literary works actually what Deleuze and Guattari call "lines of flight"?

The novels of Pynchon, Wallace, and Sebald not only adopt positions close to Deleuze and Guattari, they also question whether their characters' "lines of flight" are viable responses to the psychological tensions in modern society. In *Vineland*, Zoyd takes flight from bourgeois society yet is still beset by paranoia. In *Infinite Jest*, Hal's attempt to break out of the constraints of his tennis career lands him in a state of catatonia that makes real escape impossible. The protagonist of *Austerlitz* declares at the end of his lengthy narrative that he will continue searching for traces of his personal history, but nothing suggests that this search can be satisfactorily concluded. In the final analysis, none of these novels supports the optimism that accompanies the French theorists' notion of rhizomatic existence.

Conclusion

Talking Back to Theory

My major argument in this book has been that some of the most significant and subtle negotiations with theory have taken place in novels. Indeed, to some extent the dialogue between novelists and theorists accompanied the unfolding of theory, in the sense of French poststructuralist theory, starting as early as Marguerite Duras's first narrative response to Lacan in her 1966 novel *The Vice Consul*. Theorists like Eco and Kristeva came to novel writing after they were well established as thinkers, yet it was not as if this form put an end to their more academic work: rather, their novel writing accompanies and amplifies their development of theory. Kristeva insists: "I still feel as if I'm doing the same as before."[1] It was even rumored that before his untimely death, Roland Barthes was intending to write a novel—or was it to be a poem?[2]

The "theory wars" of the 1980s impacted many of the writers who were not themselves theorists. Against a backdrop of passionate and sometimes acrimonious debate, they took an unusual tack. Not unlike the postcolonial novelists who "wrote back" to empire, writers touched by the disputes over theory used the novel to challenge current theoretical ideas. But they did so in a sophisticated way, often allowing a small number of suggestions to conjure up an entire system of thought. Unlike the "novels of ideas" written by Thomas Mann, Aldous Huxley, and Robert Musil in the 1920s and '30s, the "novel after theory" does not, in the main, subordinate traditional novelistic elements to the presentation of ideas. Nor does it depict characters engaged in detailed discussions about ideas or include essayistic passages that trace the arguments of discursive philosophy.[3] Its method is one of allusion rather than exposition. It functions by means of a two-track strategy that allows those familiar with theory to recognize its presence yet largely refrains from spoiling the pleasures of reading. It ranges from playfulness and parody to the highest caliber of moral reflection.

In the sense in which I use the term here, the "novel after theory" also differs from earlier postmodern fictions like those of Vladimir Nabokov. Although the life of the mind is also at issue in his novels, he does not systematically assign philosophical questions to specific characters in the manner of Thomas Mann in *The Magic Mountain*. Nabokov's characters do have ideas, of course, but they usually profess them in ways at once serious and extravagant. Whether the deeper topic be love, identity, or death, the presentation is perennially on the cusp of parody, if not already transformed into parody. Flamboyantly self-reflexive, Nabokov's texts reflect not on poststructuralism but on narrative itself. He experiments with narrative strategies drawn from close knowledge of how novels work. He explores problems of biography and autobiography, reliable and unreliable narration; he tests the boundaries of parody, forgery, and translation. He shows how playfulness can be combined with more serious reflection. In short, Nabokov's works show an unusually fine understanding of narrative techniques and their functions. Yet this is very different from the French poststructuralist theory that is taken up by the novels we have looked at here.

Nonetheless, the modernist novel of ideas and the postmodern metafictional novel represent stages in a significant breaking down of generic boundaries. The French avant-garde journal *Tel Quel* (1960–82) participated in this project when it explored the relation of literature to social and political thought.[4] Julia Kristeva described it as a place for "writing-thinking."[5] Most of the French poststructuralists published in *Tel Quel* consolidated the force of this new, more capacious understanding of textuality that no longer distinguished sharply between text as fiction and text as cultural discourse. The historic shift from influence studies to studies of intertextuality is part of this movement. Conceptions of textual relations as a genealogy of like texts give way to a broader conception of what is eligible to be called a text and how such diversified texts relate to one another. From this perspective, the response of literary to theoretical texts is a subcategory of intertextuality.

Thinking in terms of intertextuality permits us to be less fixated on whether a novelist is actually informed about a specific theory or whether theory enters the novel by means of more amorphous cultural discourses that cannot be spelled out with the same clarity as a set of ideas developed by a single thinker. Where evidence exists that a novelist had read theory, I have of course included this information. Although I trace the similarities between novels and the theories to which they relate, my main aim has been to identify moments where the novels challenge theory. The differences between the abstract quality of theory and the concrete detail of fictional narratives reveal weaknesses and sometimes even blind spots in theory. Marguerite Duras's exposure of gender problems in Lacanian theory is a good example. Perhaps the most striking instance where novels advance a critique of theory can be seen in the fiction of Sebald and Coetzee, which explores at close range an extension of Foucault's ideas to which the theorist himself had only gestured: the relevance of the history of carceral systems to twentieth-century regimes like those of National Socialism or apartheid. Through the juxtaposition of theory and fiction we can see more precisely the specific contribution literary texts make to our understanding of the psychological, social, and political conditions of contemporary life.

Our novelists engage with a wide range of French theory. It is perhaps not surprising that Barthes's counterintuitive concept of the "death of the author" sparked the largest number of narrative responses. Looking back at the many novels treated under this heading, I would like to single out Margaret Atwood's ingenious *Blind Assassin* and John Banville's hallucinatory *Shroud*. Concepts of simulation drawn from or in the mode of Baudrillard were also explored by many novelists, largely because of their resonance with modern society. We have seen, for example, how Don DeLillo's ironic *White Noise* not only exposes the soullessness of media-saturated life, but also evokes sympathetically its protagonist's vain search for some sort of epiphany. Foucault's historically informed and detailed study of institutional systems of constraint inspired major authors ranging from Umberto Eco to J. M. Coetzee and W. G. Sebald. Perhaps most astonishing were the fictional engagements with the difficult thought of Deleuze and Guattari. The close attention novelists like Thomas Pynchon and David Foster Wallace paid to the complex theories of *Anti-Oedipus* is quite remarkable.

Looking back at the "novel after theory," we can trace several phases in its chronology. In the early period, poststructuralist theory was an arcane science, known only to adepts who attended Lacan's seminars, listened to the public lectures of Derrida, Foucault, and Barthes, or read the French journal *Tel Quel*. As we have seen, Duras was one of a very few novelists writing back to theory in the 1960s and 1970s. Once the poststructuralist thinkers began to receive increasing public attention, however, a new phase began. In the 1980s, as their work entered course syllabi at colleges and universities outside France and the debates over theory exploded beyond the borders of academia, novelists picked up the discussion. In the 1990s and at the turn into the twenty-first century, a more somber mood settled on some of these novelists, who became less concerned with maintaining a light touch and more troubled by the implications of theory for contemporary life. Major writers like J. M. Coetzee and W. G. Sebald began to see how theories of control and power might play out in narratives with complex characters, elaborate social networks, and sophisticated concepts of time and space. Novels like Coetzee's *Waiting for the Barbarians* (1980), Ransmayr's *The Dog King* (1995), Wallace's *Infinite Jest* (1996), and Sebald's *Austerlitz* (2001) wrestle with questions of political and social responsibility and do not hesitate to do so in complex and intellectually challenging textual forms. In a rethinking of her earlier ideas on "women's time," Kristeva moves beyond her more transparent early novels in her dense and history-laden *Murder in Byzantium* (2004), adapting their setting to a more threatening global environment.

The main wave of "novels after theory" may now be over. If so, it is an opportune moment to reflect on what these novels have accomplished. As Kristeva pointed out in an interview, "things are often more complex than our understanding of them."[6] The novel is an excellent vehicle for reflecting that complexity. At the peak of the theory debates and the broader cultural discussions in which they were embedded, factions were often starkly drawn; yet the novelists kept their sense of humor, took things with a grain of salt, and never lost sight of the subtleties at work in human situations. They neither became mindless acolytes of "master thinkers" nor did they resort to bromides about the importance of narrative and imagination. As the "novel after theory" became more intense and challenging, it still retained flashes of wit and flights of inspiration. Throughout the entire span of the narrative engagement with theory, novels emerged that are richly satisfying in all the ways we expect a novel to be. While fulfilling their contract as novels, these works also add detail, nuance, and energy to the scaffolding of theory. In contrast to the teachers and students who used theory as an interpretive paradigm or grid through which to understand literary texts, these novels wrestle with the issues posed by theory and in doing so, reveal its fault-lines and limitations. Had we attended to this dialogue more closely, the debates about theory might have been less reductive and possibly also less raucous.

The Novel After Theory redresses the balance by highlighting the contribution of narrative fiction during the theory decades. Not surprisingly, only a subset of the novels produced in those years engaged with theory, but the spectrum covered by this group was remarkably broad. Leaving aside some of those aimed at a highly theory-conscious readership or the cybernetic fiction that appealed to a niche audience, most of these novels offered pleasure and enrichment to readers of different kinds. It was not necessary to be an academic specialist to profit from the best of the "novels after theory."

Authors like Margaret Atwood, J. M. Coetzee, Marguerite Duras, Graham Swift, Thomas Pynchon, W. G. Sebald, and Christa Wolf are widely acknowledged as important writers of our day. Marilynne Robinson has established an undisputed reputation based on her three remarkable novels. To this list, I would add Christoph Ransmayr—although he is not as well known outside Germany as he should be—and, in terms of quality, David Foster Wallace, even though his work is mainly familiar to a group of devotees. Even when they infuse their texts with humor, as is often the case, all of these writers respond to serious questions about how we conceive our position in society today. Readers often like to think in universal terms, as if human beings had remained the same throughout history. But we also know that there are differences at work, too. We need to be able to take the measure of what separates Sebald's *Austerlitz* from Camus' *The Stranger*, Swift's *Waterland* from Dickens's *Our Mutual Friend*, or Wallace's Hal from Shakespeare's *Hamlet*. My thesis is that poststructuralist theory is an intrinsic part of what constitutes the distinguishing feature of a particular set of late twentieth-century novels. The specialized and often pretentious terminology of French theory does not need to trip easily off our tongues, but the ways in which those theorists understand human relations are more than a mere wrinkle in the fabric of our time. While the "novel after theory" is not identical with postmodern novels altogether, it does articulate some of the stresses at work in the postmodern age.

The brief history of theory that I have traced here lays the foundation for a set of second-generation theories that are more widely represented in recent fiction: Orientalism, postcolonialism, gender theory, cultural theory, globalization. Elements of French poststructuralism underlie many of these theories: to name just a few examples, Edward Said's *Orientalism* builds on ideas first developed by Foucault; Gayatri Chakravorty Spivak translated Derrida before going on to explore the predicaments of subaltern people, particularly non-Western women; Homi Bhabha inflects Lacanian theory in new ways in his discussions of postcolonialism; and Judith Butler's theories of gender and oppression take their starting-point in a critical dialogue with French poststructuralist thinkers. While these theories retain the kind of specialized vocabulary characteristic of the earlier poststructuralists, they are more explicitly linked with history and more obviously related to familiar social contexts. The relation of novels to the second generation of theory takes less the form of dialogue than of intertwining coexistence.

To locate at least a partial stimulus for some recent novels in their involvement with poststructuralist theory may help us understand our unease about aspects of recent texts more generally, such as the slipperiness of identity, temporality, history, and social relations. In an essay of 1980, Umberto Eco refers to a widespread notion that "reason can no longer explain the world in which we live and we now have to rely on other instruments."[7] The problem with this view, he goes on to say with his usual élan, is that it does not specify the instruments we would need, "leaving the reader free to imagine: feeling, delirium, poetry, mystical silence, a sardine can opener, the high jump, sex, intravenous injections of sympathetic ink."[8] Each of these might be appropriate, but in each case, the opposition between reason and its antidote would be a different one and "would imply a different definition of reason."[9] The puzzle, but also the charm, of the "novel after theory" is its fundamental acceptance of this unsettling state of affairs. From the thoughtful jesting of Eco's *Foucault's Pendulum* to the ironic seriousness of Sebald's *Austerlitz*, these late twentieth-century novels can best be understood when we take into account the poststructuralist impulse that sets these fictions in motion and to which they respond with questions and challenges.

Notes

Introduction

1. I adopt here Peter Brooks's happy formulation in the title of his important study *Reading for the Plot: Design and Intention in Narratives* (New York: Random House, 1984).

2. Nor does this book look back at Russian Formalism, Structuralism, or the theories of Northrop Frye, among others.

3. David Lodge, *Small World: An Academic Romance* (New York: Warner Books, 1984).

4. Malcolm Bradbury, *Doctor Criminale* (Harmondsworth: Penguin, 1992).

5. On the campus novel, see Elaine Showalter, *Faculty Towers: The Academic Novel and Its Discontents* (Oxford: Oxford University Press, 2005).

6. Gregory S. Jay and David L. Miller, eds., *After Strange Texts: The Role of Theory in Literary Study* (Tuscaloosa: University of Alabama Press, 1985).

7. In his chapter on "theoretical fiction," Mark Currie focuses primarily on books by critics turned novelists and novelists who are in some sense also critics (*Postmodern Narrative Theory* [Houndmills: Palgrave, 1998], 51–70).

8. Patrick Süskind, *Das Parfum: Die Geschichte eines Mörders* (Zurich: Diogenes, 1985); in English, *Perfume: The Story of a Murderer,* trans. John E. Woods (New York: Knopf, 1986). In the early 1980s, the concept of "postmodernism" was articulated in Charles Jencks, *The Language of Post-Modern Architecture* (New York: Rizzoli, 1977), Jean-François Lyotard, *The Postmodern Condition: A Report on Knowledge*, trans. Geoffrey Bennington and Brian Massumi (Minneapolis: University of Minnesota Press, 1984; original French 1979), and Ihab Hassan, *The Dismemberment of Orpheus: Toward a Postmodern Literature* (New York: Oxford University Press, 1971; 2nd ed. 1982, including "Postface 1982: Toward a Concept of Postmodernism"). *Perfume* is remarkably close to Hassan's description of postmodernism in his 1982 postface to *The Dismemberment of Orpheus*.

9. This book also differs from Slavoj Žižek's *Looking Awry: An Introduction to Jacques Lacan through Popular Culture* (Cambridge, MA: MIT Press, 1991), which adduces a number of films and popular novels in order to illustrate and explain Lacanian theory.

10. A. S. Byatt, *The Biographer's Tale* (New York: Knopf, 2000), 305.

11. A. S. Byatt's *On Histories and Stories* was first published in England (London: Chatto and Windus, 2000). The American version was published by Harvard University Press some five months later with a 2001 publication date; I cite the Harvard version.

12. Byatt, *Histories and Stories*, 6.

13. Kathy Acker, "Devoured by Myths: An Interview with Sylvère Lotringer," in *Hannibal Lecter, My Father* (New York: Semiotext(e), 1991), 10.

14. Daniel Punday, *Narrative After Deconstruction* (Albany: State University of New York Press, 2003), 4.

15. The talk bore the title "Structure, Sign, and Play in the Human Sciences." Reprinted in *The Languages of Criticism and the Science of Man*, ed. Richard Macksey and Eugenio Donato (Baltimore: Johns Hopkins University Press, 1970), 247–272.

16. Mark Tansey, "Derrida Queries de Man" (1990), oil on canvas. Collection of Mike and Penny Winton. For Derrida's own reading of this painting, see Sylvère Lotringer and Sande Cohen, eds., *French Theory in America* (New York: Routledge, 2001), 13–15.

17. Camille Paglia, *Sex, Art, and American Culture* (New York: Vintage, 1992), 211.

18. Paglia takes issue with "today's prevailing academic style, which sneers and condescends, rends and tramples, all in the name of chic politics and cockamamie theory." *Sex, Art and American Culture*, 84.

19. Herman Rapaport, *The Theory Mess: Deconstruction in Eclipse* (New York: Columbia University Press, 2001), 13.

20. Terry Eagleton's *Literary Theory: An Introduction* (Oxford: Oxford University Press, 1983), while showing a preference for Marxist theory, nonetheless gives a fair hearing to other sets of ideas. The best example of "theory as approach" is represented by the series Case Studies in Contemporary Criticism (Boston: Bedford Books).

21. One series is produced by Totem Books (Icon Books, U.K.). Another series is published by Writers and Readers Publishing.

22. See, for example, David Damrosch, Natalie Melas, and Mbongiseni Buthelezi, eds., *The Princeton Sourcebook in Comparative Literature: From the European Enlightenment to the Global Present* (Princeton: Princeton University Press, 2009).

23. Emily Eakin, "The Latest Theory Is That Theory Doesn't Matter," *New York Times*, April 19, 2003.

24. Paul de Man wrote of "some satiation or disappointment" that had set in "after the initial enthusiasm" ("The Resistance to Theory," *Yale French Studies* 63 [1982]: 5). Stanley Fish declared that "theory's day is dying; the hour is late; and the only thing left for a theorist to do is to say so, which is what I have been doing here, and, I think, not a moment too soon" ("Consequences," originally in *Critical Inquiry*, 11, no. 3 [March 1985]: 433–458; reprinted in W. J. T. Mitchell, ed., *Against Theory: Literary Studies and the New Pragmatism* [Chicago: University of Chicago Press, 1985], 128.)

25. John M. Ellis, *Against Deconstruction* (Princeton: Princeton University Press, 1989), vii. See also Mitchell, *Against Theory*, which includes Steven Knapp and Walter Benn Michaels' essay "Against Theory" in *Critical Inquiry* (1982) and responses to it by several other authors in *Critical Inquiry* (1982, 1983, and 1985).

26. Barbara Johnson, *The Wake of Deconstruction* (Oxford: Blackwell Publishers, 1994), 17.

27. Judith Butler et al., eds., *What's Left of Theory? New Work on the Politics of Literary Theory* (London: Routledge, 2000) and Elle Leane and Ian Buchanan, "What's Left of Theory?" in *Continuum: Journal of Media & Cultural Studies* 16 (2002): 253–258.

28. Jean-Michel Rabaté, *The Future of Theory* (Oxford: Blackwell, 2002), concludes by calling for theory to return to philosophy (151); Valentine Cunningham, *Reading After Theory* (Oxford: Blackwell, 2002), urges that theory should be replaced by close reading and tact.

29. Terry Eagleton, *After Theory* (New York: Basic Books, 2003), 1 and 222.

30. Michael Payne and John Schad's *Life. After. Theory* (London: Continuum, 2003) presents a series of interviews with famous theorists asking them to think about the question, "what are we after?" Two books look at different aspects of the "narrative turn": Daniel Punday, *Narrative After Deconstruction* (Albany, NY: State University of New York Press, 2003); and Colin Davis, *After Poststructuralism: Reading, Stories and Theory* (London: Routledge, 2004).

31. David Bordwell and Noël Carroll, eds., *Post-Theory: Reconstructing Film Studies* (Madison: University of Wisconsin Press, 1996). It should be noted that, since I am not a specialist in film, I have refrained from entering this very rich field.

32. Martin McQuillan, Graeme MacDonald, Robin Purves, and Stephen Thomson, eds., *Post-Theory: New Directions in Criticism* (Edinburgh: Edinburgh University Press, 1999).

33. Ernesto Laclau, preface to McQuillan et al., *Post-Theory: New Directions in Criticism*, vii.

34. See Kwame Anthony Appiah's famous essay, "The Postcolonial and the Postmodern" (1992), reprinted in Bill Ashcroft, Gareth Griffiths, and Helen Tiffin, eds., *The Post-Colonial Studies Reader* (London: Routledge, 1995), 119–124. See also Simon During, "Postmodernism or Post-Colonialism Today," originally in *Textual Practice* 1, no. 1 (1987); reprinted in *Post-Colonial Studies Reader*, 125–129.

35. Eventually, a combined volume in the series presented Baudrillard's "Forget Foucault" together with Foucault's riposte, "Forget Baudrillard." See Sylvère Lotringer, "Doing Theory," in *French Theory in America,* ed. Sylvère Lotringer and Sande Cohen (London: Routledge, 2001), 146.

36. Lotringer cites evidence that Baudrillard was familiar to the art world by the mid-1980s (Lotringer, "Doing Theory," 148).

37. Sande Cohen, "Critical Inquiry, October, and Historicizing French Theory," in *French Theory in America*, esp. 200.

38. Cohen, "Critical Inquiry," 200–201.

39. Ibid., 204–206.

40. F. R. Leavis, *The Great Tradition: George Eliot, Henry James, Joseph Conrad* (London: Chatto and Windus, 1955), 111.

41. Peter Barry, *Beginning Theory: An Introduction to Literary and Cultural Theory* (Manchester: Manchester University Press, 1995), 49.

42. See Cunningham, *Reading After Theory*, esp. 140–164.

43. One of the few German titles to use the term is quite recent: Oliver Simons, *Literaturtheorien zur Einführung* (Hamburg: Junius, 2009).

44. See, for example, Jürgen Fohrmann and Harro Müller, eds., *Diskurstheorien und Literaturwissenschaft* (Frankfurt a.M.: Suhrkamp, 1988).

45. For details of the American development, see Lotringer and Cohen, *French Theory in America*, esp. 128–129 and 200–204.

46. Dorothee Kimmich, Rolf Günter Renner, and Bernd Stiegler, eds., *Texte zur Literaturtheorie der Gegenwart* (Reclam: Stuttgart, 1996; rev. 2003).

47. For example, Terry Eagleton's *Einführung in die Literaturtheorie* (Stuttgart: Metzler, 1997) and Jonathan Culler's *Literaturtheorie. Eine kurze Einführung* (Ditzingen: Reclam, 2002).

48. Most recently, Jochen Hörisch, *Theorie-Apotheke: Eine Handreichung zu den humanwissenschaftlichhen Theorien der letzten fünfzig Jahre, einschließlich ihrer Risiken und Nebenwirkungen* (Frankfurt a.M.: Eichborn, 2005, reprinted Frankfurt a.M.: Suhrkamp, 2010).

49. Hans Ulrich Gumbrecht notes that once theory had been finally accepted in Germany, it was treated with excessive seriousness (in Fohrmann and Müller, *Diskurstheorien*), 96–113.

50. Kimmich et al., *Texte zur Literaturtheorie*, 11. François Cusset, *French Theory: Foucault, Derrida, Deleuze & Cie et les mutations de la vie intellectuelle aux Etats-Unis* (Paris: Découverte, 2003).

51. Gérard Genette, "Sketching an Intellectual Itinerary," in Lotringer and Cohen, *French Theory in America*, 71–86.

52. Cusset, *French Theory*.

53. Lotringer and Cohen, "Introduction," *French Theory in America*, 1. Nonetheless, the American view of these thinkers is not entirely unjustified. The new bodies of ideas shared several components: their authors saw themselves as conducting thought experiments, they emphasized the workings of language, and they focused on difference rather than unity and uncertainty rather than certainty (Lotringer, *French Theory in America*, 4–9).

54. Antoine Compagnon, *Le Démon de la théorie: Littérature et sens commun* (Paris: Editions du Seuil, 1998), 10.

55. On the political scene from which French poststructuralist theory emerged, see Peter C. Herman, ed., *Historicizing Theory* (Albany: State University of New York, 2004). He also discusses other kinds of theory, for example New Historicism, Postcolonialism, and Cultural Studies.

56. See Paul de Man, *The Resistance to Theory*, foreword by Wlad Godzich (Minneapolis: University of Minnesota Press, 1986).

57. The long-lived nature of *Theory of Literature* owed much to its cutting-edge position when it first appeared. In the introduction to the first edition, the authors note their position with regard both to German and Russian literary theory of the time, stating that they were "not eclectic like the Germans nor doctrinaire like the Russians." René Wellek and Austin Warren, *The Theory of Literature*, 3rd ed. (New York: Harcourt, Brace and World, 1956), 7.

58. I cite Knapp and Michaels from the reprint of their essay in Mitchell, *Against Theory*, 2.

59. Subsequently collected in Mitchell, *Against Theory*.

60. John Ellis, *Against Deconstruction* (Princeton: Princeton University Press, 1989), 154n1.

61. Ellis, *Against Deconstruction*, 157.

62. Daphne Patai and Will H. Corral, eds., *Theory's Empire: An Anthology of Dissent* (New York: Columbia University Press, 2005). A volume of responses to this anthology also appeared: John Holbo, ed., *Framing Theory's Empire* (West Lafayette, IN: Parlor Press, 2007).

63. In the fourth competition (1998), for example, a sentence by Judith Butler received first place and one by Homi Bhabha came in second. Jonathan Culler comments that although the prize was awarded by a journal concerned with philosophy and literature and edited by the analytical philosopher Denis Dutton, the prize was

never awarded to analytical philosophers "but always to someone involved with Marxist, feminist, or postcolonial theory." *The Literary in Theory* (Stanford: Stanford University Press, 2007), 205.

64. Hans Ulrich Gumbrecht, "Die neue Wörtlichkeit: Leise verabschiedet sich die ehrgeizige Literaturtheorie," *Frankfurter Allgemeine Zeitung*, February 16, 2005.

65. See, for example, Ian Hunter's "The History of Theory," *Critical Inquiry* 33 (2006): 78–112, and W. J. T. Mitchell's "Dead Again," his introduction to the special issue in memory of Jacques Derrida, *Critical Inquiry* 33 (2007): 219–228.

66. *Journal of Literary Theory* 1, no. 1 (2007): 1.

67. *PMLA* [*Publications of the Modern Language Association of America*] 125, no. 4 (October 2010).

68. Robert Klein, "The Future of Literary Criticism," *PMLA* 125, no. 4 (October 2010): 920–923.

69. The allusion is to the final sentence of Breton's *Nadja*, "La beauté sera CON-VULSIVE ou ne sera pas" (Paris: Folio, 1964), 190 ("beauty will be convulsive or it will not be").

70. Breton, *Nadja*, 921.

71. Jonathan Culler, "Introduction: Critical Paradigms," *PMLA* 125, no. 4 (October 2010): 907. This formulation is a variant of his definition of "theory" in *Literary Theory: A Very Short Introduction* (Oxford: Oxford University Press, 1997), 3. In his book *The Literary in Theory* (Stanford: Stanford University Press, 1997), he spells out his ideas on theory at greater length (see esp. 38).

1. The Death of the Author

1. Marcel Proust, *Contre Sainte-Beuve*, ed. Pierre Clarac in collaboration with Yves Sandre (Paris: Gallimard, 1972), 221–222.

2. See Roland Barthes, "To Write: An Intransitive Verb?" in *The Rustle of Language* (Berkeley: University of California Press, 1989), 11–21.

3. Roland Barthes, "The Death of the Author," in *The Rustle of Language*, 49.

4. Ibid., 49.

5. Ibid., 55.

6. John Ellis argues for an opposing position in his essay "Is Theory to Blame?" in *Theory's Empire: An Anthology of Dissent*, ed. Daphne Patai and Will H. Corral (New York: Columbia University Press, 2005), 92–109. There Ellis states that "the imported idea of the 'death of the author' was crude compared to the results of the debate that had already taken place in America on the intentional fallacy" (94). In *Against Deconstruction*, he claimed that Derrida's thought showed "lack of originality" (39). John Ellis, *Against Deconstruction* (Princeton: Princeton University Press, 1989).

7. W. K. Wimsatt Jr. and Monroe C. Beardsley, "The Intentional Fallacy," in *The Verbal Icon: Studies in the Meaning of Poetry* (Lexington: University of Kentucky Press, 1954), 3–18.

8. "The Intentional Fallacy," 4. Italics in the original.

9. Ibid., 10.

10. Ibid., 14.

11. Wayne C. Booth, *The Rhetoric of Fiction* (Chicago: University of Chicago Press, 1961), 67–77.

12. Booth, *Rhetoric of Fiction*, 155; for his entire discussion of this topic, see 155–159.

13. For a discussion of some paradoxes in Barthesian theory and practice, see J. C. Carlier (translated by C. T. Watts) "Roland Barthes's Resurrection of the Author and Redemption of Biography," *Cambridge Quarterly* 29 (2000): 386–392. Cedric Watts confirmed my hunch when he stated in an electronic message of August 2005 that he "translated J. C. Carlier from the nineteenth century to the present."

14. Alain Robbe-Grillet, *Ghosts in the Mirror*, trans. Jo Levy (London: John Calder, 1988), 13.

15. Roland Barthes, *Writing Degree Zero*, trans. Annette Lavers and Colin Smith, with preface by Susan Sontag (New York: Hill and Wang, 1977), 77.

16. Albert Camus, *The Stranger*, trans. Matthew Ward (New York: Everyman's Library, 1993), 3.

17. He was also uneasy about what he sensed might be Barthes's self-interest in the latter's admiration of the "blank style." At a conference on Barthes at Cérisy in June 1977, Robbe-Grillet expressed his suspicion that Barthes's flattering reviews had been, in essence, a way of laying the groundwork for Barthes's own ambitions as a novelist. See Jean-Michel Rabaté, *The Ghosts of Modernity* (Gainesville: University Press of Florida, 1996), 71.

18. I employ Philippe Lejeune's term, advanced in *Le pacte autobiographique* (Paris: Le Seuil, 1975).

19. In this connection—and in connection with Marguerite Duras's *The Lover*, which I also discuss in this chapter—see Jacques Derrida, "The Law of Genre," *Critical Inquiry* 7 (1980): 632–670. See also Raylene L. Ramsay, *The French New Autobiographies: Sarraute, Duras, and Robbe-Grillet* (Gainesville: University Press of Florida, 1996) for an insightful treatment of this genre. See also Julia Waters, *Intersexual Rivalry: A "Reading in Pairs" of Marguerite Duras and Alain Robbe-Grillet* (Bern: Peter Lang, 2000).

20. It is not clear just how Barthes sees the relation between the impersonal style and the impersonal scriptor. The two concepts belong to different periods—the first to the 1950s and the second to the late 1960s.

21. Ultimately, this narrative goes back to Phlégon de Tralles's *La Fiancée de Corynthe*, a tale retold by several other writers, notably Goethe and Michelet. On the

intertextual connections at work in the motif of Corinthe, see Ramsay, *French New Autobiographies*, 85.

22. Some French readers saw the name Henri de Corinthe as an anagram of *rien de cohérent* (nothing logical). See Ramsey, *New French Autobiographies*, 86.

23. For a recent discussion of Stendhal's legacy in literature from the nineteenth century to the present, see Morris Dickstein, *A Mirror in the Roadway: Literature and the Real World* (Princeton: Princeton University Press, 2005).

24. Both authors also engage Barthes's ideas on photography; see Barthes, *La chambre claire: Note sur la photographie* (Paris: Cahiers du cinema, 1980); in English *Camera Lucida: Reflections on Photography* (New York: Hill and Wang, 1981). For an insightful comparison of the two novels from this perspective, see Waters, *Intersexual Rivalry*, 123–155.

25. In fact, Duras had never fully accepted Barthes's theories, even in 1958 when her novel *Moderato Cantabile* was awarded the Prix de Mai by a jury that included Barthes himself and that regarded Duras as another variant of the new novelist exemplified by Robbe-Grillet: see Laure Adler, *Marguerite Duras* (Paris: Gallimard, 1998), 325.

26. Barthes, "The Death of the Author," 50.

27. See Adler, *Marguerite Duras*, 514 and photographs 23 and 24. See also Yann Andréa, *Cet amour-là* (Paris: Editions Pauvert, 1999), where he describes how he took down the first page of *L'Amant* at dictation while sitting with Marguerite Duras at a large table in Neauphle (60).

28. Betty Fernandez-Van Bowens was arrested, shorn, and paraded in the street after the liberation of France from the Nazis (Adler, *Marguerite Duras*, 232). Adler tells of a version of *L'Amant* that was to be called *L'Amant: histoire de Betty Fernandez* and was to begin with the war, the story of Marie-Claude Carpenter's salon in the winter of 1942, and the couple Ramon and Betty Fernandez (Adler, *Marguerite Duras*, 517). For more about the collaborator Ramon Fernandez, see his son's biography of him: Dominique Fernandez, *Ramon* (Paris: Grasset, 2008).

29. Laurens is a pseudonym: her real name is Laurence Ruel-Mézières.

30. There is a discrepancy between the British and American titles of the book, though both use Ian Monk's translation of the text. The British version stays closer to the French original: *In Those Arms* (London: Bloomsbury, 2003); the American version makes a change and even adds a subtitle: *In His Arms: A Novel* (New York: Random House, 2004). By defining the genre, the Random House edition reduces the ambiguity of the original.

31. Barthes, "The Death of the Author," 54.

32. This problem is addressed more explicitly in *In His Arms*, where the pseudo-autobiographical narrator Camille has a sister with an equally gender-ambiguous name, Claude.

33. I have left *c'est moi* in the original in order to highlight the allusion to Flaubert's famous remark about Madame Bovary.

34. Roland Barthes, *The Pleasure of the Text*, trans. Richard Miller (New York: Hill and Wang, 1975).

35. Barthes, *Pleasure*, 6.

36. Barthes, "The Death of the Author," 50.

37. Ibid., 53.

38. Ibid., 49.

39. Ibid., 54.

40. Margaret Atwood, *The Blind Assassin* (New York: Random House, 2000), 250. Although the feminist Iris rejects this motif, it bears tantalizing similarities to Margaret Atwood's confessed fascination with an early science fiction film called *Love Slaves of the Amazon* in which "the love slaves were male, and the Amazonians were female, clad in fetching potato sacks dyed green and bent on depriving the poor love slaves of every ounce of bodily fluid they contained." Atwood, *"The Handmaid's Tale* and *Oryx and Crake* in Context," *PMLA* 119 (2004): 514.

41. Helen Darville, *The Hand That Signed the Paper* (St. Leonards, NSW, Australia: Allen and Unwin, 1994).

42. Barthes, "The Death of the Author," 52.

43. Dylan Thomas, "The Hand That Signed the Paper," in *The Poems of Dylan Thomas*, ed. Daniel Jones (New York: New Directions, 1971), 66.

44. The manuscript version of *The Hand That Signed the Paper* used Demidenko as the name of both author and narrator.

45. An earlier version of these ideas can be found in Judith Ryan, "After the 'Death of the Author': The Helen Demidenko Affair," in *Cultures of Forgery: Making Nations, Making Selves*, ed. Judith Ryan and Alfred Thomas (London: Routledge, 2003), 169–185.

46. Michael Krüger, *Himmelfarb* (Salzburg: Residenz, 1993); in English, Michael Krüger, *Himmelfarb*, trans. Leslie Willson (New York: George Braziller, 1994).

47. Barthes, *Rustle of Language*, 50.

48. I like to imagine that the missing word might be *Verzeihung* (Sorry).

49. Paul de Man's essay on Barthes, written in 1972 but not published until after his death, does not specifically engage with Barthes's notion of the "death of the author." See de Man, "Roland Barthes and the Limits of Structuralism," *Yale French Studies* 77 (1990): 177–190.

50. A note at the end of the novel acknowledges its debt to Louis Althusser's *The Future Lasts a Long Time*, ed. Olivier Corpet and Yann Mouiler Boutang, trans. Richard Veasey (London: Chatto and Windus, 1993), from which *Shroud* adapts one passage and picks up several themes.

51. Lene Yding Pedersen, "Revealing/Re-Veiling the Past: John Banville's *Shroud*," *Nordic Irish Studies* 4 (2005): 141.

52. Samuel Taylor Coleridge, *Biographia Literaria*, ed. Nigel Leask (London: Everyman, 1997), 175.

53. Banville's novel is cited according to the following edition: *Shroud* (New York: Alfred A. Knopf, 2003).

54. See Rabaté, *Future of Theory*, 43.

55. Roland Barthes, "Textual analysis: Poe's 'Valdemar,'" in *The Semiotic Challenge*, trans. Richard Howard (Berkeley: University of California Press, 1994), 274.

56. Barthes, "Poe's Valdemar," 274.

57. Ibid., 293.

58. Paul de Man, *The Rhetoric of Romanticism* (New York: Columbia University Press, 1984), 78.

59. The concept of "defiguration" occurs in the title of a book by de Man's most distinguished student, Barbara Johnson, *Défigurations du langage poétique: La seconde révolution baudelairienne* (Paris: Flammarion, 1979). In Banville's *Shroud*, two of Vander's essays are titled "Effacement and Real Presence" (100) and "Shelley Defaced" (184).

60. America, Vander says, is a place where "no ideology would require my commitment" (*Shroud*, 183).

61. Paul de Man did raise moral objections to Rousseau, who exalted the state of childhood while claiming to have placed all his children in orphanages. Banville's novel alludes to this through Cass's unfinished thesis, which takes up the issue of Rousseau's offspring (*Shroud*, 204).

62. Coetzee is one of today's most theoretically informed writers. In subsequent chapters, I will look at two other novels of his, *The Age of Iron* and *Waiting for the Barbarians*.

2. Structure, Sign, and Play

1. Jacques Derrida, "Structure, Sign, and Play in the Discourse of the Human Sciences," in *Writing and Difference*, trans. Alan Bass (Chicago: University of Chicago Press, 1978), 278–293.

2. Lee Morrissey, "'Nostalgeria' and 'Structure, Sign, and Play in the Discourse of the Human Sciences,'" in *Historicizing Theory*, ed. Peter C. Herman (Albany: State University of New York Press, 2004), 99–111.

3. Derrida, "Structure, Sign, and Play," 278.

4. Ibid., 279.

5. Morrissey, "'Nostalgeria,'" 102.

6. For a detailed account of Derrida's relation to the Algerian War that delineates his intellectual trajectory and his gradual willingness to speak more openly about this matter, see Edward Baring, "Liberalism and the Algerian War: The Case of Jacques Derrida," *Critical Inquiry* 36 (Winter 2010): 239–261.

7. Derrida, "Interview with Jean-Luc Nancy," *Topoi* 7 (1988): 113–121; this quotation, 20.

8. See Derrida, *Of Grammatology*, trans. Gayatri Chakravorty Spivak (Baltimore: Johns Hopkins University Press, 1974), 65.

9. One should not forget another important mediator of Derrida, Gayatri Spivak, whose translation of *De la grammatologie* (Paris: Les Editions de Minuit, 1967), *Of Grammatology*, first made Derrida's foundational book accessible to English-speaking readers (see note 8).

10. Morrissey, "'Nostalgeria,'" 100.

11. See Barbara Johnson's books *A World of Difference* (Baltimore: Johns Hopkins University Press, 1987) and *The Feminist Difference: Literature, Psychoanalysis, Race, and Gender* (Cambridge, MA: Harvard University Press, 1998), where she uses Derrida's terms to explore questions of race and gender in literary texts.

12. Barbara Johnson, "The Surprise of Otherness: A Note on the Wartime Writings of Paul de Man," in *Literary Theory Today*, ed. Peter Collier and Helga Geyer-Ryan (Ithaca: Cornell University Press, 1990), 21.

13. Derrida, "Structure, Sign, and Play," 282.

14. Ibid., 289.

15. Ibid., 291.

16. Ibid., 292.

17. Ibid., 293.

18. See Mary Louise Pratt, *Colonial Eyes: Travel Writing and Transculturation* (London: Routledge, 1992), 169 and passim.

19. For a detailed account of the decolonization of Algeria, see Todd Shepard, *The Invention of Decolonization: The Algerian War and the Remaking of France* (Ithaca: Cornell University Press, 2006; 2nd ed. 2008). On Indochina, see Eric Jennings, *Vichy in the Tropics: Pétain's National Revolution in Madagascar, Guadeloupe, and Indochina, 1940–44* (Stanford: Stanford University Press, 2001).

20. Derrida, "Structure, Sign, and Play," 279.

21. Jacques Derrida, *Monolingualism of the Other; or, The Prosthesis of Origin* (Stanford: Stanford University Press, 1998). The original French was: *Le monolinguisme de l'autre, où La prothèse d'origine* (Paris: Editions Galilée, 1996).

22. The motif of the "photo not taken" is doubtless a nod to Roland Barthes, who opens the second part of his *Camera Lucida* with a discussion of his search for a photograph of his mother that captured his idea of her. See *Camera Lucida: Reflections on Photography*, trans. Richard Howard (New York: Hill and Wang, 1981), 63–72.

23. Derrida, "Structure, Sign, and Play," 289.

24. The incest taboo is one of the things Derrida comments on in his discussion of Lévi-Strauss (see "Structure, Sign, and Play," 283–284).

25. This motif clearly alludes to Lacan's statement that "the woman does not exist." For more on Lacanian thought in *The Lover*, see chapter 3.

26. This is yet another allusion—here to Barthes's "death of the author."

27. Derrida, "Structure, Sign, and Play," 280.

28. Ibid., 282.

29. Ibid., 292.

30. Marilynne Robinson, *Housekeeping* (New York: Farrar, Straus and Giroux, 1980; Noonday paperback, 1997). Page numbers in parentheses refer to the Noonday edition.

31. Marilynne Robinson, *The Death of Adam: Essays on Modern Thought* (Boston: Houghton Mifflin, 1998), 12, 76, and 77 respectively.

32. Robinson, *The Death of Adam*, 9.

33. Ibid., 7. Robinson's own university studies at Brown and the University of Washington, Seattle, took place in the mid-sixties to the late seventies, before the theory boom of the 1980s. A year's teaching in France and later positions at Amherst College and the University of Massachusetts at Amherst may well have brought her into contact with poststructuralism, but there is little evidence of specific engagement with theory during that period. Following the publication of *Housekeeping*, Robinson received several positions as writer-in-residence and teacher of creative writing at various universities and colleges, eventually becoming a faculty member in the Writers' Workshop at the University of Iowa.

34. Regan Good, "An Interview with Marilynne Robinson," *Tin House*, no. 16 (2003): 20–29, here 24.

35. See, for example, Joan Kirkby, "Is There Life After Art? The Metaphysics of Marilynne Robinson's *Housekeeping*," *Tulsa Studies in Women's Literature* 5, no. 1 (1986): 91–109, and Martha Ravits, "Extending the American Range: Marilynne Robinson's *Housekeeping*," *American Literature: A Journal of Literary History, Criticism and Bibliography* 61, no. 4 (1989): 644–666. In an interview with Thomas Schaub, Robinson refers several times to Thoreau and Emerson, highlighting their approach to metaphor and commenting on the way in which Emersonian method also involves awareness of the inadequacy of method. See Thomas Schaub, "An Interview with Marilynne Robinson," *Contemporary Literature* 35, no. 2 (1994): 231–251, esp. 240.

36. Tace Hedrick, "'The Perimeters of Our Wandering Are Nowhere': Breaching the Domestic in *Housekeeping*," *Critique: Studies in Contemporary Fiction* 40, no. 2 (1999): 137–151.

37. Ibid., 138, 139, and 141 respectively.

38. Ibid., 138.

39. Ralph Waldo Emerson, "Circles," in *Selected Writings*, intro. Charles Johnson (New York: Signet, 2003), 320.

40. Emerson, "Illusions," in *Selected Writings*, 442.

41. Emerson, "Circles," in *Selected Writings*, 324.

42. See, for example, David Leverenz, "The Politics of Emerson's Man-making Words," *PMLA* 10, no. 1 (Jan. 1986): 38–56. Leverenz suggests that Emerson's "Experience" may be "a deconstructive masterpiece" (52). For an earlier discussion of proto-Derridean elements in Emerson, see David M. Wyatt, "Spelling Time: The Reader in Emerson's 'Circles,'" *American Literature* 48 (1976): 140–151. Wyatt focuses on "Circles" as, among other things, a "'central' event in Emerson's career," akin to the rupture or decentering moment so important for Derrida (150). A broad account of revisionist criticism of Emerson over the past fifty years can be found in J. Trevor McNeely, "Beyond Deconstruction: America, Style and the Romantic Synthesis in Emerson," *Canadian Review of American Studies/Revue Canadienne d'Etudes Américaines* 22, no. 1 (1991): 61–82. Leonard N. Neufeldt and Christopher Barr argue for a crucial difference between Emerson and Derrida in their article "'I Shall Write Like a Latin Father': Emerson's 'Circles,'" *The New England Quarterly* 59, no. 1 (March 1986): 92–108. They observe that "present-day deconstructionists would part company with Emerson, for the principal goal of their agenda is to expose and loosen our deeply rooted habit of invoking or discretely smuggling into our analytic . . . versions of a transcendental signifier" (93). As for Emerson's apparent proto-deconstructionism, Neufeldt and Barr insist that it is tested and found wanting in "Circles" itself (108). Eduardo Cadava uses Derridean terminology when he claims that the "situation of undecidability" is the moment when the ethical moment emerges in Emerson; see *Emerson and the Climates of History* (Stanford: Stanford University Press, 1997), 69.

43. Lawrence Buell, *Emerson* (Cambridge, MA: Belknap Press of Harvard University, 2004), 224–225.

44. Ibid., 224. As Buell observes here, Stanley Cavell sees Emerson as an anticipation of Nietzsche: "Cavell is one of Emerson's most Emersonian readers, himself an artist in the medium of sinuously self-reflexive prose that, like Emerson's, models active thinking" (ibid.). Cavell's two essays on Emerson, "Thinking of Emerson" and "An Emerson Mood," appended to his *The Senses of Walden: An Expanded Edition* (Chicago: University of Chicago Press, 1981), 121–160, pose the question of Emerson's heritage as a philosopher. In his article, "Aversive Thinking: Emersonian Representations in Heidegger and Nietzsche" (*New Literary History* 22, no. 1 [Winter 1991]: 129–160), Cavell shows how Emerson can be understood as a precursor of Heidegger and Nietzsche.

45. Cited in Ravits, "Extending the American Range," 651n13.

46. Robinson uses this term to explain to Regan Good how she began writing *Housekeeping*. Good reports that while Robinson was writing her dissertation, she longed to revive the nineteenth-century use of extended metaphor. From time to time, she would write a passage in this form and put it away for later. Eventually, she

realized that these passages cohered and were, in essence, the germ of *Housekeeping*. She wrote a great deal of the novel while in France. See Good, "Interview with Marilynne Robinson," 20.

47. Emerson, "Circles," in *Selected Writings*, 320.

48. Ibid., 323.

49. For a nuanced discussion of transience in *Housekeeping*, see Jacqui Smyth, "Sheltered Vagrancy in Marilynne Robinson's *Housekeeping*," *Critique: Studies in Contemporary Fiction* 40 (1999): 281–291. Smyth shows that Robinson avoids any simple opposition between home and homelessness, patriarchal or matriarchal structures. In particular, she points out that both the transient life and the life of civil order are deconstructed. She notes as well that Lucille's period of vagrancy, when she plays hooky from school along with Ruth, is too often overlooked by critics.

50. Hedrick compares Ruth's idea about the floating house with Emerson's claim in "Montaigne; or the Skeptic" that "we are . . . houses founded on the sea" (Hedrick, "Perimeters," 1).

51. Emerson, "Nature," in *Selected Writings*, 181.

52. For the latter, see Hedrick, "Perimeters," 3.

53. In this connection, see Sinead McDermott's rereading of *Housekeeping* in "Future-Perfect: Gender, Nostalgia, and the Not Yet Presented in Marilynne Robinson's *Housekeeping*," *Journal of Gender Studies* 13 (2004): 259–270. Adopting a key term from Svetlana Boym's *The Future of Nostalgia* (New York: Basic Books, 2001), McDermott characterizes *Housekeeping* as a narrative of "reflective nostalgia." Nostalgia functions in the novel, she argues, as a revolutionary gesture that constructs the future by looking toward what might have been.

54. On this, see Amy S. Gottfried, *Historical Nightmares and Imaginative Violence in American Women's Writings* (Westport, CT: Greenwood Press, 1998). Chapter 5, "Beneath a Layer of White: Violence and Nature in Marilynne Robinson's *Housekeeping*," uses the image of the white paint with which the girls' grandfather covered pictures he had previously painted on his furniture as a metaphor for the "submerged" violence beneath "Ruth's imperturbable narrative" (89).

55. See the Kristevan readings by Thomas Foster, "History, Critical Theory, and Women's Social Practices: 'Women's Time' and *Housekeeping*," in *Contemporary American Women Writers: Gender, Class, Ethnicity*, ed. Lois Parkinson Zamora et al. (London: Longman, 1998), 67–86; and Kristin King, "Resurfacings of the Deeps: Semiotic Balance in Marilynne Robinson's *Housekeeping*," *Studies in the Novel* 28 (1996): 565–580. Rosaria Champagne, "Women's History and *Housekeeping*: Memory, Representation, and Reinscription," *Women's Studies: An Interdisciplinary* Journal, vol. 20 (1992): 321–329, places *Housekeeping* in the broad context of postmodernism without referring to specific feminist theorists.

56. Graham Swift, *Waterland* (New York: Random House, 1983), 8–9.

57. Hayden White, *Metahistory: The Historical Imagination in Nineteenth-Century Europe* (Baltimore: Johns Hopkins University Press, 1973).

58. Linda Hutcheon, *A Poetics of Postmodernism: History, Theory, Fiction* (London: Routledge, 1988).

59. The second epigraph is a quotation from Dickens's *Great Expectations*, "Ours was the marsh country..."

60. Derrida, "Structure, Sign, and Play," 279.

61. In his 1824 history of the Latin and Teutonic peoples, Ranke had defined the task of history as an attempt to establish the past "wie es eigentlich gewesen" (as it actually had been). See Leopold von Ranke, *Geschichten der romanischen und germanischen Völker, 1494–1514* (Leipzig: Duncker & Humblot, 1885), vii.

62. *The Compact Edition of the Oxford English Dictionary: Complete Text Reproduced Micrographically*, vol. 1, *A–O* (Oxford: Oxford University Press, 1971), 675. For clarity, I have abbreviated the entry by omitting the historical examples.

63. Derrida, "Structure, Sign, and Play," 280–281.

64. White, *Metahistory*, 29 and 70.

65. In *A Poetics of Postmodernism*, Linda Hutcheon comments on the novel's attempts to negotiate postmodern contradictions (xi), its belief that social meaning is historically constituted (15), and its narrator's lack of confidence in his ability to know the past with any certainty (117). In these ways, *Waterland* is a paradigmatic model of what Linda Hutcheon terms "historiographic metafiction." In her later book, *The Politics of Postmodernism* (London: Routledge, 1989), Hutcheon gives a more sustained discussion of *Waterland* (54–56) in which she reads Tom Crick as "in many ways an allegorical representation of the postmodern historian who may well have read" series of theorists including Hayden White (56).

66. In his later book, *The Content of the Form: Narrative Discourse and Historical Representation* (Baltimore: Johns Hopkins University Press, 1987), White includes a sophisticated chapter on Foucault's discourse and the question of Foucault's position on the Structuralist-Poststructuralist spectrum (104–141).

67. I adapt this phrase from the title of Rachel Blau DuPlessis' *Writing Beyond the Ending: Narrative Strategies of Twentieth-Century Women Writers* (Bloomington: Indiana University Press, 1985).

68. Frank Kermode, *The Sense of an Ending: Studies in the Theory of Fiction* (Oxford: Oxford University Press, 1966), 39. Kermode's chapter, "The Modern Apocalypse" (93–124) is a significant intertext for Swift's *Waterland*.

69. In this respect, Dick is modeled on Joachim Mahlke in Günter Grass's novella *Katz und Maus* (Neuwied: Luchterhand, 1961; Cat and Mouse).

70. See Luc Nancy, "'This Strange Institution Called Literature': An Interview with Jacques Derrida," trans. Geoffrey Benningston and Rachel Bowlby, in *Acts of Literature*, ed. Derek Attridge (New York: Routledge, 1922), 34.

3. *The Mirror Stage*

1. Shoshana Felman, *Jacques Lacan and the Adventure of Insight* (Cambridge, MA: Harvard University Press, 1987), 4.

2. Malcolm Bradbury, *Doctor Criminale* (Harmondsworth: Penguin, 1992), 241. The passage alludes to Baudrillard's "Forget Foucault"; see Sylvère Lotringer and Sande Cohen, eds., *French Theory in America* (New York: Routledge, 2001), 152.

3. David Lodge, *Nice Work* (Harmondsworth: Penguin, 1989), 177–178. See Elaine Showalter's reading in *Faculty Towers*, 83–86.

4. A. S. Byatt, *Possession* (New York: Vintage, 1991), 153.

5. Ibid., 155.

6. Jacques Lacan, *Speech and Language in Psychoanalysis*, trans. Anthony Wilden (Baltimore: Johns Hopkins University Press, 1981).

7. For example, Juliet Mitchell and Jacqueline Rose, *Feminine Sexuality: Jacques Lacan and the école freudienne* (New York: Norton, 1982); Jane Gallop, *Reading Lacan* (Ithaca: Cornell University Press, 1985); and Shoshana Felman, *Jacques Lacan and the Adventure of Insight* (Cambridge, MA: Harvard University Press, 1987).

8. Marguerite Duras, *The Ravishing of Lol Stein*, trans. Richard Seaver (New York: Pantheon, 1966). This translation omits Lol's middle initial, but I suspect that the initial is important, and prefer to keep it in the discussion that follows.

9. Jacques Lacan, "Hommage fait à Marguerite Duras, du ravissement de Lol V. Stein," *Cahiers Renaud-Barrault* 52 (1965): 7–15.

10. "Me voici le tiers à y mettre un ravissement, dans mon cas décidément subjectif" (Lacan, "Hommage," 9).

11. Kimberley Philpot van Noort, "The Dance of the Signifier: Jacques Lacan and Marguerite Duras's *Le Ravissement de Lol V. Stein*," *Symposium: A Quarterly in Modern Literatures* 51 (1997): 186–201.

12. Van Noort, "Dance," 188.

13. On the position of the reader, see Carol Murphy, *Alienation and Absence in the Novels of Marguerite Duras* (Lexington, Kentucky: French Forum, 1982), 101–102.

14. Sharon Larson, "Quand la folie se tait: La Psychanalyse et la construction de la voix féminine dans *Le Ravissement de Lol V. Stein*," *thirdspace; a journal of feminist theory & culture* 4, no. 2 (2005): 22–31.

15. Susan Rubin Suleiman, "Nadja, Dora, Lol V. Stein: Women, Madness and Narrative," in *Discourse in Psychoanalysis and Literature*, ed. Shlomith Rimmon-Kenan (London: Methuen, 1987), 126.

16. Suleiman, "Nadja, Dora, Lol V. Stein," 129.

17. Raynalle Udris, *Welcome Unreason: A Study of "Madness" in the Novels of Marguerite Duras* (Atlanta: Rodopi, 1993), 45.

18. Leslie Hill, "Lacan with Duras," in *Writing and Psychoanalysis: A Reader*, ed. John Lechte (New York: Arnold, 1996), 150.

19. The French original reads "Je prends des notes imaginaires sur cette femme"; see Marguerite Duras, *Le vice-consul* (Paris: Gallimard, 1966), 157. The English translation is less vivid: "That woman stirs my imagination. I note down my thoughts about her"; see Marguerite Duras, *The Vice Consul*, trans. Eileen Ellenbogen (New York: Random House, 1968), 124.

20. See Jean Pierrot, *Marguerite Duras* (Paris: Corti, 1986), 216.

21. Jacques Lacan, "Aggressiveness in Psychoanalysis," *Ecrits: The First Complete Edition in English*, trans. Bruce Fink (New York: W. W. Norton, 2002), 81–101 (here 86). The original of this essay appeared as "L'Aggressivité en psychanalyse," *Revue Française de Psychanalyse* 12, no. 2 (July-September 1948): 367–388.

22. The melody itself probably changed as well. Duras stated before the film was actually made that whatever music was used would henceforth be the "real" tune of the song associated with the vice consul, which Duras renamed "India Song." In the event, that music was composed by Carl d'Alessio. There does exist an eighteenth-century minuet called "Indiana's Song," made to accompany a play by Steele, but I have not been able to find out whether Duras knew it.

23. I use here Jacqueline Rose's apt formulation, "Introduction II," in Mitchell and Rose, *Feminine Sexuality*, 31.

24. Marguerite Duras, *L'Amante anglaise* (Paris: Gallimard, 1967). The title, deriving from a homophony between two French terms: *la menthe anglaise* (English mint) and *l'amante anglaise* (the English woman lover), is virtually impossible to render in English. Barbara Bray's translation (New York: Grove Press, 1968) leaves the title in the original French to retain its ambiguity. Quotations from the novel are from her translation.

25. See Marguerite Duras, *Les Viaducs de la Seine-et-Oise* (Paris: Gallimard, 1958), 10.

26. "Lorsque Lacan a trouvé dans Lol V. Stein l'application de certaines de ses théories, je suis restée dans l'ombre, je ne me suis pas dit: Ah, Lacan pense que je suis géniale. Pas du tout. Je n'ai pas besoin de la critique pour savoir que je suis géniale." Marguerite Duras, Interview by Sinclair Dumontais. No date given, www.dialogus2.org/DUR/interview1.html.

27. See Colin Davis, *After Poststructuralism*, 147.

28. Kristeva regards narrative as more significant than does Lacan. See Colin Davis, "Psychoanalysis, Detection, and Fiction: Julia Kristeva's Novels," *Journal of Twentieth Century Contemporary French Studies* 6, no. 2 (2002): 294–306; here 297.

29. Julia Kristeva, *Possessions* (Paris: Fayard, 1996), 212. This passage is complicated in the French original by a play on the words *seul* and *seule* ("alone" in the masculine and the feminine form respectively) and *seul à seul* ("one on one").

30. Julia Kristeva, *Possessions*, trans. Barbara Bray (New York: Columbia University Press, 1998), 178. My comment is meant simply as an acknowledgment of the inevitable problems of translation. Page numbers in parentheses refer to this edition.

228 3. THE MIRROR STAGE

31. "Il n'y a pas d'amour, il n'y a que des preuves d'amour" (Camille Laurens, *Dans ces bras-là* [Paris: P.O.L., 2000], 293).

32. Camille Laurens, *Romance* (Paris: Gallimard [Folio], 2001), 273. Translations from this novel are my own.

33. Lacan, "Aggressiveness in Psychoanalysis," in *Ecrits: The First Complete Edition in English*, 99. The French edition of *Ecrits* does not include this essay; instead, the page mentioned in the footnote to *Romance* contains an attack on an unnamed competitor of Lacan, in other words, an example of aggression on the part of the psychoanalyst rather than the patient. The vigor with which Lacan pursues this attack is actually quite funny. See *Ecrits* I (Paris: Editions du Seuil, 1966), 122.

34. Jacques Lacan, "The Insistence of the Letter in the Unconscious," in *Modern Criticism and Theory: A Reader*, ed. David Lodge, 2nd ed., revised and expanded by Nigel Wood, (Harlow: Pearson, 2000), 68.

35. The allusion is to *Le Séminaire de Jacques Lacan*, ed. Jacques-Alain Miller (Paris: Seuil, 1973).

36. Jacques Lacan, *Ecrits I* (Paris: Editions du Seuil, 1966), 146. I quote here the English version in Jacques Lacan, *The Language of the Self* (Baltimore: Johns Hopkins University Press, 1968), 31.

37. Lacan, "Aggressiveness in Psychoanalysis," 84.

38. The term derives from Lacan, "The Insistence of the Letter in the Unconscious," 68.

39. On this phenomenon in Lacan's theory, see Anthony Wilden, in Lacan, *Speech and Language*, 162–163.

40. Lacan, "Aggressiveness in Psychoanalysis," 89.

41. Ibid., 90. I might note in this connection that Lacan deeply regretted having refused to treat Louis Althusser, who did in fact strangle his wife in an attack of delirium.

42. Teresa Dovey, *The Novels of J. M. Coetzee: Lacanian Allegories* (Cape Town: AD. Donker, 1988), 9. More recently, Yuan Yuan has also explored the presence of Lacan in Coetzee in "The Subject of Reading and the Colonial Unconscious: Countertransference in J. M. Coetzee's *Waiting for the Barbarians*," *American Journal of Psychoanalysis* 60, no. 1 (2000): 71–84.

43. Dovey, *Novels of J. M. Coetzee*, 10.

44. Ibid., 12.

45. Ibid., 11.

46. J. M. Coetzee, *The Age of Iron* (New York: Penguin, 1998). Page numbers in parentheses refer to this edition.

47. This violence led to the declaration of a State of Emergency in precisely the years that are given at the end of the novel as the period of its composition: 1986 through 1989. See Dominic Head, *The Cambridge Introduction to J. M. Coetzee* (Cambridge: Cambridge University Press, 2009), 67.

48. In Jacques Lacan, *The Four Fundamental Concepts of Psycho-Analysis*, ed. Jacques-Alain Miller, trans. Alan Sheridan (New York: W. W. Norton, 1978), 144.

49. "Cast a cold eye/ On life, on death./ Horseman, pass by!" William Butler Yeats, *Collected Poems* (London: MacMillan, 1961), 401.

50. Derek Attridge, *J. M. Coetzee and the Ethics of Reading: Literature in the Event* (Chicago: University of Chicago Press, 2004), 96.

51. Ibid., 95.

52. One might think here of Goethe's *The Sorrows of Young Werther*, in which a fictive editor states in an opening note that the protagonist's "mind and character can't but win your admiration and love, his destiny your tears." See *Goethe, The Collected Works*, vol. 11, ed. David E. Wellbery, trans. Victor Lange (Princeton: Princeton University Press, 1995), 3. In distinction to Goethe's *Werther*, however, there are no editorial intrusions or additions to Mrs. Curren's letter in *The Age of Iron*.

53. On this point, see Ato Quayson, *Postcolonialism: Theory, Practice or Process?* (Malden, MA: Polity Press, 2000).

54. David Attwell, *J. M. Coetzee: South Africa and the Politics of Writing* (Berkeley: University of California Press, 1993), 121.

55. Samantha Vice, "Truth and Love Together at Last: Style, Form, and Moral Vision in *The Age of Iron*," in *J. M. Coetzee and Ethics: Philosophical Perspective on Literature*, ed. Anton Leist and Peter Singer (New York: Columbia University Press, 2010), 293–315. Here, 294.

56. Ibid., 306.

57. Ibid., 310.

58. Ibid., 312.

4. Women's Time

1. Julia Kristeva, "The Ethics of Linguistics," in *Modern Criticism and Theory: A Reader*, ed. David Lodge and Nigel Wood (Harlow: Pearson, 2000), 207.

2. Alice Jardine, "Introduction to Julia Kristeva's 'Women's Time,'" *Signs: Journal of Women in Culture and Society* 7, no. 1 (1981): 6.

3. Jardine, "Introduction to 'Women's Time,'" 7–8.

4. Julia Kristeva, "Women's Time," trans. Alice Jardine and Harry Blake, *Signs* 7, no. 1 (1981): 13–35, here 27. Subsequent quotations from "Women's Time" refer to this version, indicating page numbers in parentheses.

5. They differ in this respect from her first novel, *Samouraï* (1990), essentially a memoir of her political activities in the 1960s and 1970s, which depicts her own attempts to reform social power structures.

6. Colin Davis comments that this city "may recall, but should not entirely be identified with, the Californian city" called Santa Barbara. "Psychoanalysis, Detection,

and Fiction: Julia Kristeva's Novels," *Journal of Twentieth Century Contemporary French Studies* 6, no. 2 (2002): 294–306, here 299.

7. Brigitte Huitfeldt Midttun, "Crossing the Borders: An Interview with Julia Kristeva," *Hypatia* 21, no. 4 (2006): 172. In the novel, the old man is explicitly linked to the narrator's father, who had to leave Santa Barbara because he was unwelcome there under communism. See *Le vieil homme et les loups* (Paris: Fayard, 1991), 221; in English, *The Old Man and the Wolves*, trans. Barbara Bray (New York: Columbia University Press, 1994).

8. Julia Kristeva, *Murder in Byzantium*, trans. C. Jon Delogu (New York: Columbia University Press, 2006), 66–67 and 167.

9. Julia Kristeva, *Possessions*, trans. Barbara Bray (Columbia University Press, 1998), 51.

10. See Davis, "Psychoanalysis, Detection, and Fiction," 304.

11. Ibid., 299–300.

12. Christa Wolf, *Cassandra: A Novel and Four Essays*, trans. Jan van Heurck (New York: Farrar, Straus, Giroux, 1984). "Conditions of a Narrative" is included in this volume (141–305); it omits, however, the lengthy bibliography that had been appended to the German version of "Conditions of a Narrative," *Voraussetzungen einer Erzählung: Kassandra* (Frankfurt a.M.: Suhrkamp, 1983), 156–160.

13. Kristeva makes an amusing reference to Christa Wolf in her novel *Possessions*. There, Stephanie Delacour describes her ideal of a relaxing Sunday afternoon as "a hot bath, some Vivaldi, and an early bed with a Christa Wolf novel to kid myself that I'm clever, the world is grim, and that I can sleep without having to take any pills" (*Possessions*, 37).

14. In French, *écriture féminine*. Note that the French word *féminine* does not have the somewhat negative cast of its English cognate.

15. See entry for July 8, 1980, Christa Wolf, *Cassandra*, 228–230.

16. Christa Wolf, *Kindheitsmuster* (Berlin: Luchterhand, 1976); in English, *Patterns of Childhood* (formerly *A Model Childhood*), trans. Ursula Molinaro and Hedwig Rappolt (New York: Farrar, Straus and Giroux, 1980).

17. Luce Irigaray, *Speculum of the Other Woman*, trans. Gillian C. Gill (Ithaca: Cornell University Press, 1985), 135.

18. This fragment, "Too Near," opens Ernst Bloch's *The Spirit of Utopia*, trans. Anthony Nassar (Stanford, CA: Stanford University Press, 2000), 7. Nassar notes that Bloch's German phrase, "Ich bin an mir," has several meanings: "I am *right next to* myself," "I am by myself," and "I exist or come into being through or by means of myself" (284n1). I personally would have opted for the first choice, which captures some of the strangeness of Bloch's formulation.

19. Monika Maron, *Animal Triste*, trans. Brigitte Goldstein (Lincoln: University of Nebraska Press, 2000).

20. When the tracks were first discovered, they were held to be the claw prints of "Noah's Raven," a bird that Noah had sent out from the ark but that failed to return. See Anthony J. Martin, *Introduction to the Study of Dinosaurs* (Hoboken: Wiley, John & Sons, 2005), 63.

21. For this reason, I am not entirely convinced by Gabriele Eckart, "Ost-Frau liebt West-Mann: Zwei neue Romane von Irina Liebmann and Monika Maron," *Colloquia Germanica* 30, no. 4 (1997): 315–321. Alison Lewis presents a more nuanced and accurate reading of the novel in her article "Re-Membering the Barbarian: Memory and Repression in Monika Maron's *Animal triste*," *German Quarterly* 71, no. 1 (1998): 30–46.

22. Julia Kristeva, *Possessions*, trans. Barbara Bray (New York: Columbia University Press, 1998), front flap.

23. Kristeva, *Murder in Byzantium*, 12.

24. The original says *son roman de Byzance*, which might also be translated as "romance" in the sense of the medieval romance. See *Meutre à Byzance* (Paris: Fayard, 2004), 167.

5. Systems of Constraint

1. In the body of this chapter, I give the dates of the first publication in French for Foucault's works; English translation publication dates appear in the notes.

2. Michel Foucault, *Discipline and Punish: The Birth of the Prison*, trans. Alan Sheridan (New York: Vintage, 1977, 2nd ed. 1995), 308.

3. Paul Rabinow, ed., *The Foucault Reader* (New York: Pantheon, 1984), 115.

4. Rabinow, *Foucault Reader*, 108.

5. Andrew Bennett, *The Author* (New York: Routledge, 2005), 20.

6. It is important to recognize the distinctive arguments of the two essays. Neither is simply a restatement of what in English is called the "author-narrator distinction" (see Bennett, *The Author*, 76–77).

7. In the English translation, "The Discourse on Language" appears as an appendix to Michel Foucault, *The Archaeology of Knowledge*, trans. A. M. Sheridan Smith (New York: Pantheon, 1972), 215–237.

8. Foucault, "Discourse on Language," 233.

9. See Foucault, *Discipline and Punish*, 304–311.

10. Ibid., 310.

11. Ibid., 304, 308.

12. Ibid., 311.

13. Patricia Duncker, *Hallucinating Foucault* (London: Serpent's Tail, 1996), 4–5. The novel won the Dillons First Fiction Award and the McKitterick Prize.

14. Rabinow, *Foucault Reader*, 106.

15. Roland Barthes, "The Death of the Author," in *The Rustle of Language*, trans. Richard Howard (Berkeley: University of California Press, 1984), 54.

16. I am grateful to Verena Conley for her helpful exchange with me about this issue.

17. One might note, however, that the literary letter-novel may take precisely the form of a one-sided set of letters that include responses to the recipient: Goethe's novel *Die Leiden des jungen Werthers* (1774; *The Sorrows of Young Werther*) is structured in this manner. See Johann Wolfgang von Goethe, *The Sorrows of Young Werther*, trans. Victor Lange, in Goethe, *The Collected Works*, vol. 11, ed. David E. Wellbery (Princeton, N.J.: Princeton University Press, 1995).

18. This English translation, supplied by the narrator within the fiction, is preceded in the text by the French "original": "Qui es-tu point d'interrogation?/Je me pose souvent des questions./Dans ton habit de gala/Tu ressembles à un magistrat./Tu es le plus heureux des points/Car on te répond toi au moins."

19. Amusingly, one of Patricia Duncker's scholarly books on women's writing bears the title *Writing on the Wall: Selected Essays* (London: Pandora, 2002).

20. This recalls Tristan Tzara's recipe for a Dada poem: by taking words cut out of a newspaper and assembling them to make a poem, one will find that the result "resembles you."

21. Umberto Eco, *The Name of the Rose*, trans. William Weaver (New York: Warner Books, 1984), 387.

22. Brian McHale gives several other sources for the plan of the library: as visual sources, he suggests Piranesi's prisons and Escher's paradoxical architectures; as textual sources, he proposes Borges and Kafka, as well as a number of postmodern examples of labyrinthine spaces. He does not mention Bentham's Panopticon, however. See Brian McHale, *Constructing Postmodernism* (London: Routledge, 1992), 157–158.

23. Umberto Eco, *Foucault's Pendulum*, trans. William Weaver (Houghton Mifflin Harcourt, 2007). Page references refer to this edition.

24. The name Casaubon is a dual reference to the historical sixteenth-century scholar Isaac Casaubon and the character by that name in George Eliot's *Middlemarch* (1872).

25. Brian McHale reads this part of the plot—the notion that the Templars may be engaged in a conspiracy—as an example of "paranoia," linking it with other "postmodern paranoid fictions" like those of Burroughs, Pynchon, Robbe-Grillet, Barth, and McElroy (*Constructing Postmodernism*, 178–180).

26. Eco also alludes here to his own study of the text and the reader in *The Role of the Reader: Explorations in the Semiotics of Texts* (Bloomington: Indiana University Press, 1984).

27. Foucault, *Archaeology of Knowledge*, 49.

28. Michel Foucault, *L'ordre du discours* (Paris: Gallimard, 1971). The English translation, "Discourse on Language," is included in Michael Foucault, *The Archaeology of Knowledge*, 215–237.

29. "The Discourse on Language," 231–232.

30. Ibid., 233.

31. Ibid., 234.

32. Unfortunately, the novel has not been translated into English.

33. The figure of the narrator is based in part on Sascha Anderson, the informer who infiltrated the Prenzlauer Berg group. For an account of the Prenzlauer Berg group, see Karen Leeder, *Breaking Boundaries: A New Generation of Poets in the GDR, 1979–1989* (New York: Oxford University Press, 1996) and Stephen Brockmann, *Literature and German Reunification* (Cambridge: Cambridge University Press, 1999), 80–108.

34. See Manfred Frank, *Was ist Neostrukturalismus?* (Frankfurt: Suhrkamp, 1984); in English, *What is Neostructuralism?* (Minneapolis: University of Minneapolis Press, 1989). In this book, Frank treats such theorists as Derrida, Lacan, and Deleuze.

35. Peter Cooke, *Speaking the Taboo: A Study of the Work of Wolfgang Hilbig* (Amsterdam: Rodopi, 2000), 205.

36. J. M. Coetzee. *Waiting for the Barbarians* (London: Vintage, 2004), 76.

37. Images from the various colonized territories in Africa during the last years of the nineteenth and the early years of the twentieth centuries show troops with an eclectic mixture of weaponry. See, for example, an engraving in Thomas Pakenham, *The Scramble for Africa: White Man's Conquest of the Dark Continent from 1876 to 1912* (New York: Avon Books, 1991), located on a double-spread plate on pp. 454 and 455. This engraving depicts "Demorbida's last stand at Adowa, 1 March 1896," in which the white soldiers, some of them on horseback, fight with rifles and a cannon, whereas the black soldiers, also armed with rifles, carry heavy round metal shields as well.

38. Matt DelConte, "A Further Study of Present Tense Narration: The Absentee Narratee and Four-Wall Present Tense in Coetzee's *Waiting for the Barbarians* and *Disgrace*," *Journal of Narrative Theory* 37, no. 3 (2007): 427–446; here, 430.

39. Ibid., 440.

40. This passage is drawn from J. M. Coetzee, "The Harms of Pornography: Catharine MacKinnon," in *Giving Offense: Essays on Censorship* (Chicago: University of Chicago Press, 1996), 67. Coetzee gives a more extensive and substantial discussion of Foucault in another chapter of this book, "Erasmus: Madness and Rivalry," 83–103. I refer to both chapters in my treatment of Coetzee's understanding of Foucault.

41. My quotation from Coetzee's Erasmus essay is drawn from Coetzee's *Giving Offense*, 87. Derrida's critique, "Cogito and the History of Madness," is included in *Writing and Difference*, trans. Alan Bass (Chicago: University of Chicago Press, 1978), 31–63.

42. I do not agree with Michael Valdez Moses when he suggests that the "indeterminacy of literal meanings, the fact that the magistrate creates them rather than discovers them, illustrate a poststructural understanding of interpretation from which follow troublesome political implications." See "The Mark of Empire: Writing, History, and Torture in Coetzee's *Waiting for the Barbarians*," *Kenyon Review*, n.s., 15, no. 1 (1993): 115–117; here 122.

43. On torture in *Waiting for the Barbarians*, see Barbara Eckstein, who brings Elaine Scarry's *The Body in Pain* to bear on the novel. See "The Body, the Word, and the State in Coetzee's Waiting for the Barbarians," *Novel: A Forum on Fiction* 22, no. 2 (1989): 175–198. Eckstein's discussion of body and voice in *Waiting for the Barbarians* is of particular interest.

44. Derek Attridge, *J. M. Coetzee and the Ethics of Reading* (Chicago: University of Chicago Press, 2004), 42.

45. Ibid., 47.

46. W. G. Sebald, *The Rings of Saturn,* trans. Michael Hulse (New York: New Directions, 1998); *Austerlitz,* trans. Anthea Bell (New York: The Modern Library, 2001). The genre of these two works, like those of all Sebald's creative writings, is problematic. *The Rings of Saturn* ostensibly takes the form of a travel narrative, but it is by no means a straightforward one. Interwoven in the narrator's eccentric account of his walking tour through county Suffolk, England, are multiple digressions that recount information from reading of various kinds and even from a television program during which he fell asleep. The first edition of *Austerlitz* (Munich: Carl Hanser, 2001) does not include the genre designation "Roman" (novel), normally de rigeur in German publications. Some later paperbacks do include it, although some do not. This may be the result of editorial slippage following Sebald's death in December, 2001, not long after the book had appeared. In any event, I prefer to exercise caution about the genre of these two works.

47. When Sebald refers to Foucault in his essays on literature, it is to his *History of Sexuality (1976–1984)*. See W. G. Sebald, *Die Beschreibung des Unglücks: Zur österreichischen Literatur von Stifter bis Handke* (Frankfurt a.M.: Fischer, 1994), 188, and *Unheimliche Heimat: Essays zur österreichischen Literatur* (Frankfurt a.M.: Fischer, 1995), 37. However, he clearly had read Foucault closely, as his narrative texts indicate. The Deutsches Literaturarchiv in Marbach contains those books by Foucault that he owned, but he also consulted books in the library at the University of East Anglia, where he taught.

48. See H. G. Adler's *Theresienstadt, 1941–1945; Das Antlitz einer Zwangsgemeinschaft. Geschichte, Soziologie, Psychologie*, 2nd revised and expanded ed. (Tübingen: Mohr, 1960).

49. Foucault, *Discipline and Punish*, 205.

50. It also subtends the scene in Coetzee's *Waiting for the Barbarians* where the word "enemy" is written on the captives' backs and then beaten and washed away by their own blood (114–119).

51. Foucault, *Discipline and Punish*, 205.

52. Ibid., 209.

53. Ibid., 308.

54. The fisherman, surrounded by many onlookers, stands among an abundant catch of fish on the floor of a large hall. Taken at Lowestoft, one of the towns the narrator of *The Rings of Saturn* visits on his walking tour, the photograph appears to be from the early twentieth century.

55. Ann Laura Stoler, *Race and the Education of Desire: Foucault's History of Sexuality and the Colonial Order of Things* (Durham: Duke University Press, 1995), 1.

6. Simulacra and Simulation

1. Jean Baudrillard, *Simulacra and Simulation*, trans. Sheila Faria Glaser (Ann Arbor: University of Michigan Press, 1994), 29. The French original was published by Editions Galilée in 1981.

2. Julian Barnes, *England, England* (New York: Random House, 2000), 4–6.

3. Jean Baudrillard, *The Mirror of Production*, trans. Mark Poster (St. Louis: Telos, 1975).

4. On the "Foreign Agents" series, see Sylvère Lotringer, "Doing Theory," in *French Theory in America*, ed. Sylvère Lotringer and Sande Cohen (London: Routledge, 2001), 128–129. The first Baudrillard volume in this series was *Simulations*, trans. Paul Foss, Paul Patton, and Philip Beitchman (New York: Semiotext(e), 1983). It contained "The Precession of Simulacra" and "The Orders of Simulacra."

5. Jean Baudrillard, *The Ecstasy of Communication*, ed. Sylvère Lotringer, trans. Bernard and Caroline Schutze (New York: Semiotext(e), 1988). This volume included not only the title essay but also "Rituals of Transparency," "Metamorphosis, Metaphor, Metastasis," "Seduction, or the Superficial Depths," "From the System to the Destiny of Objects," and "Why Theory?".

6. Lotringer, "Doing Theory," 147.

7. The English version of Baudrillard's *L'Echange symbolique et la mort* did not appear until the late 1990s under the title *Symbolic Exchange and Death*, trans. Iain Hamilton, intro. Mark Gane (London: Sage, 1998).

8. Jean Baudrillard, *Agonie des Realen* (Berlin: Merve, 1978); *Der symbolische Tausch und der Tod* (Munich, 1982); a German translation of his *Oublier Foucault* (retaining the French title) in Munich in 1983; and *Die fatalen Strategien* (Munich: Matthes & Seitz, 1985); *Amerika* (Munich: Matthes & Seitz, 1987). Wolfgang Welsch includes a section on Baudrillard in *Unsere postmoderne Moderne* (Weinheim: VCH Acta humaniora, 1988), 149–154.

9. Bodo Morshäuser, *Die Berliner Simulation* (Frankfurt a.M.: Suhrkamp, 1983). To the best of my knowledge, this novel has not been translated into English; none-

theless, for the convenience of English-speaking readers, I refer to it here as *The Berlin Simulation*. The German word *Simulation* is more technical than its English cognate; it refers to such simulations as used in air pilot training and the like, and also to the kinds of simulations created by modern media.

10. The genre designation on the title page of this one-hundred-and-thirty-page text terms it a "story" rather than a novel.

11. Baudrillard is discussing Philip K. Dick's science fiction novel *Simulacra* (1964), from which he may have derived the term "simulacra."

12. My translation here and in all following quotations from Morshäuser's novel.

13. In addition to the Broadway musical, a film version, *Sweet Charity: The Adventures of a Girl Who Wanted to be* Loved, directed by Bob Fosse and with Shirley MacLaine in the principal role, came out in 1969.

14. Later included in Christopher Isherwood, *The Berlin Stories* (New York: J. Laughlin, 1946).

15. Georg Klein, *Barbar Rosa: Eine Detektivgeschichte* (Berlin: Alexander Fest Verlag, 2001), 35. The novel has not yet been translated into English. Quotations that follow are taken from this edition and given in my own rendering.

16. He was awarded the *Brüder Grimm Prize* in 1999 and the Ingeborg Bachmann Prize in 2000.

17. Reinhart Koselleck, *Zeitschichten: Studien zur Historik* (Frankfurt a.M.: Suhrkamp, 2000).

18. Klein, *Barbar Rosa*, 35.

19. See, for example, Sascha Preiß's negative opinion of the novel, which he regards as a piece of "charlatanry." See Sascha Preiß, "Mr. Charles La Tane" [a review of *Barbar Rosa*], www.u-lit.de/rezension/georg-klein-barbarrosa.html.

20. Ingo Arend, "Endkampf der Aufklärung: Georg Klein und sein neuer Roman *Barbar Rosa*," *Der Freitag*, June 8, 2001, www.freitag.de/2001/24/01241602.php. *Der Freitag* was founded in 1990 in order to further dialogue between the newly unified eastern and western parts of Germany.

21. These forms have come to be called "Erikative," on the model of such grammatical terms as "imperatives." The term honors Erika Fuchs by using her first name.

22. Fuchs's first Disney translation was a Mickey Mouse comic book that appeared in 1951. She continued to produce translations until the 1980s, when her eyesight began to fail. She died in April 2005. See Klaus Bohn, *Das Erika Fuchs Buch* (Lüneburg: Dreidreizehn, 1996).

23. See in particular Marc Schuster, *Don DeLillo, Jean Baudrillard, and the Consumer Conundrum* (Youngstown, NY: Cambria Press, 2008). His chapter on *White Noise* (9–29) is titled "Shopping for Its Own Sake: Don DeLillo's System of Objects."

24. Douglas Kellner, *Jean Baudrillard: From Marxism to Postmodernism and Beyond*, (Stanford: Stanford University Press, 1989), 66.

25. Andreas Huyssen, "In the Shadow of McLuhan: Baudrillard's Theory of Simulation," *Assemblage*, no. 10 (Dec. 1989): 6–17; here, 10.

26. Amy Hungerford, *Postmodern Belief: American Literature and Religion since 1960* (Princeton: Princeton University Press, 2010): 57–58.

27. Huyssen, "In the Shadow of McLuhan," 9.

28. Peter Knight, "Delillo, Postmodernism, Postmodernity," in *The Cambridge Companion to Don DeLillo*, ed. John. N. Duvall (Cambridge: Cambridge University Press, 2008), 27–40; here 30.

29. The entire book did not appear until 1998 (see note 4, this chapter).

30. See Tom LeClair, *In the Loop: Don DeLillo and the Systems Novel* (Urbana: University of Illinois Press, 1987), 213.

31. Randy Laist observes the "pervasive tendency of everyday things to radiate unusual meanings" in *White Noise (Technology and Postmodern Subjectivity in Don DeLillo's Novels* [Bern: Peter Lang, 2010], 67).

32. Don DeLillo, *White Noise* (New York: Penguin, 1986), 3.

33. See also Baudrillard's essay, "Crash" (on J. G. Ballard's 1973 novel of the same title), in *Simulacra and Simulation*, 111–119.

34. Jack Gladney's response to the Dylar "plot" can also be understood in terms of his paranoid mentality. On this topic, see Steffen Hantke, *Conspiracy and Paranoia in Contemporary American Fiction* (Frankfurt a.M.: Peter Lang, 1994), 47–49.

35. John Dietrich, *The Morgenthau Plan: Soviet Influence on American Postwar Policy* (New York: Agora, 2002), 55. The phrases quoted come from a memorandum by Winston Churchill in which he reluctantly speaks in favor of the Morgenthau plan, which he had originally opposed. In the end, however, the plan was never put into effect.

36. Christoph Ransmayr, *The Dog King*, trans. John E. Woods (New York: Vintage, 1998), 24; line breaks corrected to accord with the German original, *Morbus Kitahara* (Frankfurt a.M.: Fischer, 1995; reprinted in Fischer Taschenbuch Verlag, 1997), 33. References in the text are to the English version.

37. Unfortunately, the English translation of Ransmayr's novel cannot properly represent this equivalence because the English word "moor" does not refer to marshy or swampy land. I am grateful to one of my anonymous press readers for pointing out this problem of translation.

38. I would like to thank John Hamilton for information about this geographical feature.

39. His name alludes to George Smith Patton Jr., an American general in World War II.

40. Baudrillard, *The System of Objects* (London: Verso, 1996), 62.

41. Baudrillard, "The Reversal of History" in *The Illusion of the End*, trans. Chris Turner (Stanford: Stanford University Press, 1994), 10–13.

42. See James Young, *The Texture of Memory: Holocaust Memorials and Meaning* (New Haven: Yale University Press, 1993).

43. For a discussion of memory and memorialization in Austrian literature and film, see Fatima Naqvi, *The Literary and Cultural Rhetoric of Victimhood: Western Europe, 1970–2005* (New York: Palgrave Macmillan, 2007).

44. Leonard Wilcox, "Baudrillard, DeLillo's 'White Noise,' and the End of Heroic Narrative," *Contemporary Literature* 32, no. 3 (1991): 346–365. Wilcox's thesis is that the contemporary world throws into question the "heroic narratives" that provided the underpinning of earlier twentieth-century literature.

45. Wilcox, "End of Heroic Narrative," 363.

46. Baudrillard, *Symbolic Exchange and Death*, 127.

47. Baudrillard, "The Ecstasy of Communication," in *The Anti-Aesthetic: Essays on Postmodern Culture*, ed. Hal Foster (Port Townsend, WA: Bay, 1983), 127.

48. Those who set the car on fire during Bering's absence in Brand mock at the idea that they are to blame: "Begging your pardon ever so much, but it looks like the Crow flew a little too high. Must have got too close to the sun. Suddenly caught fire. Burned like a can of gas, that car did. Like a can of gas" (*Dog King*, 295).

49. I adapt here the title concept of Rachel Blau DuPlessis's *Writing Beyond the Ending: Narrative Strategies of Twentieth-Century Women Writers* (Bloomington: Indiana University Press, 1985).

7. Lines of Flight

1. John Diebold and Michael Goodwin, *Babies of Wackiness: A Readers' Guide to Thomas Pynchon's* Vineland, www.mindspring.com/~shadow88/chapter7.htm.

2. According to Gwyneth Jones, the genre known as "cyberpunk," pioneered by William Gibson and Bruce Sterling, is an attempt to present fantasies about "the future of now" that use "close extrapolations from the present, contemporary referents, political and emotional realism." See "Art, Forward Slash, Science," *PMLA* 119 (2004): 526. A British science fiction writer and critic, Jones writes of her own fascination with "information theory, which binds the visible and the invisible, the material and the immaterial worlds" (528). A similar privileging of information theory is at the root of cyberpunk fictions.

3. Félix Guattari, *La Révolution moléculaire* (Paris: Encres, Editions recherches, 1977); first English translation, *Molecular Revolution: Psychiatry and Politics*, trans. Rosemary Sheed, intro. David Cooper (New York: Puffin, 1984).

4. Guattari, *Molecular Revolution*, 154–162. Another relevant essay, "Machinic Propositions," is also included in this volume (144–153).

5. Gilles Deleuze and Félix Guattari, *Anti-Oedipus: Capitalism and Schizophrenia*, trans. Robert Hurley, Mark Seem, and Helen R. Lane (New York: Viking Press, 1977).

6. Samuel R. Delany, *Nova* (London: Gollancz, 1968), 163.

7. For an amusing account of its status, see Marc Laidlaw, "Dhalgren: The City Not Yet Fallen, the Novel Still Unread," *Review of Contemporary Fiction* 16, no. 3 (1996): 136–141.

8. Delany's description of his series *Return to Nevèrÿon* as "a Child's Garden of Semiotics" is telling (the series consists of four volumes published 1979–87). The influence of theorists such as Barthes, Derrida, Eco, Foucault, and Lacan makes itself felt throughout these novels. He has taught at the University of Massachusetts in Amherst, the University of Buffalo, and Temple University. He was also a writer in residence at the University of Minnesota.

9. Samuel R. Delany, *Dhalgren* (New York: Vintage, 1996), 11. "There is clearly a gap between Bellona and the real world, and, to get from one to the other, you literally have to cross a bridge" writes Robert Elliot Fox in "This You-Shaped Hole of Insight and Fire: Meditations on Dhalgren," *Review of Contemporary Fiction* 16, no. 3 (1996): 130. Fox interprets the gap represented by the bridge as "chaos," a gap between "two worlds" (130). It might be worth drawing a parallel here between *Dhalgren* and Kafka's *The Castle*, where the protagonist also has to cross a bridge before arriving in the village below the castle.

10. François Cusset, *French Theory: Foucault, Derrida, Deleuze & Cie et les mutations de la vie intellectuelle aux Etats-Unis* (Paris: Découverte, 2003), 266, 269.

11. See Brian McHale, "Elements of a Poetics of Cyberpunk," *Critique: Studies in Contemporary Fiction* 33 (1992): 165. McHale is especially interesting on the narratological implications of cyberfiction novels and on their relation to postmodern narrative in general.

12. *Neuromancer* initiates a trilogy that continues with *Count Zero* (1986) and *Mona Lisa Overdrive* (1988). The later novels depend on some of the same technological ideas first introduced in *Neuromancer*.

13. Brian McHale compares this use of "simstim" with split-screen cinema or television and multiple point-of-view fiction; see *Constructing Postmodernism* (London: Routledge, 1992), 260.

14. See Punday, *Narrative After Theory*, 118, and McHale, *Constructing Postmodernism*, 233–234. McHale describes *Empire of the Senseless* as "cyberpunk recycled as postmodernism" (233) and notes the existence of a "feedback loop" between science fiction and mainstream postmodernism (235).

15. "Devoured by Myths: An Interview with Sylvère Lotringer" (October 1989–May 1990) in Kathy Acker, *Hannibal Lecter, My Father* (New York: Semiotext(e), 1991), 1–24.

16. Ian Pindar, "A Very Long Scream with the Odd Couple," *Times Literary Supplement*, January 2, 1998, 7–8. Pindar adduces as evidence "the meditations on lines and territories in *Mason & Dixon*," 8. On the connections between Pynchon and Deleuze & Guattari, see Stuart Moulthrop, "Rhizome and Resistance: Hypertext Theory and

the Dreams of a New Culture," in *Hyper/text/ theory*, ed. George P. Landow (Baltimore: Johns Hopkins University Press, 1994), 299–319. Moulthrop comments: "Thomas Pynchon's nod to Deleuze and Guattari in *Vineland* may seem trivial . . . , but it suggests deeper connections between their work and his own subversive fictions" (301–302).

17. Thomas Pynchon, *Vineland* (New York: Penguin), 170. Page numbers in parentheses refer to this edition.

18. See James Berger, "Cultural Trauma and the 'Timeless Burst': Pynchon's Revision of Nostalgia in *Vineland*," *Postmodern Culture* 5, no. 3 (1995): no pages, par. 16.

19. Max Horkheimer and Theodor W. Adorno, *Dialektik der Aufklärung* (Frankfurt a.M.: Fischer, 1969); English translation *Dialectic of Enlightenment*, trans. John Cumming (New York: Seabury Press, 1972).

20. For an astute reading of the "television world" in *Vineland*, see McHale, *Constructing Postmodernism*, 115–141. He observes, for example, that the presence of television in everyday life tends to blur boundaries between the world of television and the world we inhabit, so that viewers often "behave towards TV figures as though their space were continuous with ours" (118).

21. James Berger regards *Vineland* as "an 80s parody that approaches Fredric Jameson's notion of postmodern 'pastiche'—a parody that has lost its moral axis and become indistinguishable from what it presumably had set out to satirize" ("Cultural Trauma and the 'Timeless Burst,'" par. 37). In contrast to Berger's view, my description of the novel as "simultaneously serious and parodic" does not imply that the novel has "lost its moral axis."

22. Here they elaborate on an idea first presented in a very different context by Lacan, who used the term "territorialization" to refer to the infant's investment of desire in certain parts of the mother's body, notably her breast. Deleuze and Guattari extend this notion to the ways in which capitalism invests itself in the social organism as a whole.

23. Gilles Deleuze and Félix Guattari, *A Thousand Plateaus: Capitalism and Schizophrenia*, trans. Brian Massumi (Minneapolis: University of Minnesota Press, 1987); in French, *Mille Plateaux*, vol. 2 of *Capitalisme et schizophrénie* (Paris: Editions de Minuit, 1980).

24. Pynchon's interest in the debates about the map, which began in the 1960s and continues to the present, is not surprising. Even in *Gravity's Rainbow* (1973), territory was at issue in his depiction of colonialism in German Southwest Africa (modern Namibia).

25. On this connection, see Stephen Burn, *David Foster Wallace's* Infinite Jest: *A Reader's Guide* (New York: Continuum, 2003), 24. Burn's discussion of the Eschaton episode and the relevance of the map motif for the book as a whole (23–36) is very helpful.

26. Mark Currie, *Postmodern Narrative Theory* (New York: Palgrave Macmillan, 1998), 36.

27. David Foster Wallace, *Infinite Jest* (New York: Little, Brown and Company, 1996). Page numbers in parentheses refer to this edition.

28. At the same time, however, the word "map" has also become, in this world of the near future, a slang expression for a person's face. To be "demapped" means to be killed (e.g., *Infinite Jest*, 823). An even more intriguing usage is that of the term "click" to refer to a unit of distance, as if real travel were somehow identical with internet navigation (e.g., *Infinite Jest*, 808). It is also possible that the term is equivalent to the military slang "klick," meaning a kilometer and possibly derived from the sound of an odometer turning over (my thanks to Christopher Pitts for this suggestion).

29. The word "waggling" is also used to describe the body movements of the Canadians who sell Michael Pemulis the drug DMZ. Due to the fact that Pemulis speaks no French and his drug suppliers speak no English, their negotiations look like "some kind of group psychomotor seizure, with different bits of whipping and waggling heads" (*Infinite Jest*, 215). The admissions officers at the University of Arizona seem to think Hal has had a seizure of some kind during his interview with them.

30. At one point, "Madame Psychosis" is given as an alternative name for the drug. This is not only an internal reference to the fictive radio personality of the same name, but also no doubt an allusion to the motif of "metempsychosis" in Joyce's *Ulysses*. The opening chapter of *Infinite Jest* can thus be read as an allusion not only to Joyce (we ask ourselves whether Hal has undergone some kind of metempsychosis), but also, by extension, to Kafka's "Metamorphosis" (we ask ourselves whether Hal has metamorphosed into some kind of animal-like being).

31. For some other possible explanations, see Burn, *Infinite Jest: A Reader's Guide*, 36–38.

32. Toward the end of *2001: A Space Odyssey*, HAL confesses, "Dave, I'm afraid. My brain is growing empty."

33. A British report states that "dimetridazole (DMZ) has never been properly evaluated for safety. Scientific committees disagree about its safety, but it is suspected of being able to induce both cancer and birth defects." See Richard Young and Alison Craig, *Too Hard to Swallow: The Truth about Drugs and Poultry; The Use and Misuse of Antibiotics in UK Agriculture—part 3. Residues of Dangerous Drugs in Intensively Produced Chicken Meat and Eggs* (Bristol: Soil Association, 2001), 7. In the United States, dimetridazole is not permitted for use in food animals under any circumstances; see National Research Council [U.S.] Board on Agriculture, *Drugs in Food Animals* (National Academies Press, 1999), 97.

34. Hal has had something chicken-like about him from an early point: when playing competitive tennis, for example, he is said to "probe, pecking, until some angle opens up" (*Infinite Jest*, 260).

35. Thomas Pynchon, *Mason & Dixon* (New York: Henry Holt, 1997), 56. Page numbers in parentheses refer to this edition.

36. Jacques de Vaucanson's famous mechanical duck, constructed in 1739, was able to flap its wings and, by means of separate chambers for grain and "feces," gave the impression that it could digest food.

37. See Eugene W. Holland, *Deleuze and Guattari's* Anti-Oedipus*: Introduction to Schizoanalysis* (London: Routledge, 1999), 115.

38. Sebald read Deleuze and Guattari's book on Kafka in the German translation, *Kafka: Für eine kleine Literatur*, trans. Burkhart Kroeber (Frankfurt a.M.: Suhrkamp, 1976). Sebald cites the book in "Eine kleine Traverse: Das poetische Werk Ernst Herbecks" in his volume of essays on Austrian literature, *Die Beschreibung des Unglücks: Zur österreichischen Literatur von Stifter bis Handke* (Salzburg: Residenz Verlag, 1985), 197. I am grateful to the German Literary Archive in Marbach for the opportunity to view Sebald's markings in his personal copy.

39. In due course, it may be possible to discover other works by Deleuze and Guattari that Sebald read. It is well known that Sebald underlined and annotated books he borrowed from the University of East Anglia library: his characteristic underlinings and marginal lines may help identify these volumes.

40. W. G. Sebald, *Schwindel. Gefühle.* (Frankfurt a.M.: Eichborn, 1990); in English, *Vertigo*, trans. Michael Hulse (New York: New Directions, 2000). One of the most perceptive studies of Sebald's relation to Kafka with particular reference to *Vertigo* is Eric Santner's *On Creaturely Life: Rilke, Benjamin, Sebald* (Chicago: University of Chicago Press, 2006).

41. W. G. Sebald, *Die Ringe des Saturn: Eine englische Wallfahrt* (Frankfurt a.M.: Eichborn, 1995; Fischer Taschenbuch, 1998. The subtitle is omitted from the English translation, *The Rings of Saturn*, trans, Michael Hulse (New York: New Directions, 1998).

42. I cite the definitions given in *Webster's Third New International Dictionary of the English Language*, ed. Philip Babcock Grove and the Merriam-Webster editorial staff (Springfield, MA: Merriam-Webster, 1993).

43. Richard T. Gray maps this structure in "Sebald's Segues: Performing Narrative Contingency in *The Rings of Saturn*," *Germanic Review* 84, no. 1 (2009): 26–58. After demonstrating how one can see the various layers of the narrative in terms of concentric rings, he concludes that the best way of understanding the book's structure is to think in terms of the European emblem for the Jakobswege, an irregular eleven-spoke diagram used to indicate the paths that can be followed by pilgrims as they make their way from Eastern or Central Europe to Santiago. On pilgrimage in *The Rings of Saturn*, see also Claudia Albes, "Die Erkundung der Leere: Anmerkungen zu W. G. Sebalds 'englische Wallfahrt' Die Ringe des Saturn," *Jahrbuch der deutschen Schillergesellschaft* 46 (2002): 279–305. A contribution of my own, written before Richard

Gray's article but for technical reasons not published until later, also discusses the question of pilgrimage at some length: "'Lines of Flight': History and Territory in *Die Ringe des Saturn*" in *W. G. Sebald: Schreiben ex patria/Expatriate Writing*, ed. Gerhard Fischer (Amsterdam: Rodopi, 2009), 45–60.

44. W. G. Sebald, Interview with Christian Scholz: "Der Schriftsteller und die Fotografie," Manuskript des Radio-Features, Erstsendung am 16.2.1999 im WDR, Köln (cit. Heiner Boehncke, "Clair obscur: W. G. Sebalds Bilder," *Text + Kritik*, no. 158 [IV / 03]: 51.

45. See James Cowan, "W. G. Sebald's *Austerlitz* and the Great Library: History, Fiction, Memory. Part I," *Monatshefte* 102, no. 1 (Spring 2010): 51–81. Note especially the map (75).

46. Gilles Deleuze and Félix Guattari, *Kafka: Toward a Minor Literature*, trans. Dana Polan (Minneapolis: University of Minnesota Press, 1986). In Polan's translation, the relevant formulations read: "affected with a high coefficient of deterritorialization" (16) and "the individual concern thus becomes all the more necessary, indispensable, because a whole other story is vibrating in it" (17).

47. See Sylvère Lotringer and Sande Cohen, eds., *French Theory in America* (London: Routledge, 2001), 142.

Conclusion

1. Kristeva is responding to an interviewer who was intent on separating her work into different periods and projects. See Birgitte Huitfeldt Midttun, "Crossing the Borders: An Interview with Julia Kristeva," *Hypatia: A Journal of Feminist Philosophy* 21, no. 4 (2006): 166.

2. Barthes's last lecture course seemed to be moving in that direction. The course was published as *La Préparation du roman I et II: Cours et séminaires au Collège de France 1978–1979 et 1979–1980* (Paris: Seuil, 2003). See Antoine Compagnon's accounts of this question in "Le Roman de Roland Barthes," *Revue des sciences humaines* ("Le Livre imaginaire") (2002): 266–267 and "Roland Barthes's Novel," trans. Rosalind Krauss, *October* 112 (Spring 2005): 23–34. See the English translation of Barthes's last lecture courses: *The Preparation of the Novel: Lecture Courses and Seminars at the Collège de France (1978–1979 and 1979–1980)*, trans. Kate Briggs (New York: Columbia University Press, 2011).

3. In Aldous Huxley's *Point Counter Point* (1928), the fictional Philip Quarles defines the "novel of ideas" as one where "the character of each person must be implied, as far as possible, in the ideas of which he is the mouthpiece." *Point Counter Point*, intro. Nicholas Mosley (Normal, IL: Dalkey Archive, 1996, 2nd ed. 1999), 294. While Huxley's novel is itself usually characterized as a "novel of ideas," this opinion from Quarles's notebook nicely reflects on the problematic nature of the genre.

4. Graham Allen, *Intertextuality* (London: Routledge, 2000), 31.

5. Cited in Allen, *Intertextuality*, 31.

6. Midttun, "Crossing the Borders," 172.

7. Umberto Eco, "On the Crisis of the Crisis of Reason," in *Travels in Hyperreality: Essays*, trans. William Weaver (New York: Harcourt Brace, 1986), 125.

8. Ibid., 125.

9. Ibid.

Index

Castle, 239n9; "Hunter Gracchus," 201; "In the Penal Colony," 151, 202; "Metamorphosis," 241n30; *The Missing Person (Amerika)*, 151

Kafka: Toward a Minor Literature (Deleuze and Guattari), 200, 242n38

Kassandra (Wolf). See *Cassandra*

Katz und Maus (Grass), 225n69

Kermode, Frank, 12; *The Sense of an Ending*, 73, 170

Kittler, Friedrich, 13

Klein, Georg: *Barbar Rosa: A Detective Story*, 161–165, 236n19; *Libidissi*, 161, 236n16

Klein, Robert, 16

Knapp, Steven, 15

Koselleck, Reinhart, *Zeitschichten*, 162

Kristeva, Julia, 5, 208; autobiographical material, 106–107, 108, 230n7; and *Critical Inquiry*, 12; on fiction writing, 205, 243n1; and *Housekeeping*, 67; and setting, 90–91, 108, 122–123, 229n6; on *Tel Quel*, 206. Works: "The Ethics of Linguistics," 105–106; *Murder in Byzantium*, 108, 109, 120–124, 231n24; *The Old Man and the Wolves*, 108; *Samouraï*, 229n5; "Women's Time," 105, 106–108, 117, 121, 124. See also *Possessions*; women's time

Krüger, Michael: *The End of the Novel*, 41; *Himmelfarb*, 41–44, 219n48

Kubrick, Stanley, *2001: A Space Odyssey*, 195, 241n32

Kuznetsov, Anatoli, *Babi Yar: A Documentary in the Form of a Novel*, 39

Lacan, Jacques, 5, 79–104; and *Age of Iron*, 99–104; and Althusser, 228n41; and *L'Amante anglaise*, 86–88, 89; and Bhabha, 210; and *The Lover*, 88–89, 222n25; and *October*, 12; and *Possessions* (Kristeva), 89–92; and psychoanalytic establishment, 79–80; and *The Ravishing of Lol V. Stein*, 81–83, 84, 88; and *Romance*, 92–98, 228n33; on territorialization, 240n22; and *The Vice Consul*, 83–85. Works: "Analysis and Truth or the Closure of the Unconscious," 99; "The Insistence of the Letter in the Unconscious," 93; review of *The Ravishing of Lol V. Stein*, 81–83, 88

Laist, Randy, 237n31

language: in *Age of Iron*, 102–103; blank style, 25–30, 36, 48–49, 217nn17,20; in *Cassandra*, 113, 115–116; and deconstruction, 52–53; in *Foucault's Pendulum*, 137; in *Hallucinating Foucault*, 132, 232n18; in *Housekeeping*, 67; in *The Lover*, 60; in *The Old Man and the Wolves*, 108; in *Possessions* (Kristeva), 89–91, 111, 227nn28,29; and resistance to theory, 8, 16, 80, 212n18, 215–216n63; in *Romance*, 93, 95, 98; in *Waiting for the Barbarians*, 147–148; in *Waterland*, 69, 70, 74

The Last World (Ransmayr), 176

Laurens, Camille, 218n29; *Avenir*, 34; *Index*, 30–34, 218n33; *In His Arms*, 31, 34, 92, 218nn30,32. See also *Romance*

Leavis, F. R., 7, 9, 12

Leavis, Q. D., 12

Die Leiden des jungen Werthers (Goethe), 229n52, 232n17

Lejeune, Philippe, 170

Die letzte Welt (Ransmayr), 176

Leverenz, David, 223n42

Waiting . . . (continued)
   Sebald's work, 234n50; torture in,
    148–149
Wallace, David Foster. *See Infinite Jest*
The War: A Memoir (Duras), 29–30
Warren, Austin, 15, 215n57
Warren, Robert Penn, 12
The Wasteland (Eliot), 179
Waterland (Swift), 67–74; and Grass,
   225n69; history in, 68–70, 72–73, 74,
   225n65; meaning in, 69, 70–71, 74;
   occlusions in, 71; realism in, 71–72
Wellek, René, 15, 215n57
"What Is an Author?" (Foucault),
   128–129, 130, 231n6
White, Hayden, 6, 225nn65,66;
   Metahistory, 68, 72–73
White, Peter, 165
The White Goddess (Graves), 112
The White Hotel (Thomas), 39
White Noise (DeLillo), 165–172, 180–181;
   death in, 165, 170–171, 237n34;
   doubling in, 168; ecstasy in, 180–181;
   and intellectual climate, 6; nostalgia
   in, 170; operational negativity in,
   168–169; television in, 166–168;
   theoretical influences on, 165–166

Wilcox, Leonard, 181, 238n44
Wilden, Anthony, 80
Williams, Raymond, 12
Wimsatt, W. K., Jr., 12, 24
Wolf, Christa, *Cassandra*, 112–117, 120
women's time, 105–108; and *Animal
   Triste*, 117–120; and *Cassandra*, 112–
   117, 120; and *Murder in Byzantium*,
   108, 109, 120–124, 231n24; and
   Possessions (Kristeva), 109–112, 121
"Women's Time" (Kristeva), 105,
   106–108, 117, 121, 124
Woolf, Virginia, *A Room of One's Own*, 112
wordplay: in *Possessions* (Kristeva), 90,
   227n29; in *Romance*, 93, 95
Wordsworth, William, *Prelude*, 61, 65
World War II. *See* Nazi Germany
Writing and Difference (Derrida), 52–53
Writing Degree Zero (Barthes), 25–26
Wyatt, David M., 223n42

Yale School, 12, 44. *See also* de Man, Paul
Yeats, W. B., 100
Youth (Coetzee), 49

Zeitschichten (Koselleck), 162
Žižek, Slavoj, 12